STO

ACPL ITEM
DISCARDED

3 1833 00257 1245

P9-BHW-167

NOV 13 '78

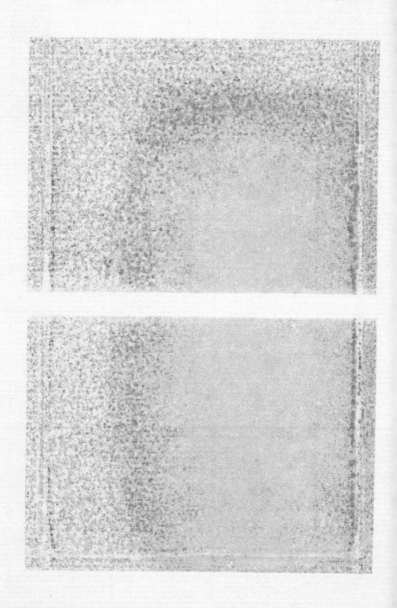

ENGLISH RECUSANT LITERATURE
1558–1640

Selected and Edited by
D. M. ROGERS

Volume 388

BONAV O'HEOGHUSA
Dan do Rinne
[c. *1614*]

A Shorte Declaration
1615

NINIAN WINZET
Certane Tractatis
1562

NINIAN WINZET
The Last Blast of the Trompet
1562

BONAV O'HEOGHUSA

Dan do Rinne

[c. *1614*]

The Scolar Press

1978

ISBN 0 85967 507 6

Published and printed in Great Britain by
The Scolar Press Limited, 59-61 East Parade,
Ilkley, Yorkshire and
39 Great Russell Street,
London WC1

2022834

NOTE

The following works are reproduced (original size) with permission:

1) Bonav O'Heoghusa, *Dan do rinne*, [c. 1614], from a copy in Cambridge University Library, by permission of the Syndics.

References: Allison and Rogers 581; STC 18791.

2) *A shorte declaration*, [anon.], 1615, from a copy in the Folger Shakespeare Library, by permission of the Trustees.

References: Allison and Rogers 763; STC 20451.

3) Ninian Winzet, *Certane tractatis*, 1562, from a copy in Edinburgh University Library, by permission of the Librarian.

References: Allison and Rogers 903; STC 25860.

4) Ninian Winzet, *The last blast of the trompet*, 1562, from a copy in Edinburgh University Library, by permission of the Librarian. Both surviving copies of this work consist of only five leaves: apparently no more was printed.

References: Allison and Rogers 904; STC 25861.

OAN

DO RINNE AN BRATH-
A bos dóro S. PROINSIAS
bonabentúra ó Hēōasa gā-
dián brátar néiuoñać lobáin
dpioréapaid ğide ōó,
do tuit a neipiceṡ, lé
mhiğō an tro-
gail, ⁊ aimmian
a cholna.

Cuio de tꞃas, ꞅ leiġsꞃ dorḃáꞃa ⁊
ambẽgra, a inclẽgra, ma bproill-
ꞃğéthi lé nꞃumaib roi ene (ꞅ naċ
éroin pneaẑ do ċabainc) con-
daꞅ, incomiaꞅ, coiréiñe, abſoal-
caꞅ, ⁊ gaċ iomláme oile, da mbẽ-
nać go dilioꞅ ꞃé piꞃꞇglaiꞅ ndé
do beiċ amáin, agan ꞇglaiꞅ Ro-
máñaiẑ, ⁊ a ccoráꞃꞅa nó a ccon-
A   tꞃáꞃóa

cu$\dot{g}$óa $\int$in, do beit a$\int$ $\dot{g}$a$\dot{c}$ coi$\dot{m}$-
$\dot{b}$onól enie$\dot{c}\dot{o}$ ma$\dot{o}$ luat, no mall
tainig, nó tioccay. Cuid oile an
teigio$\int$ an$\int$ma$\int$a, ┐ ainmiana a to-
lo, do neir mc ay léin ran dán,
┐ a ccuiy$\int$m (do $\dot{b}$eóin dé) $\dot{g}$lúai$\int$
$\dot{m}$in$\dot{g}$te do $\dot{b}$ $\dot{g}$ $\dot{g}$a$\dot{b}$ món de a-
tá cu$\dot{n}$ai$\dot{o}$ ┐ an bpobal ccoit$\dot{c}\dot{g}\tilde{n}$.

Tnua$\dot{g}$ liom$\int$a a $\dot{c}$ompáin do $\dot{c}$o-
tnua$\dot{g}$ an mo$\dot{o}$ ┐ a $\dot{b}$ry$\dot{l}$ ri$\dot{b}$;
ní léin doit rola$\int$ rán $\dot{g}$néin
an don$\dot{c}$ac$\dot{h}$d rein ní léin $\dot{o}$it,
Ar ériiceac$\dot{h}$d do t$\dot{h}$riéi$\dot{g}$ tú,
'Oiana no$\dot{u}$l, i$\int$ crerdo$\dot{m}\dot{h}$ 'Dé:
m$\dot{b}$o an rle$\int$i tánla $\dot{o}$h$\dot{o}$i$\dot{b}$h;
mór de an maoit ní tui$\dot{g}$e réi$\dot{n}$.
'Dá $\dot{b}$hrc̣ict̃e$\dot{a}$, mc $\dot{o}$o $\dot{c}$$\dot{i}$d each',
an$\int$roilly$\int$i acā $\dot{o}$$\int$$\dot{i}$$\tilde{u}r\dot{g}\dot{o}$ ont,
bhun noon$\dot{c}$a$\int$ do ba léin li$\dot{b}$,
do trg$\int$d̃ó ri$\dot{b}$ réin $\dot{b}$ur ccor.
·Do

Do dhruinge gūn ghníanac glan,
do dall adh í dā toil rém,
trúag nách tērla nibh ó tús
líaigh do fóirfeō tū ód fém.

Do tſuntaſ do nachain rém,
aſ go cclōin mé (meiſoi g̃ ndóig)
otha neimhníx nibh dā naoh,
nách léig lámh líga dā chóm.

Alo ghoime ó nách féadrim dol
crinri chrigam g̃ ron Dé,
ſar tāirdſr na ſinſhi róm,
eſr tſſſlāinte dod dóig rém.

An dall atā an trigri niamh?
nó an í an toil lé miain an crirp
do chuir an ebóra g̃ dho céill
ſoilſe an ctervm̃ nác lér duit.

Maſ í an tuigſi, maſ í an toil,
aſ cionntach nī cōr tſ céill,
bíod oramſa an tuigſi do cōig
rbíod coſg na toile oirt fém.

a 2   Maſ

Már i an tuigs as cionta sinb,
ag so dhuit a leighis riú,
creid onsglais briatra Dé,
ór di nosas sém a rún.

Dise tra nosas a rún,
Eom ta thibað dúm is Pól,
Sbiorað té ré a hais to gnát
ni bi a mhspall, gattám dhó.

An Pápa sa ngabhan leis,
as i an tglas a dein mé;
ni phoil tglas oile as so,
agam a bhus an biot cé.

Do ghell Dia, ta thibhað sm,
i emtha sgroptúir sib va sað
tglas shoisaissona Críost,
nách crnsiti síor go brát.

Don tglais Romanta a máin,
to cómltch so, táil go bsios,
atá anuas ó aimsis Chríost;
gan tlaeclóð, gan tiot, gan
sgos.   gać

Gac einicigḟ tánig riamh,
mall do tall, no as glún do mhíl,
má an nác eglas do Chríosd,
biéro díobh, ná labhrad é.

Ná habrad é Cailbín claon,
nó Lúithin na claon ó bhreit,
nó gibé dronng libhar díobh,
gab oeglais Chríosd iad féin,

Gibé heglas libhar riad,
ní tánig niamh no npa féin,
már i rm an eglas chíon,
cionas frorraio éosd g bréig?

Do réin a naomála féin.
cúig céd bliadain ter éis éosd
an eglas Rómánta cáid,
bá hi a mám an eglas fíor.

Ionam di an ugrm ra nor,
roóbact saémainte moo rbhí,
creroim, chgasg, cumair, bríg,
uir aicing ri a soaio do gnír.

a 3   Fan

Fán naimpom do bádan án,
    aitpe naomta clann do tías,
    gaca bfoil agam a noir,
    ap iad poim do tígaise piad,
Fán naimpion tainig on Norm.
    Patraig naomta iji côn sgil,
    gac a bfoil agám a noir,
    ap iad poim do tígaise trín.
An cretim, do tígaise trín,
    Patruig trió teisgiobal dé,
    má do trpéigpim pioñam uaib,
    cia hi anuán do téigpim é?
Signe pemeagailpi Dé,
    ap ap ngglair, léim do các,
    atá ap long na nh bal paop,
    coñda, coitcéñ, naom do gnác.
Ap long na nh t al atá,
    ni tfg ám ta dh bad po,
    antbad céirtglar Criosd,
    gac ni ticb to nipe anop.
                        A tús

Oltáid h̃ brigh ṁte fós,
   tṡrbað oile ar lén ꝗ rũ,
ꝗ long a ceile to ḡnáit,
   ó ló p̃hteꝗ zur an lá á níu.

Oltá ꝗ ntglus tonóa leis,
   tortcorp cumaiſz zan teilt ĩ,
tortceañ,ꝗ an tconpſa atá,
   na boill trá to néiṅ an cĩ.

Toittceañ,aſ zrò zhiṁnurò í
   zabirò rí zaċ tbĩ lẽn toil,
atá ingaċ aimſin añ riaṁ:
   to bí ingaċ tín tiꝗ iſ toiṁ.

Naṁẽã fós ꝗ ntglus fron,
   bẽ há a naẽ ,a tṡgaiſz óṡn,
iomaò a mioŕbal,ſa pãò,
   lón,to tác tá óṡh bãò fuò,

Na ſiẽniſ maſt acciall,
   zã ntgluſſie riaṁ atáit,
ſiꝗne cotaſſia, aſ ole briòz,
   zã nſ tcáiŕtib biós na náit.
        s 4   iomõa

Iomdha dhaoine nach iad féin,
mun buð fada beit gá níomh,
dhchibhar gurab í ro amháin
antglas táið do tog Críoṡð

Mairim gurab creiðte dhuit
gach ní ruib ðá nabrann fúð;
creiðthe uaithe briaṫra Dé
ór ði nochðar féin a rún.

Lᵃᵉjthi, Cailbin taoib ré taoib,
ran ṁerð gabaṡ ðattaoib rúð,
mó aṡ inchreiðte ᵴglaṡ Dé,
ór ði nochðaṡ féin arún.

Mairg chríṡṡ lᵃᵉjthi na noic,
olc a ċoinghell, olc a chiall,
olca na tᵴáiᵴᵴ tuᵴ uaiðh,
raṡ olc antoiðe obhſaᵴ iað,

Doṁnne bhréiᵴ ré Dia móṡ;
miᵴ do ċreiðᴘteð ðó ða éiṡ;
biᵴ ré ðaoinibh aṁlaiðh ṡin,
coṡṁail ṡiṡ go nðiongnᵴᵴh ſé.
boᴛᴀṡ

bofᵃf, ógohuf, umhluf néiōh,
do dhiᴅ féin do ghᴇllfᴅn iᴅō
do bhᴉfⱬō leᴉf bⱬⱬ dhá ulc,
nᴅ ꞇfí móꞇoe ꞇuⱬ do dhiᴅ.

Tuⱬ bofᴅf ⱬ fᴅoᴅhbuᴉf mbof,
do ꞇféᴉⱬ umhlᴅ ⱬ ᴅ ꞇhoᴉl féim,
cᴅᴉll bō dhubh ᴅᴉⱬe nᴅ mᴉᴅoᴉ,
nᴅ mhᴅnᴅᴄh ⱬe dho bhi fé.

Ofoe foⱬhlᴅmᴅ fuⱬ fem
ᴅn oᴅbᴅl (mⱬ ᴅ oeᴉf féᴉm)
ⱬᴉbé mⱬ ɲn chnefoᴉf oō,
oon oᴉᴅbhᴅl fof chnꞇf fé.

Ill ᴅᴉnⱬ do ꞇꞇꞇfō Cᴅᴉlbᴉn fóf,
plᴅnnꞇᴅ oile ᴅ póf nᴅ loꞇō
ofoe lⱬꞇéᴉf lⱬꞇh féᴉm,
do fhᴅfᴅᴉⱬh féᴉᴅo ⱬ olc.

U ghoⱬ ⱬᴅᴄh ɲlc do ɲí fo,
do oᴉᴅ ⱬlóɲꞇⱬ olc ᴅn chiᴅll:
ᴉonᴅñ oófᴅn ⁊ foᴉn,
ᴅ fᴅoh ᴅch foᴉl Oᴉᴅ ᴅᴅ ohiᴅ,
    ᴅⱬ   ⱬuf

Gur fhéchaid Críosd corñac té
a deir re ní fém an chiall:
ionañ tógan 7 rom,
a fáth nac foil Dia na thid.
Atá g brgle táin a ciall,
no ní hionañ Dia atá róim:
Dia oile cosmail ris fém
ar bó athrar ré tg móigh.
Air an ndia tá nathrañ fein
ole labhrar gibé ar Dia dó:
an Dia fíre athrar cách
ní cherite trá g aghlór.
Ní abraim go nteanna rom
athaltías ir roir go lór:
ar gibé tho fhacth iat.
ñhaim ñg cherite g dia a glór
Na comthe fá rh a g tér
Sotoma ro tl óth go láir,
ní roirfañ rác th na riañ,
fhéčibeich fér na ro fnač.

Fhaffaig

Fiafruig dá fhlaithbhruidh féin,
    fiafruig dá bhuachaill séim slim
    rdo bhéraðtá dhalta ril,
    anabruid an cneirtpith gñ.
Alr airmhing ronn anoir,
    ra ccló urtail ré a ccoir rið,
    mhrtha g an nóir to móðh iað
    nác tóib to norrað Dia anún.
Mi ti tá fór nác bioð ré a nair,
    an Sbioraið nacm an plait rior
    tá ccoimhto mg tzlair ntré
    g fhzhán rg bhréig to rióp.
Ni chnercpló ár Dunne lm.
    ton dirrm ir tá lbh iað;
    míle bntz a nazhairh Dé,
    fia nazaid rém to móðh rað
. Mi cneirte ðaibh; a ré athioð,
    rúntiamhra an riog uatá rið
    creirte ónthzlairbhriatra Dé
    ór ti norar rém a rún.
                            Atáið

Atá bríathra Dé 7 ḋá ṁoḋh.
creidte ontglais gaċ moḋ ḋíob
cuid ḋíob san sgríoptúir atá
cuid 7 cuiṁne ag cáċ do fíór

An sgríoptúir gid líónṁ ḋo,
a ċneroiṁ ngab lóir líṫ:
iomḋa neiṫe a doḃaint críosa
ng cuirẻo aṁ ror fá rẻ.

Aiṫẟaisg ṁioncá gaċ laoi,
anoiṁa ingaċ trobh ng gaḃ;
cia an sgoptúir mga ven éoin
naṫuilẟẟo fa ḃeoig a líṫh.

An ṁéiṫẟn ng rgniobaḋ ḋiob
bríaṫra críosa gḋoriog nanoúl
gnáṫċuiṁne 7 sin viaig anviaig
coiṁḋoas gan ċiaig iao vúṁ.

Gan sgríḃ ne mg rin vognaṫ.
ḋo toimbir cáċ bríaṫra Dé
ó Aḋaṁ go Ṁroiri a nuar,
gaċ vroing nua von vroing vá
héir.   Do

'Do bí fós antiomna nua,
rglad anuas tᵹéis Chríosd,
gan sgríbne ⁊ cuimne to gnát,
rda creitᵽ ag cáć to fíor.
Gibé aden náć cryeatᵽ ré,
aᵹ ton sᵹoptᵽr fém amáin,
fiafᵹigim te an ccréidtᵽ leif
mas é an sᵹoptᵽr sem na láim
'Da nabratᵽ náć creidtᵽ fém,
sᵹoptᵽr 'Dé ᵹab é rem,
fiafᵹigim teirᵹu aᵹíf,
cry rá ccryᵽn an ní a teirᵹ
'Da nabratᵽ go ccry (ᵹattᵽ)
ᵹab é ríud sᵹoptᵽin De;
an trᵹf fᵹr fiafᵹigim te;
naᵹ lᵹ rem ran sᵹoptᵽr fém
An braratᵽ ran sᵹoptᵽr ryatᵽ
nó má to tᵽnᵹe cia an ball;
soisᵹél lúcáiᵹ to beit fíóᵹ,
Soisᵹél Tomaiᵹ gan boᵹ aᵽ;
                    bheitᵽ

bheit do ghmuire riam nahóigh,
  bairrcfó lámh gcóir do ghréin,
beit ar an ndoomnaé don cáisg,
  ran rcniopttiin fór caic ng
gibe le ccneirdéin iad ro, (Ltg
  cneirdte dó nó atá gan cerll
naé lón an rgniopttiin a máin
  gan curmne ngnaic bnéir dé
Cia an sgniopttiin ar cneirdti tná,
  cia an gnácér,miin a tá fiór?
  a cciall ancon muin an mhuin,
  cneirdti ónsglair gaé curd diob
Már i an tuigsg buaidónlsr tá;
  ag ro a leigior gáttu dó,
muna fognd a nábnaim dhi
  dó géába aruf ní ra mó
Már ian toil ar cionteé uib,
  flán lib, ní bhnabra dhi:
  a leighlf ní geb ne hairf;
  aidnid daimfa go maic i,

                              An

An toil óg ab reir an corp
buain uimpe ní bog an céim;
péiro ar doideanra má sein,
nír delb ort ní foil pan grein;
An fulaindh riog na ndúl,
fruit lonoam a ccúil do tall,
a gnineall do nor an muin,
oá gluarar dosgum an grian;
An pobul óg choisg mq ruc,
gluarar náouita dúl mbalb,
anmanna attoile do chosg;
ní frainrin uatha a lor am.
Iomao mionbal, iomao plág
bagq gnát báir 7 pian;
cosg anmnan choruin an riog;
ní táng oiob, nín phéo rao.
Tionól lenm an corr duib,
tiglat nnne a brul pan rbéin
ní b'rooir uile a lor gléoró;
buanána toile ar oa. oom re-
₩.   each

Each piaghta ó nach faghthar fos,
a los fgla ná a los gnaid;
ní leig as da mgcach féin,
gid glacadh a spiem amáin.

Meince a cách do tspgnadh le,
a mgcach féin gidh é an;
Solam Samson Daibioth naomh,
aitnidh dóibh a trom náspan;

Samson ar ghi chalma a nisc,
Solam ghi gmc chr a chiall,
ghi naomtha daibioth go ngmis;
anmrana a ttoil do chlaoriad.

leigsr na toile do láimh,
ní gelsa chnáning drn
ag ro rísr duitsi gitte;
chgasg tsg na hagard rit:
Do chérdneitib sgnidh go gan,
an chr fsg crutaigh tia an toil
iónar go ttugadh to gnáth;
fuath ton ule is gradh ton mhait.

Maithe

Maire an domhuin leth ⁊ leth,
dá mbí teoi lim pá ré rao,
maic fine gan cumasg nuile,
tiéb uile ní puil ar Dia,

Thé comhair aca tá bfuil,
gan a hurduil uile né chair,
a nuile uatá pém atáro,
ó Dia amháin ruasseeo a maic.

Man rm gabé Dia amháin,
ar con curbóin gró von toil,
ní hiongnáró ar ⁊ sun Dé,
comhí oile pán gnem glem.

An maic mbréige nác buan né,
trigáro Dé to ba vióc naic,
an maic gan poncgg gan cric
an maic fine ó mbi gác maic,

Más to chéiztró Dia na ngg,
tobg lán rillp to rión,
⁊ an raxál, laz na hprin,
⁊ an ccum cácró céiz antigg,
            b   Solar

Solar an bgéa míg tuc
g príortín ndub g uaim ccbó:
anchoncoir coibhnir do hfgm,
mág do tréig g gleañ nantbó:
gleañ na ndobn an rcogal bof,
gan añ ár gol nó páth guil:
priórtín don ti thuigfr é
uaiṁ donca don té náč tuig.
Ní ðiol gnárð abfaghtg uað,
ðiol g puath an rcoghal féin.
ðfoč neiṁe áčioblaigté čná,
lomnán don bár ir ðfeing ó.
lán do bočða a thoice mór,
a coibhlr pór lán do mhcoith,
an méið ar milir ðá ghnáð,
ní bi ar lán do ðhomlár coi.
Mág chgar a rhatóbair bof,
bg argða ag ðol ran nuaig:
areaðb rantrcoghaira péin,
mó ðho péin ðon forpín cuf
                              fprioc

Fuioċ lé Solaṁ raiṡḃneṡ móa
aiznió ṡó náċ món a bhuiġ.
viomhaoinṡ ve ġoinṡ ré
reaṡóh ṁcine ancé zá mbí
béġ cháinṡ an bhéċ vá ṁil,
aḃheníoch liḃh ⁊ ċṡó vo ré
ṡoċhṡ a chnuṁṡgċhe onc,
a⁊ġhṡ ro ni léċ réin,
Oá cron⁊ṁċe a⁊ac vo ṁaoin,
bhuó béġ a⁊ġbhṡ vroibh réin,
aconṁéṡo onc⁊ṡ vo ghnáċh
a caichṁí a⁊ cáċh c⁊ héiṡ,
Au vho ⁊ġroibh ⁊ vo chloinn,
vo bíavh c⁊ḃhṡ na ꝛoinn ꝛúo
an ohiṡi ꝛhion cuille ġaꝛon
cá béṡoċhá m⁊ ꝛo a ꝛoṁ ꝛúú
Oá bha⁊ȯcá m⁊ náċh ꝛíȯ cú,
an ꝑiái criónꝑa ꝛúú vo ꝛoṁ,
ꝛoinn vin niċhéḃhṡvh ꝛávȯ
m⁊⁊vo ċꝛe⁊g⁊vȯ v⁊⁊ ⁊an ꝛo⁊
oin⁊.   b 2   Oioṁ-

Díoshraine nátoice do chí,
tá mazh léin toit í on toil,
coibhilr bréige an bétha cé
tiomheaine tná é ma rom
Ar n cáoibhilrra (gattám tí ó)
ghin mhaunlr ní món a bríog
an rian toilltlh g a rhon,
mgrith ro tné bhiotha ríon,

TRUALGH.

AN

An bráthair
céadna

Ag tréagadh an tṡaoġail dó, aṡ
an mbaiṡb ṫaiġm ⁊
chríochnaiġh
a láéte.

Ḋaḃh aiṫreaċhas
a cominc oil dé;   (uaim,
na tréig mn an coi
da mháio do ṁill mé.

Do ṁill mé go lón
a ḟlaiṫ niṁe nroi;
da mháio do ṁill mé
na tréig mn an coi.

Oló ⁊ ττurmíḋ tná
aτá(τη aġh an τníomh)
gaċh o'c náη ná uιcnḋ
ag τoṙ aḋḃ ḋhioη.

Nír chuir Ézld orm
éag am chéio a ccurp.
biothpomn to bí rézh cchzc.
zézh iopnoimn rém uz.

Mo chronze nír chealz
cairrém amzeal rézh
zéi nimze na nacmh,
cho ar mire mór.

Uch mo níire nzór,
mo mhíne riom mill.
uch oram zré rleill
an cholann to chmn.

Uch ar zruazh mo zcirz,
ní r zl airz né anl eic zó
cmnézh er an ccli
no gun milézh mé.

Cainzéz ní olc bízhearo
rch ir zézza zhímo,
caoizrzh mire nzorn
no go zle ar rúil.

No

No go síe ⁊ srín
na sruch tiochta dbi
a cuibhreach a cnámh,
go fuighibb a fréam.

An teangara tug
tú a bfeing riompa aní,
uch fuil to mharbh mé,
uch nách balbh to bhí.

An bél to bhnord sfeing
uch uch is olc leinn,
gan é ⁊ uladh luim,
nó ag cnumaib gá chremn.

U ch uch gan an ful.
lé fillinn go sobh,
na cann cl firchrum chriad
na clichall tgb tol.

U ch uch gan an ccoir,
cor na ccémeann cclan.
marbh na criathan chriadh
ag biathadh taribh tol.

Truag

Truagh nach táinig an lámh,
lámh do loitthi a chlaith
reongla an mball ga mbréit,
na ccnámh nó na ccloich

Na hairm ruadas uait
(dohbhal uaim an tolc)
iad milim né tucd,
iad do iminnn ort

An imneas ort duic,
ní hé do thuill tú
ag loighe rán lia
roo chnorde gan chnú.

Na boillg aníoc mhuile
iodhbnuim buaheacha daoib:
má an ciad dhlighe dhinn
achaidh nimhe naoimh

Na boill charaohra a chríoro,
cuma amodbainc uáin,
cnú an dhgofa dhinn,
my cobanca uaibh.

An

An mo ghon tug tú
    an troighthe ran taobh,
    an dá dhírghbhoir dúinn;
    do fóbrair ancon.
Iodhbairt mhanm in duit,
    duitfi ní diol é,
    uait rán ruanar í
    ʒan dualáir a dhé.
Gabh am ule ʒróʒó
    irra bheirar uaibh,
    mó ʒ ccom (cairgill dúinn)
    abhfoil agann uann.
                    gabh

                s a n

        b 5

s. beɑrrɑ́ʁt ʁo cum ɑn ʁɑ́ɲʁɑ,
ʁɑn ʁʰʁʒuʁ̃ó lɑ̃ʁ̃e ɑ ʁʁɑʁ-
ɑʁʁe ɑn ʁʁɑ́ʒ̃ʁeɑ̃, ɲ́ ʁɑ
liʁʁ̃ɑ́ʁe ĩɑ́ ʁ̃ʒ ɑʁɑ́
ɑʁ̃ ʁo. Ɑn bʁɑʁʒ̃
buʁ̃ ʁ̃ʃ̃ɑ́ʁo-
ʁe ʁo cum ɑ
ʁʒɑʁʁ̃ʁ̃ʒ
ɑn ʁ̃ɑ́ʁo-
ʁʃ ʁ̃e.

Tʁuɑʒ̃ coʁ cʃcʃʁ̃e tɑ́ʁ̃-ʁɑ̃ʁ̃,
ɑʁ̃ʒ̃ʁlic ceiʁo ɑn ʁ̃oʁ̃lɑ́ɲ;
ʁioʁ̃̃ɑom ʁʃʁ̃ɑ ʁeiʒ̃ʁ̃eiʁ,
ʒlóiʁ ʁ̃ʃcʁ̃ɑom ɑʁ ʁomʁ̃uɑin;
Ɑ̃ ɑiʁ̃iʁʃ ɑʁ ʁɑ́ʁ̃ ʁuʁʁʃ,
ʁoice bʁoʁ̃ ɑn ʁ̃ʁ̃ʁɑ,
ʁéiʁ ɑ ʒɑl ʃɲ ʁɑ̃ɑʁ̃ɑ,
ʃʒ ʒʁoil ʁ̃é ccuʁ ccʁ̃ʁ̃e;
                                        NI

Ní fuil inte as leram,
nó bít g leic oiʒhuđ;
nó brúʒ fóiʒ ném fiobhlaiʒ,
a ttoiplém ó thoirniʒh.

T fuaʒ truaʒ ron tí ṁʒllas,
moil bréizi as bʒʒ ttoncuð
ʒnáč tiombuuđ na tʒʒaiđ,
bláč tiombuan an toṁáin,

Ʒlóin đíomhaom an toṁáin,
tuille a nʒđoit ʒ ʒluafaf
treall tá bfaʒʒčá a iafef,
ʒačča ʒrliu né a ʒuafaf.

As ainʒ to ʒeib an nʒlóirfi;
ʒhin ṁuirfi a meađuir,
fbiuiʒ ʒo cian fá a coṁair,
an fhian na viaiʒ viłʒair.

Cuite aroif nʒit Sáṁóin,
nó Scoinh cul fluiffiǔ,
nfizʒoil cun an chuistin,
ʒoṁ Eafuis nó Aicil,

                              Cáit

Cáit rér abḟuil Solaṁ,
  raoi go nḟġra miomláin,
  no an ríoṁṫe reang roġró,
  ionat do bḟẟm miompáiḋ,
Caiḋe cuṁas Sḟẟrain,
  no rén Ailexanoain,
  caiḋi an eẏn ēlaṫ ccuṁṫaiġh,
  naṫ na nẏm no a nẏṫgoil,
Caiḋe áille Aḃrlón,
  ṁṫleaċṫo Aimortotuil,
  reanga ṫrén Thuil Siein,
  ó bẟul rnéṁ ẟaeh pocuil,
A cholann a cholaṁ,
  ao cḣi cealga an trioġuil,
  bíoṫ ont má nuṁan,
  a chnioch boṫ a broẟuil.
A bẟṫa híaro cciorḋuḃ,
  a chẏn luaṫa an luaẟuil,
  a bláṫ ġḃẟg an nẟnánaḋ,
  crẟṫ ar ṗúṫ do cuaḃan,

                Eḟṁ

Tsin go mbia béird tiocnach,
ag cneit to cnámh n olom,
ambnuzh énird bir cumáig,
a brath cnum achodán;

Tlin go mbia an béal concna,
na éniaid piain téir tabard;
rméoin tioméaia an troigit;
ra rionétoña an uluit;

bud iomda go haitélin;
a náit na noss rétóglan;
rrán troibreata rógeal
leaba ag orol ga dérgad;

Ag rm cricch to cumuin;
pir an ccnun a ccealgut;
ma a tioi an ti to cumduig;
ná ao cleoi aéli tá chizuib.

An una ragtd ucibhri;
umlar aignead riotbrían;
gnad coitceach gan élaoción;
bur bronéioñ bud riortnuat.

TRUAGH

A Shorte Declaration
1615

2022834

A SHORTE
DECLARA
TION OF THE LIVES AND
DOCTRINDE
OF THE PROTESTARTS
AND PVRITA.
Ns, VVHER BY
ONE OF INDIFER-
ENT IVDGMENT
MAY KNOVV THE
holinesse of then
Religion.

AS the good tree is knovven by the good fruits, fo the
Euill tree by the Euill fruits. *Math.* 7.

A ROVEN,

PRENTET IN THE PRNT HOVS

OF MARIN MICHEL

1615.

4312534

ADMONITION TO THE
READER.

THE Sonne of God (Gentle *mat.* Reader) Sheweth vs in the 1Z. Gosoell of S. Mathewe that as the good tree is knowen by the good frutis: so the euill tree is knowen by the euill fruits Chriſt by this ſimilitude teacheth vs how wee may know and diſtingiſh the Godly Paſtours & doctours of the true Church of God, from the decitfull troupres of heretiques, which come to vs clothed in the Sheepes ſkine of pietie and ſim- plicitie but yet within are Rauening wolues killars of mens Soules for as the Godly Paſtours of the Church of God are knowen by their good workes ſo the ſeditious troups of hereiques are knowen by their Euill workes yf any man will compare the puritie of doctrine & holy Liues of the Paſtours and Doctours of the Catholique Romaire Church with the peſtilent Doccaine and abhominabll liues of our Proteſtants and Pureiane, he ſhall find as great differnce betweene

them

them as is betwene light and darkneſſe, life, and death, good and Euill.

As concerning the holy Ancient Fathers you ſhall ſee them agree amōgſt them ſelues in vnitie of doctrine, allthought thcy haue beene ſeueered one frō ane other in diuerſe places and ages of the world, adorned with rare holyneſſe of life and Innumerabll Miraclee as an Infallible teſtimonie of God approouing both their liues and doctrine as aceeptable vnto him.

But yf you will conſidder our Proteſtants and Puritans liues and doctrine you ſheall ſee ſuch a confuſion in their doctrine different one from an other, & abhominable liues without all Miracles, that it is a wonder how anie man ſetled in his naturall witts ſhould followe ſuch varullie ſellwes to Euident perdition.

As concerining their doctrine 3 thing are to be conſidered. The confeſion of their erroneous opinions. The libertie they giue to all kind of Euill. The contempt of good woorks as not profitalle to Saluation.

Toiching the confuſion of their Erroneous opinions, you muſt vnderſtand that in the ſmoeke of Luthers hereſie
more

more then tow hundreth damnable
opinions were Ingendred by diuerse
loftie braines (as Rhetius in his athei-
sms deelareth) which haue dasled the
Eyes of manie Ignorant soules with
such a thic e mist of diuerse heresies
that manie thousand soules not knowing
what they doe goe astray with a wandr-
ing foete from the way of Saluation to
Euident perditon.

As there is but one lyne to leuell rightly to the marke, a hundereth wayes to
shut a stray: so there is but one true
faith and Religion, whereby true Christians goe to Heauen but an hundreth
false faiths and Religions which lead
Ignorant soules and vn Godly men to
Eternall damnation.

when the Catholiques reprotch the
Protestants of their desagreeing in the
Chiefest heads of Religion, manie of
them now a dayes answere, that a man
may be saued in any Religin that is pre-
sessed, pouyding he beleue to be saued
in the Blood of Christ.

This is the cause wherefore they say
althought the Maesse, praying to the
Saincts, honoring of Images in Temples
be Idolatrie neuerthelesse that good
Papists may be saued in any Religion,
becaufe

becaufe they beleeue in Chrift this is ane of the greateft deceits that Sathan could inuent for the damnation of man when he persuadetd him that he may be faued in anie Religon that is profeffed in the world prouyding he beleeue to be faued in the Blood of Chrift for when a man is surely persuadetd to be faued this way, he careth not of what Relagion he be, whether he be a Proteftant or Puritane, Trinitar or Anabaptift, Caeholque or heretique beeaufe that all Reliegions are a like to him prouyding he beleeue in Chrift, and fo by this persuafion of Sathan he abideth with alfe great fecuritie in a falfe Religion, which leadeth Ignornt foules to Euident perdition as yf he were in a true Religion, which is but one. and likewife the only fure way to faluation.

Moreouer according to the falfe opinion of Proteftants all heretiques which euer were fince the birth of Chrift (how blafphemous that euere their herefies were againft God) fhould be faued, as Arrius which deny the diuinitie of Chrift, Pelagius which affrmed that man might be faued by hes owen proper vertue without the grace of God and all
other

other suchlike blasphemous heretiques, because they did belue in Christ and presesse them selues to be Christians & so euery one should goe as securely to Heauen with a false faith and blassphemous Religion, which opinion is so contrapie to the holy Scaripture and vpright Reason that it is a wonder how such an opinian should enter in the braine of man.

For S. Paule sayeth, that there is but one faith as there is but one God. so he that hath not this faith which is but one and worshipe not this God truly which is also but one can nowise be saued, for it is Impossible sayeth S. Paule to be acceptable to God without faith, where S. Paule speaketh of true faith which is but one, & not false faiths which are manie for. Turques Iewes & heretiques beleeue all in God but all by false faiths, and likewiise serue him by a false Religion. *Ephes. 4. 5. hebr. 12. 6.*

Christ to this purpose sayeth: he that will not heare the Church let him be vnto the as an heathen man and publicane. It is most sure that heathē Infidells haue no participation with Christ and his passion, nor yet heretiques and Schismatiques seuered fro m the Church of God *Mat. 18 17.*

God by Excōmunication, which Christ compareth to heathen Infidells, becaufe they will not heare or obey the Church of God as Chriſt Cōmandeth them to doe.

So a man which hath not the true faith of Chriſt which is but one, and is not within the true Church of God, which is alſo but one can nowiſe attaine to Saluation.

This opinion is alſo contrarie to vpright Reaſon. becauſe (as is mentioned, aboue) there is but one way to lenell Rightly to the marke but an hundreth wayes to ſhute by: ſo there is but one true faith and Religion togoe to Heauen, but an hundreth falſe faiths and Raliginos whereby Ignorant ſoules goe to Endleſſe miſeereie. Thus much concerning their manifolde hereſies and confuſiō of our new Goſpellers doctrine.

The ſecond point which is to be remarked in their doctrine is that they teach men to be made free from the keeping of all Lawes as much of God as of man by their faith in Chriſt & libertie of their Goſpell. ſo according to this doctrine men may adore Idolls, blaſpheme the Name of God contemne and diſobey

Inther in cap. ad Galall. in ſerm. de Moyſe et in cap. 20. exee 20. exod Cāuin. lib. 2. inſt. cap. 7. ſect. 14.

disobey their Father & Mother, cōmite Murther and Slaughter, Inceſt, fornication, & adulterie, thifte periurie or any other ſuchlike crimes without any ſcruple of conſcience, becauſe they are not bound in conſcience to keepe the Lawe of God, as Luther, Caluine and all our Proteſtants and Puritans doe teach vs whoſe proper words you ſhall ſee hereafter cited in the. 54. Chapter, wherein wee prooue that the Proteſtants and Puritans by their Peſtilent doctrine lead Ignorant ſoules to a theiſme and plaine Infidelitie.

The third point which is to by marked of their doctrine is that they teach that the beſt workes, which Iſſue from Godly Chriſtians are but deadly ſinnes, when they are weighted in the iudgement of Cod, ſo according to this rule of their doctrine it is all a like to adore God or to worſhipe an Idoll, to praiſe Cod or to blaſpheme his holy Name, to honnour his parents or contemne them to kill a man or ſaue his life, to ſleepe with his Nighbonrs wife or with his owen, to with holld his Nighbours goods or to render them, to declare in Iudgment he truth or to foreſware him ſelfe, to
keepe

Luther in aſſert. art 31. 32. 36. Cal. lib. 3 Inſt. cap. 12. ſect. 4. et cap. 14 ſect. 6.

B

keepe promise or to breach the same, to
fast and praie, or to spend his time in
wantonesse and Banqueting, to spoile
a poore man or giue him almes, for doe
what you list in all these or suchlixe
other things, all your workes are but
deadly sinns in the Iudgment of God,
whiche deserue no other reward but
damnation.

By this same rule of doctrine when
man goe to their Churches to preach
or heere the preaching, to giue or receiue the communion to fast and prair vpon
sonday to Excommunicat Catholiques
for not obeing their lawes. all these
workes of Religion are but deadly sines,
which is the seruice of Sathan and not
of God becanse sinne is from Sathan &
acceptab'e seruice done to him. as S.
Ihon writteth, and contrariwise it is
hatefull and odiouis to God as cotraria
to his holy will.

1 *Ihon.*
3. 8.

They teach by the same rule that it is
but folie to a man to paine him selfe to
doe anie good woixes, becaufe that
when he hath done all that lyeth in hi
power it is but a deadly sinne, which
can not helpe him to Heauen. wha
should a man doe then in this Religio
bu

but paffe his time in the mirrieffe, and
fo beleeue to be faue in the Blood of
Chrift, and fo he fhall goe mirrily to
Heauen without all paine and ftrife.

Now good Reader yf you will Iucge
finccrly according to the truth, all par-
tialitie, will you not fay that this Religion of the Proteftants is more like to
Epicurus Religlon, where all libertie is
giuen to fatiffie the concupiffonce of
the fleyh than the Religion of Chaift,
which reftrineth the concupiffance in
all difordained defires by prescaing of
penitence in affes and Secke Cloth, by
diligent watching in fafting & praying
to keepe vs from tentation of the flefh
the Deuill and the wordl. The Religlon
of Chrift cōmandeth to fight lawfully
againft the concupiffanee of the Eyes
the finnefull luft of the flefh, and difordained pleafours of the word: but the
Religion of the Proteftots is altogether
Effeminaate which yeeldeth obedience
to the luft of the flefh, concupiffance of
the Eyes, and worldly pleafours which
may content the concupiffance. The
Religion of Chrift cōmandeth vs to
enter vnto Heauen by the fteraite way
of vertue & penionce. But the Religion
of

of the Proteſtants leadeth wordly man
mirryly to Hell by the broad way of
carnall libertie and concupiſſence of the
fleſh to thie ſame, ſo that freely without
all ſcruple of conſcience they may cōmit
any ſinne they pleaſe, becauſe they are
mad free from all lawes by libertie of
their Goſpell.

Yf Sathan wold haue transformed him
ſelf in the ſhape of a Miniſter to preach
in a Pulpite, what Greater libertie wold
he haue giuen men to ſinne then our
Goſpellers haue giuen to their auditours
by the libertie of their Goſpell, for good
works are contemned by them as nowiſe
profitable to ſaluarion, and ſinne is
Cheeriſhed amongſt them ts nothing

Reſerie hurtfull to ſaluarion theſe are the heads
Exode of Religion which may of the Miniſters
Guliel. of England profeſſe, as VVilliame Kei-
Reginal- nold a learned Engliſh man reporteth.
dus lib.   Firſt ſuch are deceiued as thinke ro
4. pag. be ſaued by many good workes.
10. ct   Secondiy ti is not neceſſarie to worke
20. good works to attainae to Saluation,
becauſe wee are ſure thereof by faith.

     Thirdly that it is a great errour to
thinke that good workes may helpe to
Saluation,

     Fourthly ſinne doth not diminiſh the

Glorie of God, all the domage is in the
slaunder of our Nighbonr.

Fyftly Iesus Chrift by his Blood hath
deliuered vs not only from finne, but alfo from all lawes doth obliedge vs in
Confcience, thence is that wee are free
from the ten Cōmandements of the
Morall lawe & precepts of the Sacramēts

Sixtly thou ought no other thing to
God but only faith whereby thou confeffeth Iefues Chrift, and beleeueft that
he is rifen from death to life, and fo doing thou fhalt be faued.

So accordiug to this doctrine doe
what you pleafe, beleeue in Chrift and
you fhall be faued. there libertie giuen
to cōmite all crimes and mifchiefe the
world without all fcruple of confcience.

Now yf you will confider their perfons
they are conforme in their liues to this
fame doctrine.

Firft yf you will behold Luthers life
there you fhall fee his familar friendfhipe, and conference with Sathan, in
whofe fellowefhipe he did eate a bufhell
of Salt as he affirmeth him felfe in A
Dutch Sermon to the people: yon fhall
fee his breach of theie Godly vo wes,
puoertie, Chaftitie & obedience a monf-
trous comunction of a forefworne friet

with an apostatisse Nunne in an Sacrilegious bedde, and how he could no more keepe him selfe hrom venus game ahen he could doe from spitting, as he writteth of him selfe in his booke of Matrimonie, likewise he thinketh no shame to say yf the wife refuse to come, the hand maid shalbe welcome, because the fellowshipe of weemen was as needefull to him as sleepe meate and drinke.

He sheweth also his intollerable pride in so much that he sayeth that Kings, Princes and the Pope him selfe are not worthie to lose the latchets of his shoes and that a Thouand Cyprians and a Thousand Augustins are not to be compared to him.

He sheweth also his great crueltie & sedition when he did stirre vp the rude cómon people of Germanie against their Prelats and temporall Lords in such a fashion that a hundreth Thousand man of the cúmon people wer slaine, & thrie hundreth Castells ouerthrowen. in one prouince of Germanie called Franconia.

Yf you will considder the liues of Caluin and Beza there you shall see their Extreeme pride to oppose their priuie Iudgment to the whole antiquitie of the the Ancient Fathers,

You fhall fee likewife in their liues) thift Sacriledge homicide, cruell feditiom ftirred vp by them in France, adulterie, fodomie and bougrie.

Yf you pleafe to viewe Sir Ihon Knox life the holy Apoftle of Scotland there you fhall fee Inceft cõmitted by him with his owen good Mother in a cornexill or xillogie. adulterie wtih an other mans wife his Necromancie and familiar friendfhipe with Sathan, whofe Example many of the Miniffers of Scotland did follow as you fhall fee herefter in the defcription of their liues.

Confidering (Gentle Reaeer) that the tree is kncwen by the fruis (as Chrift fayetd) you may Eafely Iudge by the fruits and morall workes of our New Gofpellers, as much taught by their doctrine as practifed in their liues whether their Relegious tree be good or no when the tree it felfe is nothing elfe but a confufed mas of olde herefies patched together like an beggere olde Clocke, which were condemned long, agoe in olde heretiques by the ancient Fathers. and the fruits thereof a libertie to liue after the pleafours cf this world and concupiffance of the flefh in all pleafant voluptie of eating and drinking, and

*Mat. 7.
vngodly
doctrine
vngodly
Religion.*

Exercise of venus game, and to cōmit anie sinne that is as homicide, adulterie, thifte periurie, Sodomie, and other suchlike crimes, without scruple of Conscience, because men are made free from the keeping of all lawes by their faith in Chrift and libertie of their Gospell.

Sathan him selfe could not haue geuen a mor pernitious Religion to mortall men then to giue a confused mas of olde condamned heresies, and to teach men that they should neuer paine them selues to doe anie good worke because that all good workes are but deadly sinnes in the Iudhment of God, which can not further our Saluatiō but rather procure our damnation & that men should not be feared to cōmit any sinne that may pleasour him: because that no sinne can condemne him, prouyding he beleeue to be saued in the blood of Chrift, for so teaching all good workts are banished away as vnprofitable to Saluation and libertie giuen to man to cōmit all sinnes that may pleasour him without all feare of damnation I praie God to saue vs frō such a pestient Relinion and to graunt vs grace to abide conftantly in the bofome of the catholique Romaine Church

AMEN.

ACERTEN TREATISE
VVHERE IN ARE EVI-
DENTLY DECLARED THE
ABHOMINABLE·LIVES OF
the chiefe pellars of the newe Gospell,
their pestilent doctrine, their Incalling
of Sathan and conference·vvith him,
vvhereby they shevve them selues
Iaolaeers, lastly vvee shevve
hovv their abhominable lines
and pestiferous doctrine.

Lead Ignorant soules to manifest Infidelitie and
Euindnta perdition.

OF LVTHERS *abhominable life and*
pestiferous doctrina.
CHAP. 1

TO Beginne first at their
patriarch Luther you must
vnderstand that he was a
Monke and prossed Frier
of the order of S. Augusti-
ne, Ingendred (as Lindanus writteth)
by a Deuill called Incubus transformed
in the shape of a man.

This forelorne man did breath his 3.
Religous vewes made to God pouertie
chastitie and obedience for the disordained loue he bare to honours, riches and
volpties of this word.

He confesseth that Sathan did teach
him that the Messe was but Idolatrie &
Euill of it selfe for thus he writteth in his
booke Intitituled de *Missa priuata et vn-*
ctione Sacerdotum tom 7. *vvitinberg anno*
1558. saying: contigit me semel sub ne-
diam noctem subito Expergefieri Ibi Sathan mecum cœpit huiusmodi disputationem, audi Inquit
Luthere Doctor perdocte, nosti enim te quindecim
annis Celebrasse Missas priuatas horrenda essent
Idolatria, quid si Ibi non adfuisset Corpus &
Sanguis Christi sed tantum Panem et vinum ado-
rasses et alis adhærandum proposuisses: Cui Ego
Respondi sum vnctus Sacerdos accepi vnctionem et consecrationem ab Episcopo.

That is to say: it hapned me once about
midnight to be suddenly awakned out
of my sleepe, there Sathan begoud
this disputation with me. heare me (
said he) most learned Doctour Luther,
thou knoewest thou hast al most daylie
Celebrated Masses these 15 yeerce by
past? what yf such priuie Masses were
horible Idolatrie? what yf the Bodie &

bloo d

Blood of Chriſt were not reallie there, but only that thou dideſt adore bread and wine, & offer the ſame to by adored by others? whome to I did anſwere, that I was a Prieſt, and that I hade reciued vnction & conſecration from a Biſhope.

after theſe words Luther reharſeth the arruments which Sathat did bring in to diſprooue the Maſſe, and that the Prot-ſtarts peruſe to day for the ſame effect. this is the cauſe wherefore I can not Eſteeme but good of the Maſſe ſeeing that Sathan (which euery where doth procure the damenation of man) did diſprooue the ſame.

Now good Reader thou mayeſt eaſily ſurmiſe how this woe:ull Prophete of the Proteſtants was ſend by Sathan to diſturbe and vexe the Church of God with his hereſies and not from Ieſus Chriſt to reſrome the ſame.

He confeſſeth that he did withſtand and reſiſt his conſcience the ſpace of ten yeeres to giue aſſent to his erroneous doctrine which he did learne from Sath-an and did perſuad his Bretheren of VVitemberge to doe the ſame in aboliſ-hing the Maſſe.

Beholde this foreſworne Monke enne-mie

lib. de ſeruo ar-bitrio. Tom. 2. Luther fighteth agamſt his o ven conſciēce

Ennemie to truth condemneth as S. paul
sayeth by his proper Iudgment and light
of his owen conscience.

VVhat edification, may you receiue
by his Example, but to learne from him
to with ftond our owen consciennce
when wee haue any Euill tourne to doe.

He confesseth that he was mooued
with hatred and Enuy to depairt from
the Romaine Church, becaufe the promulgation of the Indulgences was not
graunted to the Religious order of S.
Auguftine.

he confesseth that he was citizen of
the Romaine Church and after his dep-
airting thence he sheweth not to what
Church he did retire, but grauntetd that
he was that time him felfe alone. Thus
Luther was in no Church at all.

*In prnfat
Tom. I.*

He confesseth that he was mooued to
Excogitate new Errours againft the
doctrine of the Romaine Church for
the great hatred he bare againft the
Pope of Rome.

He teacheth in his cõmentaies vpon
the. 50. of Genefis that yf the wyfe re-
fufe to come the hand maid fhalbe welcome a fine Example of Edifitation to
all fuch as are prone to abufe weemen by
their

*in cõment
in cap.
30. gsnef
pag. 455*

their wedded wiues.

Luther graunteth that yf he hade bene *his infidelitie* in the time of the Patriarch Noe that he *Tom. 6.* wold not haue beleeued God threatning *cöment in* the destruction of the world by the gen-*cap. 7.* erall flood, *Genes.*

Luther confesseth that he did hate *pag. 105* God in his heart, beholding the seuiritie of his Iustice in the punition of sinners. *præfat.*

Luther confesseth in his dispate at *Tom. 2.* Lipsia against Doctour Eckius before *his batred agaiñst God* the Duke of Saxonie that his purpose *ed agai-* was not begune for the reuerence of God *nst God* nor yet should end for his hónour.

Luther confesseth that he could no more stay him selfe from venus game then he could doe from spittinh,

This apostata Frier againe did rate him elfe so much that he thought no shame b say that a Thousand Cyprians and a Thousand Augustins were not to be bmpared to him in doctrine belonging b Saluation.

To shewe that he did climbe to the ɔpe of pride he thought no shame to y with a braisen front that he wold ɔt admite the Angells of Heauen to be dges to his doctrine althought he was ached by Sathan (according to his
owen

owen confeſſion) to abrogate the Maſſe

Thus good Reader thou mayeſt eaſily ſurmie whether this new Goſpeller was rulled with the humble Spirit of Chriſt or by the the proud Spirit of Sathan.

Luther writteth againe that good workes make no man good nor Euil workes make no man Euill, and that no ſinne how great ſo euer it be can condemne the man but only Infidelitie.

Luther writtetg againe: let vs take heede to keepe our ſelues from ſinne, but much more from good workes. beholde the councell of this new Euangeliſt to be altogether Sathanicall.

As concerning his auditours he confeſſeth that they are more auaritious vnmercifull, luxurius, ſtubborne vnGodly, and much more worſe ſince the time that the light of the Goſpell was reuealled vnto them, then men were in the time of Pope rie. Muſculus lib. de Prophetia Chriſti: and fmidelinus con clhiſ. 4. de Planetis Errantibus affirmee the ſame.

Laſtly he affirmeeth with Caluin that all the workes of Iuſt men are but deedly ſinnes. ſo according to Luthers & Caluins doctrine and Theologie it is all

lik

ike to be faithfull and deceitfull, to giue
Almes to a poore man and spoile hem of
his goods, to sleepe with his owen wife
r his nigbours, for so much that all the
worxes of lust men are but deadly sinnes,
nd their faith so Effectuall in Christ
hat it shall blotte all thir sinnes away (
they say) with the twinckling of on
ye.

when Luther did Endeuour him selfe
o driue away an vncleane spirit out of
possessed person, the Deuill terrified
m in such a fashion that he was cons-
ained to take the flight him selfe, and
ue his owen life from the daunger of
at Deuill. Staphilus his Disciple as he
we this miracle did wrote the apolog 2
And to confirme this pestiferous doc-
ine disordained life, and leud maners
eadfull death did come to him (after
: was well whitled and drunke of the
pper before) so suddenly in lying in
s bedde, to charge him to compeare
fore the fearefull Iudgment of Cod
make account of his works, that he
de not time & space to cry for meicy
his sinres, as sundrie Autors worthie
credence wrote of his finall end.

o yf Sathon hade come out of hell in
the

the shape of a man to preach in a pulpit
as Ministers doe what greater shewe
reason could he haue sette doune to giu
the raines of licentius libertie to th
vnruilled nature of man to deliuer th
selues to all kind of vncleannesse, I
nominie, malice wickednesse Enu
mischiefe murther contétion, trecheri
murmuring, backbiting, pride, dissen
tion, dissobediencc, crudelitie, and
other sinnes of like kind, and since pe
suade sillie soules that their only faith
Christ shall deface & put away all the
fromer and suchlike other sinnes in th
moment of an houre.

This is the Edification which Eue
one may learne as much from the doc
rine of Luther as from his former life.

Thus much of Luther Patriarch to
Protestants.

OF CALVINS ABHOMI
ABLE LIFE AND PEST
FEROVS DOCTRINE.

VVhat Edification and Instruction Each
may receiue from the vvholesome doctrine
and morall life of Caluin Paterne of
Perfeaion to the Puritans.

CHAP. 2

E Fore all things you muſt vnderſtand that Caluin was Borne in a Towne of France in the Prouince of Picardie alled Noyon in the yeere of God. 1599.

He was a great blaſphemer of the lame of God in his youth.

Being a ſtudent and promoted to a Cure and Chappell he was ſurpriſed in he abhominable ſinne of Sodomie, wherefore he was marked on the ſholder with an Brunt yron in the forme n Floure delyce.

Caluin being ſo defamed as much for iis bougrie as for peinition thereof by an brunt yron, he become ſacriegious n ſalling his benifice, and after went to Geneua Changing his Name from Cauing to Caluin to the end that his Infamous life ſhould not be knowen by he title of his proper name.

So ſoone as he did arriue in Geneua Incotinenent he ſtrred vp a great ſedition betwen the Miniſters and Citizens of the Towne.

For his ſedition he was Caſt in banihment and by his ſecreete Craft receued in the Towne of Geneua againe.

Of 4. thouſand franks which he did receue form the Queene of Nauarre and

two

two thousand Crownes from Monsieur
Dauid de Haynault, with much more
from sundrie others to diftibute to the
poore he did Iudas like, keepe the gra-
aeft part for his owen cōmoditie and
Impairt the reft to his owen frinds, and
corrupt some of Coūcell to aff.ft hisEnt-
erpryse againft all such as did oppone
them felues to his croftie defings and
Malitious attempts, & when the poor
Necessitous did Murmure againft hi
vngodly dealing, he caused them be caf
in banifhment, as libertins and vngodly
Chriftians.

Caluin likewife gaue councell to on
called Nicolas de ferre banquerupt t
buy with 3. Tphoufand pounds he had
in his hands Innobile goods in th
Name of his wife and Daughters, an
fo him felfe being difpoffeffed of a
fubftance his creditors fhould find n
way to conftraine him to pay the
whome to he was detfull.

Thus to receiue their cōmunion wor
hily it is not needefull to reftore or
Nighbeors goods but to defraude hi
yf wee may (according to Caluins co
ncell) for our owen cōmoditie.

Caluin gaue not this councell f
nought for this banquerupt did acknn
wled

cknowledg hes beneuolence in this ehalfe with an fomme of money, and Married one of his daughters with Calins Brother.

VVhen Caluins friends offred them elues to bring a young prouincell whih hade taken from him the the value f 4. thoufand franks after he hade fered Caluin a long time, Caluin wold ote, Condifcend the they fhould paine hem felues in that matter, which made anie fufpect that he feared the young ans accufation yf hc hade beene brouht againe to haue abufed him in the nne of Sodomie according to his olde uftome.

Caluins pride and ambition was fo great hat he wold fuffer no companion at all, Therefore the Church of Berne Nigh to Geneua, did call him by contumelie and lockrie, the Pope of Geneua.

Caluins pride and ambition was fo reat that he thought no fhame to fay penly in his preachings that he was a aophete, that he was Endued with the pirit of God, that he was fend by the ord, that he could not Erre or ftray om the truth, and yf Incace (faide he I fpeake any thing aftray it is thou o

Lord

Lord that deceiueth me, and maketh
me to Erre for the sinnes of the people

There neuer was a holy Doctour of
the Church of God that did boaſt and
brage of ſuch perfections & prerogatiue
of Grace as this ſhameleſſe Sodomite &
malitious hypocrite doth.

VVhen a Citizen of Geneua had
ſaide to his friend that they Eſteemed
more of Caluin then by good Reaſon
they ſhould doe, he could neuer be con
tented with that citizen called Pete
Amy vntill the time he ſhould be caſt in
Priſon, and thereafter come ſhirte alon
with a Light Taper or Torch in his hand
and cry him mercy before the whole
world with ſuch amend honorable.

VVhen ſome of his frends did aeprotch
him to haue pulled done the Image of
our Lord our Ladie and holy Saincts in
Heauen, and ſuffer his owen Image to
be ſette vpon publipue places of the
Towne, and to be hanged about the
necks of ſundry Inhabitants of Towne
he anſwered without any conrteſſie ſay
ing: let all ſuch as miſlike ſuch thing
burſt for malice.

VVhen he went out of Geneua to
viſic the Church of Beane, he did Ryde
vpon

vpon a Gailziart Steede accompained
with 25. or 30. horsemen well Armed
with their Pistolets like Capitaains of
warre, aud not like a Prophete or one
of Christs Apostles.

VVhen Caluin did persuade sillie
poore man for a litle some of siluer to
faine him selfe to be dead, and sine to
arise at his praiers before all the people
when he did praie God. cry vpon the
sillie poore man for to arise at his praiere
& to confirme the truth of his Euangell,
the siillie abused man was found dead in
deede, and so Caluin to confirme his
Religion did kill a quicke man when
the holy saincts of the Romaine Church
to confirme the Catholiqne Romaine
Religion by manie other miarcles did
often times restore by their holy prayers
he life agains to such as were truly depairted out of this world.

Caluin also stirred vp with pride and
imbition and vains Gloire that he could
ieur to his contentment be sufficiently
ionnored vntill the time he did writ
etteres and frame sundrie workes whe-
ein he dmit nothing that might aduace
t extoll his dwen honour and sette thes
vorks out to the whole world in the Ne-
ies of others to hide in this behalfe his
                                    sused

rufed tre cherie and deeite.

Caluin was fo proud in his owen conceite that he did not only preferre himfelfe to all the heretiques of his time. but alfo to the aneient Fatheres as acconnting nothing of their authoritie, he wold bring in his owen fentence with a maiefticall authoritie againft the holy Dectours faying Anguftine fayeth this Hierome fayeth that. *Sed Ego Vero*, as yf he hade beene the Meffias difputing againft the Iewes.

Cap. 13.

All fuch as did profeffe this new Relihion could doe Caluin no greater pleafour to purchaffe his friendfhipe, then to call him often times to dinner and fupper, where all kind of daintie meats were in aboundance, which forme of life made many poore Indigent to murmure againft his gluttonie of their carnall Gofpeller.

Cap. 14.

His Siluer Flagons with fineft wines, his bread compounded with fine floure, rofe watter Sugare Cannell & Annlfeeds were euerie where carried about with him to ferue for his dainti mouth.

cap. 14.

Since the begining of the world it was neuer hard or feene that anie of the Prophets fend from God, or Apoftles from
Chrift

Chrift did feede fo daintily as Monfieur Caluin did great Prophete of the fouri-tans, and Cherift him felfe as he did in the promulgation of his fenfuall Gofpell for he did deuore and fwallowe doune more fugred confits of Portugall and Spaine both drie and mole then manie poore fillie foules could find morfells of bread for the conferuation of this their mortall life.

Of Caluins fodomie wee haue made mention before. as concerning his Im-puidicitie there was a great murmure & flaunder of fundrie Dames and Damo-fells which did haunt familiarly with him with out any companie except a litle Infant leding in their hands, and fome times he take lodging with the faireft Damofell when her hufband wos away, and the hand maid benifhed away, be-caufe fhe faid that the print of tow perf-ons was left in the bedde after, the vpr-ifing from him of her Miftreffe. *cap.* **15.**

Caluin gaue concell to Madame Iolland de Breed to lit her hufband pine away in his difeafe witholding from him fuch things as were neceffarie for his conuale-fcens, with promife to Marie her after his death, which counfoull made the noble

noble Dame to despite him and retired
her selfe and her husband out of the
Towne of Geneua.

Because that no man in the Towne of
Genenua did oppose him selfe to Caluins
vngodly practises but the Gouernour of
the Towne called Amy Perin, he did
Imagine sundrie strategems & treasona-
ble attempts against the Gouernour,
Either to beraue him of his life or than at
the least to cast him in Banishment, which lastly he did obtane persuading falsly
the Gentle men of Frence (which were
retired to Geneua for Religio... ...use)
that the Gouernour hade cospired their
death, who with the concurrance of Caluin and his faction constrained the
that Gouernour to saue his life from
their dauger, retiring him selfe to Bern
adiaent to the lands of Geneua, in this
seditionc coused by him he made sundri
young men to lose ther liues against th
lawfull order of Iustice

OF Caluins horrible discases in his laiter day
and Execrable Death.

CAluin in hie latter dayes was by th
Iust Iudgment of Cod punishibe
with

with horrible diseases & desperate death
for his blasphemous heresies, deceitfull
hypocrisies, and Execrable life, for
Theodore Beza writteeh that he was
heauily troubled with a consumption of
the lungs, with the crampe, collicke,
difficulte of the breath, the Stonie Gra-
uell, the Gutte, hemoirods or bloodie
fluxe, the Migrame or Ache in the head,
besids these euills written by Beza, he
was cruellie tormeted with the lousie
euill the through the whole bodie, a wir-
ulent and stinching ver in the fondam-
ent, and his secreete Members cõsumed
with crewling or creeping wormes, as
Antioehus herods enemies to God were
berefte of this mortall life by consumption crewsinh or creeping worms which
did creepe like swarmes of Bees plentif-
ully abroad out of their bodies.

Mach.
99. act.
12. 23.

He was so painefull, and troublesome
to him selfe, and priuie Seruants by the
Execrable stinch of his corrupted bodie
that no man was able to abide the pestilent puanture of the same therefore he
gaue a straite cõmand that no man should gette entresſ to visie him.

He likewise was so Impatient to suffer
the great griefe, and Intollereble paine
of

E

of so manifolde diseases. which he did
feele deriue from the weightie hand of
the dreadfull Iustice of God without any
hope of mercie (as his finall end doth
testifie) that he did Incall the Deuills,
sweare disperatly detast and curse the
day and time which he did bestowe
to the knowledye of letters and setting
out of Bookes.

Now Gentle Reader beholde the
desperate end of a malitious heretique,
a trecherous Impostour and cruell killer
of mens souls worthie and conformable
of his pestiferous doctrine deceitfull
hypocrisies, and abhominable life.

Hieronimus Bollecus phisition of
Lyons affirmeth to haue heard with his
proper Eares, these things of Caluins
ouen priuie Seruants which did serue
him vnto his latter end.

Now let vs beholde Edification and
Instruction wee may receiue of his blasphemous doctrine which he writteth
against Christ our Sauoiour and Rede-
mptour.

Before all things he maketh God the
cause & author of all mischeefe hynous
Cryms & sinnefull acts by men comitted
in this world, and lay all the blame and
Charge

Charge vpon God firſt author & cauſe
of the ſame according to his doctrine,
for thus he writteth in his Inſtitutions: *lib. 1.*
man by the Iuſt Enforcing of God doth *Inſt cap.*
that thing which is not leſſe to him do. *18. ſect.*

Caluin writteth againe: that men doe *4.*
nothing but that which God hath decre-
ed with him ſelf and apporuted to be *lib. 1.*
done by his ſecreete direction. *Inſt. cap.*

Eurthermore he writteth: I omit the *18. ſect.*
generall concurrace of God whereby
each creature is vpholden and retauneth *1.*
ſtrainth to effectuat all thigs, which they
doe, I ſpeake of that only action where- *lib. 2.*
by each miſdeede may be aſcribed to *Inſt. cap.*
God, to Sathan, and to man without *4. ſect. 2*
amie abſurditie or Inconuonrencie.

Here Genitle Reader thou ſhalt morke
how Caluin aſeribeth each miſdeede as
much to God as he douh to Sathan or *lib. 1.*
to man. *Inſt. cap.*

He writteth yet more blaſphemouſly *18. ſect.*
of God ſaying: Sathan is ſaid to deceiun
and Inchant the minds of Infidells, but *2.*
whence is that vnleſſe the efficacie of
Errour deriue from God him ſelfe.

Marke here good Reader according
to Caluins doctrine that God worketh
in to the minds of men the Efficacie of
error and althought Caluin maketh Sa-

Sathan

Sathan the Inftrument, yet he maketh
God the cheefe caufe of this mifcheefe
and not Sathan and much leffe the will
of mortall man.

Caluin writteth alfo both blafphemoufly and without all reuerence or fere of
cap 2.17. our Lord thar he did vtter the words of
defpeartiō vpō the croffer & to be much
lib 2. cap. affrayed to be condamned for Euer.
Inft. fect Behold the blafphemie which this
16. malitious herctique writteth againft
Luc. 22. Chrift our Sauconr, which was as fure
69. of his owen Saluation as he was fure that
Ihon 9. he was the natuarall Sonne of God and
37. that he was to come with great Maieifte,
accompained with his Angells at the
letter day to Iudge the quicke and the
mat. 24. dead, and that his Kingdome was in the
30. fuc. other world to come.
24. 26. Thus Caluin made the Prince of
Ihon. 18. Patience and Magnanimitie, (which
26. giueth ftrainth force and courage to all
the Martoirs of the world) to faint
doubt and dfpaire of his owen Saluation
in the time of his owen Martiredome.

VVhat other thing can Caluins breth
fmell in thefe and fuchlike words, but
Godiffe Infidelitie to make men thinke
by fuch leud reafons that Chrift can not
be

e accompted natnrell Sonne of God in
uch a feruile feare & curfed defperatiō.

Likewife Caluin doth not only take
way the Fathers Limbe & Purgatorie,
which lowe places of Eartd he calleth
aine Imaginations, fained deuifes and
uerile fables, but alfo he doth (againſt
he Expeſte word of God) take cleane
way the burnig fire of hell, affirming
ieretically (efter his olde cuſtome)
hat the paines of hell are no other thing
ut a forrowfull Anguifh of the Soule
nd terrour of the mind whereby Eche
ian doth feele God wrethfull & angrie
gainſt him, as Chriſt him felfe did Ex-
eriment yet in this mortall life whan
ie was hanging on the Croſſe; which
ierefie was long agoe condamned in
rigmes. as witneſſeth S. Hierome. *Epiſt
d Auitum.*

Thus Caluins doctrine can not tend
o any other fcope to make God author
if iinne, Chriſt to doubt of his Saluatiō
nd difpaire at the houre of death, and
o take away the burning fire of Hell
Prepared for the vngodly, but to driue
ilhe Soules from the true Religion to
atheifene and Godleſſe Infidelitie.

lib. 2.
Inſt. cao.
16 *ſect.*
3. *mat.*
23. 41.
lib. 2.
Inſt. crp.
16. *ſect.*
10.

NOVV LET VS CONSIDE[
vvhat Inftruction and Edification vvee may
receiue from tbe life and doctrine of Zuinglius Prifh Prienft of Zuricke to vvne in
the Heluetian countrie of Tinurie.

CHAP. III.

AS concerning Zuinglius Parif
Prieft of Zuricke Meitrpolita
Towne of the Heluetian Countrie c
Tignrie, he did Exchange his mee
Prieftly dignitie with the fieirce offic
of an Souldier, and laftly was Killed i
warre.

He writteth him felfe (as Luthe
doth) to haue learned his doctrine fror
a Spirit in the Night, but he did nc
Know (fayeth he) whether this Spir:
was blacke or white which did teac
him Berangarius herifie Entombed lon
before, that Chrifts Bodie was not rea
lie in the Sacraament.

This Luinolius Patriarch to all th
Puritans writteth blafphemoufly tha
God is author of finne, for thefe be h
words: *Numen Ipfum eft author eft Eu
quod in nobis eft Iniuftura.* God him felfe
anthor of that thing which is Iniquit
and Iniuftice in vs.

le wiritteth likewise, that God enforc-
h men to homicide adulterie, and to
other naughtie, deeds which be wro-
h in this world.

Behold here good Reader the edific-
ion & Inftruction which all vngodly
en may learne from Zuinglius and
luin, Prince of all Puaitans to Excufe
eir finnes, when they cõmit thift, ho-
icide, Adulterie or any other nanghtie
ede faying that they can not withfta-
l the will of God, which Enforceth
em to doe all Euill deeds,

٦E *Abbominable life aud blafpemous doc-*
trine of Theodore Beza.

CHAP. IIII.

٦HEODORE BEZA Borne
in vezile Towne of France, being
tudent as forelorne fóne, was wholly
nt to lead a licertious and riotous life
the Towne of Parifh and Orleance
pinn veerely 700 crownes of the be-
ice of the Catholique Church, which
wothily he did fpend in this fafhion
ntioned before.

You fhall not find fince the memorie
man, a more vncleane, lafciuious and
fhamleffe

fhamleffe peete than he was, which hath tranfgr
efed the bounds & limits of all honeftie, as muc₁
in his naughtie words as in abhominable deeds
for that could not afford him contentmet t₁
abufe his bodie with other mans wyfe calle b₁
proper Name was called Claudiae, and in th
abhominable finne of Sodomie with abeutiful
young man calld Audebert, Vnleffe hade proc
laiued his Execrable finnes vnto the whole worl
in his booke of Epigrames.

T H E Epigrame vvhich he diē compound in the proife a₁
commenodatioon of condida the Taylers vyfe and
Audcbert his fellovv- Sodomite

A BEST *Candida, Beza quid moratis?*
Audebertus abeft, quid hic moraris?
Tenent parafij tuos amores
Habent aurelij tuos lepores
Et'tu vezeliis manere pergis
Procul Candidula amoribufque
Et leporibus audebertuloque.
Immo vezelij procul valete
Et vale pater et valete fratres
Namque vezelijs carere poffum
Et carere parente, et hic et Illis
At non Candidula Audebertuloque
Sed vtrum rogo preferam duorum?
Vtrum Inuifere me decet priorem
An quenquam tibi Candida Anteponam
Au quenquam Anteferam tibi audeberte

uid Si me Ingeminas secem Ipse partes
Harum vt altera Candidam reuisat
urrat altera versus Audebertum

At est Candida sic auara noui
t totum cupiata tenere Bezam.

Sic Bezæ est cupidus suj audebertus
za vt Gestiat Integro potiri.

Amplector quoque sic et hunc et Illam
totus cupiam videre vtrumque

Integrisq; fruj Integer duobus
æferre attamen alterum necesse est

O Duram Nimium necessitatem.
d postquam tamen alterum necesse est

Priores tibi defero Audeberte
uod Si Candida forte conqueratur,
uid tum Basiolo tacebit Imo.

Thus his Epigrame may be Englished.

) Beza why doost thou nowe make bide
From Candida, which should lye the beside
d Audebert a youth of comely grace
Vhome thou behind with Ioy did oft Imbrce
r Parish dotd containe thy paramours
And orleance the lillie of thy floures
vezile why thy Fathers duelling place
oost thou remaine ferre from the Gentle face
f Candida and Audebert thy Ioy,
Vhose felloweshipe dotd keepe me from anoy
ewell vezile my Mothers hatlhing nest

F

My Father and my Brotheren with the rest
  Your harbour now I Easily may want
My Parents and my Bretheren as I graunt
  But Candida and Audeberr by night
I may not want my haly hearts delight
  But of thele tow, which should I in this cace
Now tirst goe fee molt fweerely to Embrace
whome in this world fall I preferre to the
  My candida this time to p eafour me
Or yet to the fueil of n y fire
  Eaire Audebert my only hearts defire
VVhat yf I should deuide this corps of mine
  In Egall pairts which dotd to both Incline
VVherreof the one with carefull diligence
  Should quicxlie Ioy my Candidas prefence
The other fhould goe runne without a mifle
  To Audebert his daintie Lippes to kifle
Yet Candida molt cupid as I knowe
  Doth wifh my curps al whole and fhe below
And Audebert a greedie wanton boy
  VVold quicklie ftriue while Beza to Enioy
But with my heart I wold them thus Embrace
  That with Eche I might whole be in Eche pla
But I accunt an hard neceftitie
  One to preferre in pleafnt voluptie
To the other in this checrefull delight
  Yf I might both Embrace the winters night
But fith the force of cruell deftinie
  Doth me conftraine with fuch neceitie
That the one to other I muft preferre

To feede my luſt where pleaſantly I Erre
To Audebert the honour I will ycet
who doth adorne the flours of venus ſielde
Yſ Candida for this act will complaine
ſhe laſtly muſt her ſelfe from Sighs reſraine
    So Endeth Bezas Epigrame.

Here good Reeder you may ſee how Beza
ſiporteth him ſelfe in proclaiming his owen
bhöinable deeds to the whole world as an forel-
ane man without all feare of God in his conſcince and worldly ſhame before the Eyes of men.

So foone as Bezas booke of Epigrams com to
ne light he was ſümoned to compeare before the
ords of Seſſion at Pariſh and to Interprete his
pigrame compounded by him in the praiſe of
ndida the Taylers wyfe & Andebert his ſellowe
domite.

Beza knowing that the due punition of ſuch
ne was nothing leſſe then his life, he ſette his
miſice for the ſpace of ſiue yeers to one ſecre-
ly, and to ane other ſold it out at the ground,
d ſo tooke the ſlight to Geneua, where he was
ade Caluins Diſciple and ſucceſſour·

The Taylers wyfe by him called canedida
uld not content him being Minſter in Geneua.
leſſe he corrupted a virg in ſeruin him in the
uſe called Claudia whome to after the conce-
d he gaue a poyoned drinke to kill the Child
the womans Belly. ſo this Euangeliſt did maxe

domie and account to cōmith homicide, sodomi
and perpetuall adulerie.

The yeere of God 1560 Caluin and Beza witl
an other called ottaman conspired amongst then
selues with their assistance to Massacre the Kin
of France called Frances, the Quneene his Mot
her Queene Marie his wife daughter to Iame
the 5 King of Scotland, the King of Franc
Brother, the Lords then remaining in Court an
the good Magistrats. Thete be the fruits of thei
carnall Gospell.

As concerning Bezas doctrine he maxeth Go
author of sinne, as Caluin did teach before hi
for thus writteth: *oportut Ergo. &* It behoued Go
to open vp and ditclose that only way to him sel
which is the ordaine the fall of Adam and agai
Querenda est vtn orige wee must research the origi
all of sinne in the voluntarie motion of Instrum
nts whereby God hath luit y decreede that wor
which men doe vniustly; but then u willt say, th
could not resist the will of God, I graunt it is tr
(said Beza) their will could no otherwise doe

Thus yf the will of man be constrained to d
al naughtie deeds wrought in this world, as B
teacheth vs the man may purge him selfe of
sinnes cōmitted by him and lay the charge vp
God which constraineth him to worke the san
for as S. Austgstine sayeth: no man sinneth in tl
which he is constrainetu to doe by necssitie otl

W

wise Beasts, fooles madman and Infants without
Iudgment or Reason, should be guiltie of sinne
in the behalse, be hold now Reader the good
Edification which thou may'st reape from Bezaes
abhominable life & blasphemous doctrine against
the goodnesse of God in making him the chiefe
cause and author of sinne.

OF Bucerus *an Dominican Frier.*

CHAP. V.

Bucerus wus a foresworne Monke Dominican
frier Master to Ihon Caluin Infected with Luthers heresie, since with Zuinglius pestierous docr-
ine, which affirmeth with Caluin that Baptisme
is not necessarie to Saluation, and that Christs
Bodie is not reallie in the Sacrament.

Lastly he recanted these Errours and become
a Lutheran agine, he Expyred his furthast braith
in England, and at the houre of his death he
affirmed that Christ was not the true Messias, but
that wee should abide an other,

OF Carolrstdins *Priest*

CHAP. VI.

Carolastadius Priest and Archdeacon o
VVitemberge (who was the first of Ecclesiasticall dignitie in our time which Ioyned hem-
selfe to a Sacrilegious wyfe by the persuasion of
Luther) was banished out of all the Iurisdiction
of Saxonie and thus contemnead both by Catholiques & Lutherans for his vnGodly Imperhectiós
he

he was the first renuer of Berengarius hersie in our time Luther in Colloquns Mensalibus, fol. 367. and Erasmus Alberus Lutheran writ that he was taught and possessed with a Deuiill,

OF *œcelampadius monke*

CHAP. VII.

Ecolampadius a foresworne Monke did Sacrilegiously against his 3. Vowes of pouertie, Chastitie, and obedience Ioyne him selfe to a wife and lanstly for punition of his Sacriledge was found dead in his Bedde and as Luther sayeth he was killed by Sathans firie darts others affirme that he was put to death by his Sacrilegius wyfe others ascertaine that he did kill him selfe with his owen hande.

SIR IHON kNOX *life, the false Apostle of Scolland Extracted out of M. Nicoll Burns disputation and approoued by other Oculare vatnessis vvhich vvere liuing in his teme.*

CHAP. VIII.

SIR Ihon Knox a renegat Priest of the Towne of Hadintowne in Scotland was Incensed with the burning lust of the flesh, as the Prophete Danielf did foretell, 12. 37. that all feare of God and honnour of the world sette asside did thinke no shame at all to polute his Fathers bedde, in comitting horrible Incest with his owen Mother

in

n lawe in an cordnexill who being Excōmuni-
ated by his owen Bihope for such an horrible
rime, did in deipight by his Bilhope and censure
ised againſt him, foreſaixe at once his Prieſtly
dignitie and ſanction with the Catholeque Religion and ſo be come an heretique.

Thus as S. Paul ſayet. 1. Tim. 1 10 hauing ban-
iſhed away good conſcience from him ſelfe did
make ſhipe wrake of his faith, which looſe of
conſcience and corruption of life is alwiſe the begining of hereſie.

After that he did foreſaixe the mexeneſſe of
Priſthood, he become a cruell actour and conſpi-
ratour of the Cardinall Beatons deatd which was
cruellie Murthered by our heretiques firſt plāters
of this carnall Goſpell in Scotland, when the
Caſtell of S. Androwes was taken from our heretiques which did hold the ſame by force Againſt
the Queenes Maieſtie, Knox with the reſt of the
heretiques conſpiratours of the ſaid Cardinalls
death, were alſo taken by the frincemen. and
condemned as Slaues vnto the Galleyes.

Knex at the laſt by ſome quyet conuoy beirg
ſette at libertie from Galley Slauene went vnto
Englandwhere he did lerne the artie of Necromancie for better aduanceēt of his carnall Goſpell

The Earle of Murray in the meane ſeacn ceirg
in England, Knox did enter in conference with
him at S. Pauls Church in London, where he did
per

perſuade the ſaid Earle that God hade choſen him to be King of Scotland to Roote out Idolatrie, Eſtabliſh the light of their Goſpell and that he as a new Ioſias ſhould mantaine and defend ſir Ihon Knox the new Helias againſt all Catholique Paſtours which he calletd the Prieſts of Baal, and liekwiſe the Queens Maieſtie which he Nickna. med Ieſabeli.

VVhich things to performe and atchiue he ſette out his booke Intituled, the blaſt of the Trompet againſt the Regiment of weemen attempting therely to ſpoile the Queenes Maieſtie with all ther peſteritie of their Regall Diademe and heriatle of the the Kingdome of Scotland & ſo at one time did Endeuoure him ſelfe to Plant a falſe Renigion for a true and to Inſtall an vnlawfull King for an lawfull Princeſſe in the Realme of Scotland.

This was the Sound Intention & whole drifte of this falſe Prophete with the reſt of his ſeditious Miniſters to ouerthrowe the Spirituall and temporall Eſtate in the Realme of Scotland at one time.

This forelorne Prieſt retourning from England to Scotland againe did perſuade a Married woman with her daughter to foreſaike her haſband to follcw him, and thus ſhamefullie, !Sacrilegiouſly, and Inceſtuouſly, ſeale and proper fruits of their Carnall Gopell.

Aſte

After the death of that adulteresse he being an
ld decreeped Priest at the pits brinke he did ryde
pon a prettie Guelded horse with his Silken
carfe adorned with an Golden Ring & Pretious
tones, as yf he hade beene a young Springall and
vanton youth: an Euident Signe of an meere
vorlding full of bold presumption & Diabolicall
ride

He did also wooe an Gentle woman of the house
f Ochiltrie to Marrie in this princely forme, and
Enchant her so by his Deuillish Arte of necrom-
ncie that he did appeare to this young Gentle-
voman not in his owen shape, an olde decreeped
Priest, but as a young Strypling most beutifull to
eholde & site to fight courgiously in Venus siield
nd so did Incense such an disordained loue in hir
leart towards him selfe, that she could nowise
iue or take repose without his accursed Societie.

All the world beholding her to be a beutifull,
raue and pleasant Damosell, and Knox to be but
n olde decreeped priest of an base and obscure
ondition and of Ignoble blood, they could not
Ascribe the cause of that vehement affection.
which she did beare to such decreeped Priest but
iis Dueillish Arte of Sorcerie or Necromancie.
whereby he did bewitch the young Gentle woman
in such fashion that she could not behold the shame
ind disgrace, which she did Incurre, when she did
linke her selfe in Marriage with such a renegate
Priest

G

Prieſt and Ignoble perſon as Knox was in verie
deede.

The progreſſe of his life did ſhewe theſe thing
to be moſt true when an young wōan in the Lord
Ochiltries houſe almoſt did looſe hir life for feare
when ſhe did eſpy thraugh an clift or bore in the
doore Sathan in ſhape of a blacke men in quyer
conference ſpeaking with Knox, which was the
blacke Doctour and Maſter of Schoole whom
froe he did learne his leſſon, as much in Sorcerie
& Necromancie as in the Preaching of his carnal
Goſpell.

A Gentle woman worthie to be beleeued in thi
behalfe did ſee Knox face toure in his necke duri
ng the time of his Preaching in S. Gils Church a
Edinbrugh as truly She did relate vnto me.

As the Arrians did not ſkare with the Doctrin
of Arrians when he did ſhute his Entralls in th
Iacks with the looſe of his life publickly: Euenſ
the puritans are not affrayed at the doctrine o
Knox which was damnad by God with ſuch
Monſtrous prodige as the doctrine of Arrius w
in ages long before.

Laſtlly when he at the houre of death did aſſu
his Bretheren that the olde Religion ſhould ari
againe, they ſaide that he did but dotte and rat
in ſuch ſpeaches as a man be ſtraught in mind
Anſwerred to them ſaying : to the end you m
beleeue ſuch things to be true as I haue foretol
yo

ou, goe you Incontinently out of the house
vhere I doe lye and when you retourne in againe
ou shall find my words to be confirmed with a
rodigous signe after they hade performed his will
n this behalfe as he hade desired them to doe,
intring in the house againe where they did
eaue him giuing vp the Ghost, they did find all
he lights Extinguished and Knox him selfe lying
old dead on the floore and his face tourned in
iis Necke. This is the prodidgious end which
his forelorne Priest did make most worthie of his
leserts.

The young man which did serue him vnto his
itter end, did, relate all these things to a Gentle
nan of Estate worthie of credence which did
eherse these thinga as most true vnto his frinds as
hey are tecited abue.

) F M. *Ihon Craige a foresvvorne Dominican frier Minister*
to his Maiestie.

CHAP. IX

laister Ihon Craige apostata Frier Minister to
King Iames the sixt of Scotland, minded to retn-
irne to his Monastrie (being at time in Italie)
or laike of Moyen, after he did foresaike the same
onfesseth that the Deuill in the shape of a blacke
logge meete him passing through Italie with a
)ursefull of Gold hanging at his Necke which he
did

take from Sathan. So by the helpe of Sathan he
did continue in his apoſtuſſie and hereſie of our
New Goſpel to his liues end. Nicol Burne in his
diſputation againſt the the Miniſters of Scotland
cap. 34. pag. 175. for good angells did neuer
aeare in the ſhape of Doggs or Baſts, as the Deuill
haue doue ſeuerall times as wee Read in the liue
of holy Saincts, but in the ſhape of men Geneſ. 18
2. 19. 5. Ioſue 5. 13.

OF vellax one of the firſt Preachours of this nevve Goſpe.
in Scotland.

CHAP. X.

This willox was a Necromancer (as Nico
Burne reporteth) whoſe ſonne did reaiſ
the Deuill Doctour to the Miniſters of Scotland
in Arthurs ſeate not farrie frō Edinbrugh, whe
re firſt they did Preach their Goſpell. Burne in
his diſputation againſt the Miniſters of Scotland
CHAP. 21.

OF Paul Mephen an other of the firſt Goſpellers of Scotlan

CHAP. XI.

This Paul Mephen was a man more lire crue
Souldier, a man of warre armed with h
Piſties (as the Miniſters of France weree) the
then lire one of the ſimple Apoſthes of Chriſt,
man whole conſecrated to venus Game & feedin
of his belly God, & nowiſi adorned with Chaſtir
and ſobrietie, which are the cheefe ornaments (
the true Deſciples of Chriſt Burne Ibiden
Chap. 22. fol. 192.

OF *M. Iames Lavrsonne*

CHAP. XII.

Master Iames Lousonne Menister of Edinbrugh being banished for conspiracie aga-
nst the Kings Maiestie did make his finall end in
dispaire, Incalling Sathan for his helpe, with fore-
saiking of God.

OF *Deane Adaam, heriote.*

CHAP. XIII.

Deane Adame heriote Chanon and Renegate
Priest, fominh at the mouth did fall doune in
the streete where he did walke, that he hade not
so much time guen to him by God as to cry for
mercy and grace for remession of his sinnes,

OF *Reader in the Church of Edinbrugh called Drūmond*

CHAP. XIIII.

An Reeder in the Church of Edinbrugh called Drūmond Alias Doctour Handie being
sette vp in the Chocks (for punition of his rioto-
usnesse, and abusing of bodie with weemen,) at
the Marcat Crosse of Edinbrugh, he did stobbe &
kill him selfe to the deatd before all the people to
the Imitation of Iudas, which did hing him selfe
after he hade betrayed his Master Christ.

OF *Ihon Coynsse Reader in tle same Church*

CHAP. XV.

I Hon Coynesse Reeder in the Church of Edinbrugh in Reading the praiers one day did suddenly cry out with a loud voece: I am condemned
after such desperate words being caried home to
his house and admonished, that he did not know
well what he hade saide. but to haue recourse to
the mercies of God, he answered that he did know
very well what he hade saide- and that mercies
doore wesshute vp from him and he did end this
mortall life the Imataion of Iudas.

M. Thomas hebron Minister and Necromancer.

CHAP. XVI.

Master Thomas hehron Menister and Necromancer in East Lawdian, a litle be for
the houre of his death seated in a Chaire in
the Church yarede at his owen dsire was suddenly
killed by a horrible Tampst, which made th
Church to shake in such fashion that it was neer
eby ouerthrowed to the ground. This was the du
rewarde which he did receiue from Sathan hi
Mister for hus suruice made in a false Religon.

OF M. Thomas Ramsay Minister of S. Androvves.

CHAP. XVII.

Master Thomas Ramsay Minister of
Androwes did suffer that publicke sham
in the time of his Preaching before all the peopl
that his face did tourne in his necke to the Imitat
ion of Sir Ihon Knox likewise he did openly pro
fesse that Knox, their false Apostle was (prim
Genitu

Genitus Diaboli) & that him selfe was (secundo natus) a litle after he did yeelde vp his furthast reath in dispaire to the Imitation of Iudas pro-itor to Christ.

OF M. George Hay parsone of Raphen.

CAAP. XVIII.

MAster George Hay Person of Raphen be-ing altogether dedicated to his gluttonie nd dronknesse (as the most pairt of Minister, re) which is the dayly seruice of their belly God o confirme this New Religion with a Miracle orrespondent to the same, he did suddtuly giue p the Ghost in discharging his belly vpon the acks to the Imitation of olde heretique arriue, which did deny the diuinitiie of Christ, as the 'uritans doe when they make Christ, a the Priest n his diuenitie as will as in humanite for so ot nust be a God Inferior to his Father & not Equall vith him in deitie when he offreth vp hônour nomage seruice and Sacrifice to the Father, and onsequently as a poore creature, because there au not be a true God but one.

OF M. Patrike Lindsay Minister of kelly in Angus.

CHAP. XIX.

MAster Patrike Lindsay Minister of Kelly in Anguse at the houre of his death did cry ut with words of desperation that he was perpe-ualie condāned to hell fire, who being admonc-hed of the Brethdren that hē should desist from

suh

ſuch words of deſperation, for ſo much as theſe
words wold cauſe great ſlaunder to the Religion
and wold moue the people to like the worſe of the
ſame, when they ſhould ſee the Miniſters thereof
to die them ſelues in diſpaire, he anſwered that
they were alſe ſurely condamned as he was, and ye
he hade knowen before that Sathan ſhould haue
hade ſuch power in the world as he did know him
to haue at that time amongſt the Miniſters that
he ſhould neuer haue trubled him ſeiſe to haue
ſerued Chriſt in this new Religon as he did in
former times thus he did goe hence in diſpaire to
the Imitation of Iudas proditnr to Chriſt for
Euen as Iudas did betray Chriſt deliuiring him
with a keſſe to the Iewes, ſo the Proteſtants and
Puritane betray Chriſt in aboliſhing his hōonur
true worſhipe and Relgion, to Eſtabliſh their
hereſies vnder pretnce of true faith in Chriſt, this
is likewiſe one of the chiefeſt cauſes wherefor
calum did looſe his life, being ouer whelmed in
the horrible Gulfe of deepe diſpaire.

OF M. *Dauid Blacke miniſter of kelly in* Aagus.

CHAP. XX.

MAſtſter Dauid Blacke Miniſter of Kel
in Angus (after the foreſaide Patren
Lindſay drinking at the wine in dundie and ha
ing the cupe at his lipps yet before he could t
of the ſame God did ſumond him to compeare b
fore the fearefull Iudgment. heb. 9. 27. by dea
whi

which did beraue him so suddenly of this mortall
life, that he did obtaine not so much time & space
from God as to cry for mercy and grace with
remission of his sinnes. Therefore lette vs not
followe the Example of the Ministers which are
addicted to the Seruice of their belly God, least
perhaps wee make such an vnhappie end as these
haue done which wee haue recited before: but let
vs praie with the Catholique Romaine Church
in hir litanies from suden & vnforeknowen deatd
the Lord deliuer vs.

OF the Minister called killoch.

CHAP. XXI.

After Nicoll Burne in his disputation Chap.
22. writteth that the Minister called Killoch
did murther his wife and put hir to death, buthe
sheweth not whether it was for adulterie, or yet
that she did know anie secreete point of Ne-
romancie in him, which he feared she should
disclose. so how euer the matter be there is one
thing sure that Sathan hade power ouer him when
he persuaded him to Murther his owen wyfe
expresly against the Comandement of God.

OF Ihon Baxter Minister of Innernoth.

CHAP. XXIII.

Ihon Baxter Minister of Innernoth with in the
shiredome of aberdine after his preaching in
sunday went to an aile house which was Iames
als and there Exchanged his Strumpet which

he did peruse as an harlote before, with an man
wife called willame Rossie by Name which wyse
he did abuse in adulterie vnto her dying day: lastly he was found killed vnto the death in his ower
door, and noman did know him who did kill the
Minister, adeath foresuith which was a Iust
rewarde for such an adoulterous life: because al
their good workes are but deadly sinnes it is ar
all a like to sleepe with his Nighbours wife as with
his owen to Giue almes to the needie, or to spoil
a poore man, for all their good workes are bu
deadly sinnes as is taught by them.

Of Ihon Patersonne Minister of alsurde.

CHAP. XXIII.

IHon Patersone Minister in Alsurde did Ioy
in Marriage Ihon Tamsone a man duelling
achintoll, with an woman calle EliZab.
Robersonne in one sunday and nixt wednisd.
the after did disolue the said Marriage contracte
before, and Married these tow persons to oth
tow tuantie dayes therefter. so that their Ma
riage is nothing eles but open adulterie, for Chr
sayeth whosoeuer taxeth the womad deuorc
from her husband, althought the pairtising
made for respect of adulterie. yet he which Ioy
the him selfe to the woman diuerced comitt
adulteirie. Mat. 19. 9. 14our Ministers thinke
shame to Mareris one man to 3. or 4. wifes c
after on other all liuing together as the Laird
Balquhae may be a notable Expmple of our, da

So the Marriage of our Newe Gospellers bë euided in 3. kinds according to the practiese of heir Church, that is in Sacriledge Inceſt. and dulerier in Sacriledge as when Luther, Knox, Craige, and other ſuchlike foreſworne Monkes Prieſts and Friers Ioyned them ſelues with anie roman in an Sacrilegiorus bedde againſt their owes and promiſe made to God. 1. Tim. 5. 11. nceſt as when they Marrie within forebiden derees as Siſter and Brother Bairnes lying in their wen blood adulterie when an man thixeth the roman which is deuorced from her huſband as ree haue ſhewed aboue mat. 19. 9.

OF *Dauid Straitone miniſter of Colſtrue.*

CHAP. XXIIII.

Dauid Straiton Miniſter of Colſtane after he hade beene in anay aſſemblie in Aberdine oming home by the wae become Madde and n that raging madneſſe did looſe his life by he way in Kincarne.

This was the fruite he receiued of their ſinodoll lecrees ſet out againſt afficted catholiques to be ſpoiled of the Knowleog of God and of him ſelfe t his finall end when hade moſt to doe with the

OF *Duncane Danidſonne miniſter.*

CHAP. XXV.

Maſter Duncane Dauidſone Miniſter and Perſone of the Church of Rethen did looſe iis life in the lixe rage, which wos a juſt punituon

of God, for so much that he did take in Marriag
an othermans wife Called Ianet forbes during th
life of her first husband Laird of Auchinhoofe 8
and Auchinhoofe did take to him selfe a Sister o
the Laird Aberzeldies as his wedded wife, but ir
deede in both the Sides it was manifest adulterie
So that by the Ministers lawes oppen adulterie a
will approoued as lawfall Marrirge.

This is the light of their Gospell which can no
distingish the ane from the other that thing whic
is of God, by that then which is of Sat' .n.

OF Ihon Stroquhane Minister at the Church of Keige

CHAP. 26.

I hon Straquhane did confesse to an Gentle ma
who did relate the same to me, that Sathan di
apeare Visiblie to him a long time before h
death, and chiefely in his bedde where Sathan di
almost strangle him so that lastly he did loose th
mortall life in a Rage without any knowldge (
God or yet him selfe, This is a great curse of Go
when a man becometh witlesse at his latter en
when he hath most to doe with the same.

OF M. Ihon Messer Minister of Mellicke.

CHAP. 27.

M. Ihon Minister of Mellieke for taking
an young childs brotti tooke a litle Ch
of; 7. yeere olde and drewned him this was t
crudslitie he vsed to a witlesse creature likew
he hade a litle blacke dogge that folloed on hi

the fpace of ane yeere, fome tim it wold Roeke the crndle, and when he wold be at his fupper it wold fitte at the boord with him he on the on fide of the chandler and it on the other, and when he yeede to the watter fayde, called ythen to his prayeis, it euer accompined him. alfo Golden Chainzie being taiken away theifteoufly, the feme Minifter to obtaine the fame agane did put an Cocke vnder an Caldron, Inquiring from the Cocke hath this man taiken the Chainzie, he did fpeare rund about vntill the time the Cocke did crawe when he was Named who did fteele the Chainzie.

To fhewe that this Cocke was Sathan it is Euident, becaufe that a naturall Cocke hade no wilte nor vnderftanding to Declare where the Chainzie was. Likewife the Laird of Haddoch who was prefent at this Reuelation of Sathan did Incontinent loofe naturall wits and become beftraught in mind and did a litle after loofe this mortall life.

OF M. *Thomas Anderfone Minifler at the Church of Glaffe*

CHAP. XXVIII·

Master Thomas Anderfone in an affemblie in Elgine being perfued in the Chanrie Church by fome of his Brethere, as it was prefuppoed to make a facriffice of him to the Deuill he faued him felfe on horfebacke by fpeede of foote, his

boy being trxen by the faid Minifters was neuei
feene againe, the Lord xnoweth what they dic
with him·

OF M. Androvy or then M. VViliam? Dalachindore.

CHAP. XXIX.

THis Mafter Androw Dalachie Minifter e
Achindore being perfued by fome of hi
Bretheren in the fame Chantie Church of Elgin
being bereft of his Cloaxe fword and his be hing
ing fleaues did efchape him felfe out of thee
hands at that time, and for haftintffe to faue hin
felfe did almoft drowne him felfe in the watter o
Spey, & after his arriuing home did taxe bedde &
in few dayes thereafter did loofe his mortall life.

OF M. Alxxmdet Dovvglas Bifhope of Muray.

CHAP. XXX.

MAfter alexander Dowglas Bifhope of Mui
ray Being difeafed in his bodie could nc
obtaine his hetlth vntill the time aprotie youn
wench was brought to him at his owen defyre t
conforte him in his fickoeffe. and afaer that w;
found with bairne, he did perfuade a friend o˛ hi
to accept of the Childe as his owen to faue hir
felfe from that point of difhonnour.

This fame Bifhope being abfent from the Towa
of Elgine his owen wyfe and his Brother M. Gaui
Dowglas did fee Sathan xeping the Bifhops ftudi
in his abfence, who was fupponet to be his Doc

our. in his prefence, as he was to **Luther before**
im.

The faid Bifhope is full of crafte and deceite which
e practifed both agains Catholiques and Protef
ants, his pride is Intollerale as he did chiefly fhew
when he wold nowife be content with his Brother
Gauin vntill the time he did cry him pardon fitti-
ng vpon his knees in the Councell houfe fore a
itle diflobedience, which truly weighted in it
elfe was no fault at all his malice lichcoie, and
Gluttonie are Euident to world, which are the
proper qualities of a profaine Bifhope meete for
he proteftant Religion.

OF M. *Bartholl Robertfonne Minifter of Rynie.*

CHAP. XXXI.

MASter Barthole Robertfonne Minifter of
Rynie for the time, made a wifes Teftam-
ent after fhe was dead, more for her hufbands
Comoditie, and his owen then Iuftice require, in
caufing his owen man with fained voice to fpeake
be hind the Dead wyfe, as it hade beene the wife
her felfe for fuch diftribution of her Goods as the
Minifter hade Informed his owen man to fay.
This trecherie was prouen againft him, and him
felfe depriued. he made no confcienece likewife
to abufe Ihon Baxters wife in Elgine by his adulterie. and when he wes reprooued of that difhonef-
tie he anfwered and faid that he played but a litle
wanton ticke, and gaue her but a Checke by the

way. Beholde the fruits of this new Religion without anie Conſcience before God or ſhame before
man there be tow Reaſons wherefore they account no thing of mortall ſinnes; the firſt is that
a man hath no free will and Inherent grace to
reſiſt ſuch tentations, but when the tentation
cometh they ſay that they muſt yeelde vnto the
ſame of neceſſitie becauſe the Cõmanddments of
God are in poſſble to be kepet, & chiefely this cõ-
mandemants, which is concerning the concupiſſance of fleſh. The ſecond Reaſon is as they ſay,
that for the reſpect of faith which they haue in
Chriſt, neither the ſinne of Adulterie, homicide,
thiſte, or anie other deadly ſinne is Imputed to
them as deadly ſinnes but as veniall and Euen in
the meane time that they are Iniuſt and full of
ſuch mortall ſinnes in them ſelues that they are
made Iuſt by the Iuſtice which is in Chriſt apprehended by their faith. This in the doctrine of all
Proeſtants, and puritans, and Cheefly of the Puritans ſee caluinlib. 3. Inſt. cap. 2. ſect. 2.

VVee may adde the thrid reaſon which is a
they ſay. that they are not bound in conſcince to
keepe anie lawe that is Either of God or man, bu
that they are made free from all Lawes in thei
conſciences by theis faith in Chtiſt and libertie o
their Goſpell. ſo you may ſee how their life and
doctrine goe ſoundly together accordinh to th
hereſie of the libertins, which haue no Religio
Indeede, but an outward ſhewe of fained Godli

esse Euen in their most zealous profession tõ lecrue the world.

Of Makowvly Minister at the Church of kinnimore.

CHAP. XXXII.

MAckowly Minister at the Chuch of Kin-nimore, the Cõmunion being Ministrea-Ministreaed tõ the people, saide to some of his riends, Elders and Officers of the Church that here was a Rosted Goule in the Ailehouse and Asmuch bread and wine after the Cõmunion as was necessarie to eate and drinke with propertion :o the same, so at the Ministers persausion they :onsumed the Goose with the Cõmunion bread & wine which were resting after the action in the Church.

Now I will aske of them yf they hade faith in Christ when they did eate the rosted Goose with :he Cõmunion bread and wine, which did rest ifter the action as they hade befor? then I say that :hey eate Christ by the same faith as really with :he rosted Goose and Cõmunion briad and wine :ogether as they did before with the Cõmunion >read and wine alone, for somuch as faith Reach-:th it selfe vp to Heauen to receiue Christ there sitting at the reght hand of God the father, and not to the Cõmunion bread and wine to receiue him there with a corporall mouth within the :ompasse of their Sacrament, according to their doctrine.

Yf they will reply and say that they hade faith

I.

habitually and ot actually in Chrift, becaufe the
dead Eliments (that is the rofted Goofe with the
bread and wine) could not ftirre vp their faith
actually to beleeue in Chrift, without the word
Ioyned to them to quicken them as the foule doth
the Body.

Then I will thus argae aginft them yf the Minifter in the meane time they did eate the rofted
Goofe with the bread and wine Ioyned the word
to the dead Eliments (that is to the rofted Goofe
with the bread and wine) to quicken them as
the Soule doth the Body, faying Bretheren in the
Lord, you muft recall to memorie that Chrift did
fhedde his blood vpon the Croffe for remiffion
of your finnes & fitteth prefonly at the right hand
of God and from thence fhall come to Iudge the
quicke and the dead, who likewfe hath created &
ordained this rofted Goofe with the bread and
wine to nurifh your Bodies corporally, as the
Body of Chrift nurifheth your Soules Spirituall
eaten by faith. The muft confeffe that they receiu
the Bodie of Chrift as truly by actull faith in Eat
ing the rofted Goofe with the bread and wine a
they did before with the bread and wine alone.

For fo much as their faith is als free to goe v
to Heauen to Chrift their Spiritually in eatin
the rofted Goofe with the bread and wine, as
was in receiuing the Comumion bread and wer
alone before, aud no more ftay made to faith t
Exercife her office in their action then in the fo

mer vnlesse they Graunt some vertue to be in the
Comunion bread and wine, which maketd them
to recerue Chrilt more Effectually then is in faith
it selfe, which thing they will neuer graunt, be-
:ause that all the Purians affirme that there is no
other recciuing of Chrilt but only by faith in a
Spirituall forme without receeuing of him in the
Comunion bread and wine with corporall mauth.

Thus you see Euidently how there is no difference Indeede betweene theire Comunion and a
prophaine banquete prepared in a Tauerne or
Inne for the corporall Sustentaion of men. or a
Iewish Comunion, which is without all vertue &
grace to cure a sicke Soule, for they agree all in
that point of Religion that Sacraments giue no
Spirituall vertue or grace to the receiuer, but that
all vertue and grace of Iustification and remission
of siinnes are only obtained by faith in Iesus Chr-
st, and not by the Sacrament or good workes.

Now to conclude this purpose wee affirme that
heir faith is as Effectuall and true in Chrilt when
they eate the rofted Goose, as it wee when they
reciued the Comunion, so wee say that they receiue Chrilt by the selfe same faith as truly when
they eate the rofted Goose Ioyned with the bread(
s is recited aboue) conclifion that faith receueth
Chrilt as well with the rofted Goose as with the
Comunion braed. becaute Chrilts Bodie is no
more within the compasse of the Comuion bread
then

then within the rosted Goose, but only in Heauen where faith gooth vp to receiue him as with they eate Christ in the Cōmunion bread Ioyned with the word, for faith and her office is Euenr when a like free, therefore the fruit and the Effecr must alwise be a like fore all vertue & grace is obtained by the action of faith, and not by the Cōmunion bread, as is taught by them selues.

OF *M. George Nicoslonne Minister of Gairtely in Straithboguy*

CHA. XXXIII.

Master George Nicolsone Minister at the Church of Gairthly after that he did know surelie in an assemblie at Elgne in murray hade concluded amongst them selues to giue him vp in a Sacrifice to Sathan chiefe Doctour of their blacke diuinitie, he was so much affrayed of their conspiracie against him that Iincontinent he tooke the flight from the synodoll assemblie to saue his life from such a tragedie prepared for him, and for the greater hast to runne away he hade almost loosed his lif in passing amasedly and rashly through the watter of Spey, and so soone as he come home to his owen house he went sttraightly to bedde wher within a few dayes he gaue vp the Ghest, which fighting in the agoie of death said vnto his wyse, vf they Beetheren Chainge not their mainers and forme of life which they peruse they will lastly make all such an end as the Rea

frier

rirrs did before them This Miserable man by
iese words did declaree to vs that the Ministers
id hônonr and worship Sathan with Sacrifice &
uerthipe hônour as the Read Friers did beiore
iem, which by the cômandement of the Pope,
ith the assiitance of Christian Princes were all
ittroyed in one day, which forme of death (as
I. George Nicolsîône did fotetell) should fall
ion the Ministers for the like seruice made to
ithn. see the historie of the Read Friers, other-
iso called Templiars in the French tragicall
itories of Belfora.

An faithfull womon which did heare these words
M Georges owen wyse when he did speake of
e Ministers at the houre of his death did rehearse
em vnto me as I haue written aboue:

OF M. Ihon knox Minister of Bally in Enzie

CHAP. XXXIIII.

Master Ihon Knox Minister of Belly in En-
gzie one Spey syde being consecrated by
e Bretheren as a Sacaifice vnto Sathan in an
her assemblie at Elgine in Murray he tooke the
ght from the said assemblie to saue him selfe
om such daunyer, and for hast to Eschape most
de drowned him selfe in the watte, of Spay.
than at that time could obtaine no other thing
him but only did depriue him of an Eye which
could neuer obtaine againe vnto his dying day
ise that sawe him spoiled after the fearfull ten-

fen

fentence of the forefaide affemblie againft him d
relate this hiftorie vnto me.

OF M. Peter BlaeKeburne Bifhope of Aberdine.

CHAP. XXXV.

MaPter Peter Blackurne Bifhope of aberdi
is aceufed to be witch and Necromac
for four caufes.

Firft for fo much that he hath a Clocke fo En
haunted and Charmed by witchcraft that wh
fo euer any Gentle woman did couer her fe
with the fame, fhe was Incontinently berefte wi
loue of him, wherfore it was cōmonly fpoken th
he did purchafe to bim felfe the Laird of Cafkil
ns Daughter by his Enchanted Clocke.

Secondly there was a younhe wenche in Bud
annochie which is within the Baronie of Gig
who was fo bewitched that fhe hade no power
perufe her Members Armes and Leggs, but v
Impotena in their function, wherefore the wer
hes Fathar did carie his dangter to the Bifhope
Aberdine for the famous bruit he hade to cr
fuch dieafes as other witches doe, to the end th
by his aide and crafte the maid might recou
her health againe, which Indeede fhe hade conf
red with the Bifhope and vfed his crafte in ft
behallfe; in the meane time fhe hade a vifion wh
fhe fawe viuely one Rauening Beaft caft the fik
fe vpon her, and an other Rauening Beaft take
of her, that is one Deuill did caft the difeafe vp

r and an other Deuill take it of.

Thirdly when the witches of the North were
:cufed by the Bifhope and other Minifters
tbe cômiffion which my Lord Marques of
untly hade obtained from his Maieftie to this
fect, fome of the wtiches did anfwere to the
fhope, and faid, yf your life were alfe wold
ed in this behalfs as ours are you wold be
und more familiare with Sathan then wee are
Fourthly when an boy called williame Read
l fpy in the Councell houfe where the Minifters
re affembled in the Towne of Aberdine Sathan
fhape of a blacke dogge, M. Peter Blackeburne
oderatur for the the time did fo Enchaunt this
efaide williame Read to end he fhuld not reue-
e their fecreete confence with Sathan that the
y did loofe his naturall wits and became a foole,
l likewife did neuer ritorne to his netiue coun-
y thereafter, as you may fee in the life of M.
hame Roberrfonne Minfter of Tarland in
omare more at lenght.

Moreouer his vngodly vfurie is knowen to the
rld which taketh 15. Marks for the hundreth
erely which is a Iewfh forme of dealing againft
hriftian.

OF M. VVillame Robertfone Minifter of Tarland

CHAP. XXXVI.

Afters VVilliame Robertfone Minifter at
the Chuch of Tarland in Cromare went to
prefbutrie of aberdine with his boy called wil-

liamé Read, which being in the Councel
Houſe quyetly, did ſee Sathan in forme of a bla
cke dogge & retourning home againe did ſpeain
at his Maſter what ſuch an blacke dogge it was
his Maſter vndeſtanding that he ſawe the black
dogge, Incontinently directed the boy abacke to
M. Peter Blackburne Moderataur for the tim with
a Miſtiue letter, when M. Peter vnderſtood th
truth of the mater as is reciteh aboue, he did In
contiently caſt ſuch witchraft and ſorcerie vpon
the boy that he did looſe his naturall witts, an
euere ſince did remaine a foole, and did neuer re
ourne to his natiue Countrie.

OF *Ihon Durie Miniſter of Manroſſe*
CHAP. XXXVII.

I HON Durie a foreſworne Monke being i
Edinbrugh for ſunſrie of his owen aftaires h
wife went vp vnto his Studie where when ſhe i
Sathan like a blache man lying on a lowe Beddei
the Siuddie, ſhe was ſo perturbed with ſuch
feare and tentation of Sathan that ſhe did ſtric
her ſelfe with a ſharpe knyfe in at the ſhour
Ribbs ſo that all the Neghbours did diſpaire
her life, which Neuertheleſſe ſhe did not looſe
that time Ihon Durie being retorned home
Excuſe the matter ſaid that the peapll ſhould r
Interprete that fact of his wifes in an Euill pai
becauſe that God did permite his moſt holy S
uants to be tempted with Sathan. it is true th
God permitteth Sathan to tempt and Exerciſe
h

oly Seruantts as it is written of S. Anthon, S,
Hylarion, and manie others, but not to be ouer-
herowen with Sathans tentations, as Ihon Duries
wife was which was a manifest taken that Ihon
Durie was a Necroamancer and familair with
athan, to haue him so familiarly laidvp vpon
is law beedde in his Studdie, and that Sathan
ade power oner his wife, when at his persuasion
nd tentation she did Endeuore to kill her selfe, as
hese who did see this Miserable woman in this
light did relate vnto me.

OF M. *Thomas Meluine Minister at* kindrimie
CHAP. XXXVIII.

Master Thomas Meluine Minister at the
Church of Kindrimie being in his Chalmer
: conference with Sathan his wife perceiuing the
ime was surprised with such a horrible feare that
ie Incontinetly become madde and bestraught
i mind, which thing being truly knowen to him,
or excesse of feare that his wife should reueale his
creete conference with Sathan, he likewise be-
5madde. him selfe & bestraught in mind. This
as the Iust hire which he did receiue for his
ruice made to Sathan.

lo

OF M. *Robert Cornuell Minister at Linlothgo*
CHAP. XXXIX.

Master Robert cornuell Minister at Linlith-
go being in his Studie his Eldest Doughter
ome to seeke a booke from him. to goe to the
cheole, and because she saw a blacke dogge lying
pon boord conferring with her Father, which

K

leapt of the boord at her entring in the Studdie &
did hide him selfe from her sight, her Father bette
her for temeritie & rashnesse to come so suddenly
vpon him as she did by his Expectation. Thus
you may behold how the Deuill is Doctour to the
Ministers in teaching them their blacke diuinitie
condemned by the Ancient Fathers long agoe.

OF M. *Iames Spading Minstley and seruant to M.*
Thomas Straquhane Personne of kiucare.

CHAP. XL.

M. IAMES Spading coming an sunda
to the Church of Lumphanan and pastin
ouer the wetter of Die in the Coble of Kincarn
the Deuill apeared vnto him accompaining hi
the space of tow myles, caused him retire back t
the Persons house, and at his backe cōming wol
haue kessed the Persons wife, being refused of h
desire kissed an wench in the house, and Incont
naently therefter he became madde and raging l
his mind, bestrooue an Oxe of the Persones wh
ch he ranne to the death so that the Minister
his rage and the Oxe did both die at once. T
was the due rewarde which he obtained for l
obedience to Saahan.

OF M. *Anthony Fithie* Minister of *Inverkillevve*

CHAP. XLI.

VV HEN Certen witches. 1605. yee
were accused and burined at Brigh
they affirmed amongst other things that
artho

Arthour Fithie Minister of Inner Kissowe assisted with them when they consulted with Sathan, and Exercise their crafte.

Thus you see how the proper fruits of the Min-sters is to be Necromancers or witches to lerne their lesson by conference with Sathan.

Moreouer when some Ministers and Gentle men were drinking in Tauerne Sathan came in to hem in the forme of a blacke dogge, this same Minister Fithie tooke an shoulder of Mutton out of the plaite before the Gentle men and did cast the same in the blacke dogges mouth which suddenly went away with it, therefore a Gentleman did say vnto the Minister Fithie what was in your mind to cast the rosted Flesh which was ordained for vs in the Deuills mouth, might you not haue giuen him rawe Flesh, seing that there is fire innough in Hell to rost the same behold here how Sathan is not only familiar with ther Ministers in their priuie Studies, but also in open Ins before the whole world.

OF M. *Androw Ogstoun* Minister *of the Church of* Canesby *in* Cathnesse.

CHAP. XLII.

Master Androw Ogstoun Minister of the Church of Canesby in Cathnesse dothe ruse so much a booke of Necromancie made by Michel Iscotte that yeere of God. 1608. is accused to be an open Necromancer, that is say a man which Consulteth with Sathan, to learne

Learne from this hellish Doctour the knowleg
of such thing as he thinketh Expedient or prof
itable to his office or condion of his Estate

Of M. *Dauid Coluine Minister of Fersoch*

CAHP. XLIII.

MAster Dauid Coluine Minister at the Chu
rch of Fersoch in Cathnesse, being so wel
whitled and drouke at night that he could no
learne his Preaching for the Sunday following h
was constrained to ryse out of his bedde long be
fore day in winters Night to Studie vpon hie te
and Glosa thereof, in the mean time of his readin
and Studiing vpon his books, come in a black
dogge to helpe him, which when a young man o
twelfe yeeres olde his bedfollowe did espye, h
was so amased at the sight of the blacke dogg
that he beeome as it were benumed of his sense
and almost without all moouing and feelin
Neuerthelesse with such power as he hade t
made a litle signe with his hand (because he coul
not speake) to the Minister to helpe him out o
such a staite as he hade presently, whereof the li
he neuer felt beore, the Minister did nothing b
mocke and laugh at the sillie Boy, in his gre
anguish and distresse, who seing the Minister l
ting at him he hade recourse to God praying
his heart God helpe me Christ helpe me and a lit
after his prayer made to God the blacke dog
went away, and the Boy be good to reprotch t

m

Minifter of his vncharitable deed that he wold
not helpe him in fuch a ftraite, the Minifter anfwered and faid I beheld you to fee what you wold
loe, the boy faid againe you fhall fee what I fhall
loe, fo faying did Inueft him felfe in his apparell
and went away from the Minifter, fo that he wold
neuer be bedfellswe to him ageine.

This boy which did fuffer this Iniure from the
Minifter did declare to me this hiftorie of him
elfe, after that he become a Catholique, and how
his Minifter thereafter was paffeffed with a Deuill
hat men were conftrained to bind him hand
nd feete tofaue themfelus from his furious Rage.

OF M. Iames Read Minifter at the Church of
Banchory on Dye fyde.

CHAP. XLIIII

IHON Cheyne feruant to M. Ihon Cheyne
Laird of Petphichie, being fufpected to haue
aken away thift'oufly a Golden Chaine from the
aird of Petfichie, to purge him felfe of fuch a
aunder went to Iames Read Minifter at the
Church of Banchory on Dye fyde for the famous
eporte of his great fkill of fecreete things by the
arte of his Necrmancie, how foone the Minifter
ade receiued Eight Marks of Scots money for
is reward in this behalfe, he conuoyed Ihon
heye within a Barne or corne houfe with a Catte
o make a Sacrifice vnto Sathan and fo fone the
linifter hade made round circle with ceten
quocations of Sathan the Earth beganne to tremble

tremble and Sathan a litle after did apeare in tl
forme of a blacke Moure with curled locks, tl
Minister Incontinent thereafter his arising out (
the Earth did cast the Catte to him in a Sacrfic
since did aske Sathan where the Golden Chain
was, who did answere him with a low grosse voic
as yf he hade beene spaking out of darke deone o
hollow caue vnder the Earth, that the Golde
Chaine was in such a place where it was found i
deede, Ihon Cheyne being put foorth of barn
the Minister was much troubled to send Satha
doune againe to his former place, Ihon Cheyn
was so affrayed at the sight of this Euill Spirit a
that time that he appeared neuer to be will Satle
in his naturall witts, but to hau a souage and vild
countenance and behaueour.

OF M. VVilliame Pape Minister of Dornoch in
Sutherland.

CHAP. XLV.

MAfter williame Pape Minister of Dornoe
in Sutherland ryding home from the T(
wne of Taine to his owen house in Dornoch, w.
so assailzred by the way by a multiude of Rauen
that they did not only scratch his Body with the
Clawes and Nailles, but also did rent and tea
his apparell with their bills and becks, his wi
asking him after his ariuing in the house, wh
should be the cause of his disarryment and troub
he andwered, that it was a multitude of Raue
whi(

hich did 'rent his garmints and scratch hodie
ith their bills their furious rage in stricking and
eaking at him with such an Extraordinare power
at with great difficultie he hade saued him selfe
om the dint of their Clawes and beckes which
ing so soone his wife hade related to their Nig-
boues they did all suspect that such a multiude of Rauens was a companie of Deuills, for so
much that such a skirmish or bickring of Rauens
gainst a reasonable man was neuer hard or seene
ard or seene before, and for confirmation of this
ruth after such conflict he was so vexed & beaten
n his owen house by the same Rauens that he was
onstrained to leaue it, and goe loge in an other of
is friende, which things shewe euidently that his
rouble and vexation was caused by a companie
f Deuils which hade power ouer him, and not
y a companie of good Andells.

OF M. Andrevv Andersone Minister of
Loth Sutherland.

CHAP. XLI.

MAster Androw Andersone Minister of Loth
in Stuherland being in the morning Studi-
ng on his books in his priue Chalmer, in come
ne of his Schollers called Huchon Aikin to gette
kenning of his lessone, and there he saw beside
he Minister a litle beacke whelpe as it hade beene
new whelped. which after the sight thereof did
yith such speede retourne to the doore that he
did

did breach his head and Incontinent thereafte
did ly bedde ficke the fpace of fourteene daye
with continuall ratdring of his meate by vomite
the Minifter euer ftill Intyfing the boy not t
difclofe the caufe of his corporall difeafe. Thif
was the yeere of God 1610. in the moneth o
Deember.

OF M. Robert Bruce Minifter firft of Ediubrugh
and fince at Innerneffe
CHAP. XVII.

MAfter Rober Bruce Minifter of Innerneffi
the yeere of God 1608. was fo vexed trou
bled perfued with Sathan in forme a blecke dogg
and fome time in the fhape of a colte or fole, tha
could not know by what way he should foue hin
felfe from his daunger, and beholding that hi
Spirituall Armours of Preaching and Prayer
could Auaile him nothing in this fearefull affaul
of this potent Ennemie, he hade accoutfe to cor
porall Armour and force of mortall man, Neue
theeleffee fiixe men in Armes mour watched thi
miferable Minifter nighuly, yet could not Emp
etch this blacke dogge to oppen the doore Eueri
night wher M. Robert Bruee did abide, fo that i
is likly that this frind ehall paffeffe him as he heat
done others or he leaue him at the laft.

And the Minifters to collour this matter:
much as they could to shewe that this come not
M. R Bruce for their deferuing as yf their nauj
naught

naughtie liues and hereticall doctrine were accep-
ble to God, but by M. R. Abercromies and M.
hon Hamiltouens Sorceries and Enchantments
which did hound this hellish dogge vpon M.
Rober Bruce, to vexe & torment him according
o their desire. But this fond Inuention of theirs
s no thing else but a malitious detrction and forged lye. First becaufe M. Robert Abercromie at
hat tim was out of this Countrey in a Colledge
of the Iesuits built in the Towne of Brownsberge
n the Kingdome of pole. Secondly Catholique
Priests are aceustomed by the power of God giuen
o them to cast Deuills out of poffeffed perfons,
but not to fend the Deuill to vixe any man as the
falfly alleadge. Thridly yf the Ministers haue the
rue Religion and the true affiftance of God (as
they falfly challenge to them felues) why doe they
not chafe away the Deuill by the vertue of God
or approbation of their new Gofpell as Catholique Priests doe for confirmation of the Catholique Religion. But feing they haue noe power
ouer Sathan, as Catholique Priests haue, they muft
coufeffe that they are but heretiques & the bound
flaues of Sathan, and no true Chaiftians.

This blacke dogge at the laft (as the euent did
hew) did tranfform him felfe in a familiare fpirit,
which M. Robeart Bruce did call his God, for M.
Robert and his familiare fpirit were feene confer-
ing familiarely in his Church about twell howres

L

at euen or midnight with great lightes in his
Church, which theis familiare spirit of M. Robe-
rts did furnish, for M. Robeat being but him selfe
alon talking with this spirit did taxe no candles to
his Chich for to cause such light in his Church as
was seene M. Robert after long conference with
this familiare spirit said to his friends and nighbours that it was God that came to teach him such
heads of Religion as he should preach publickly
to the people.

But the Godly Reader may conie&ure what a
familiare spirit this was that came to teach M.
Robert about midnight by the histories of Luther
Zuinglius the firſt Pillars of this New Religion
which they reherſe of them ſelues, as M. Robert
doth preſently of him ſelfe.

For Luther thus writteth of him ſelfe in his
Booke of priuie Maſſes. *Contigit mihi ſemel ſub mediam*
noctem ſubito experge fieri:et ibi Satan mecum cæpit eiuſmodi
diſputationem audi (Inquit) Luthere Doctor perdocte,
noſti enim te quindecim annos celebraſſe Miſſas priuatas pene
quotidie. Quid ſi tales Miſſæ priuatæ eſſent horrenda Idolo-
latria. Quid ſi ibi non affuiſſet corpus et ſanguis Chriſti, ſed
tantum panem et Vinum adoraſſes, et aliis adorandum propo-
ſuiſſes, Cui ego Reſpondi, ſum Vnctus Sacerdos, accep
Vnctionem, et Conſecrationem ab Epiſcopo.

That is to ſay. it hapned me once bout midnig
to be ſuddenly awaκned out of my ſleep. Ther
Sathan begaud this diſputation with me heare m
(ſayeth he moſt Learned Doctor, Luther, Thou
κnaweſt

cnowest that thou hast almost dayly celebrated
priuie Masses thise 15 yeares agoe what yf such
priuie Masses were hoaribie Idolatrie what yf the
Bodie and blood of Christ were not realie there,
But only that thou didest adore bread and wine,
& offere the same to be adored by orhers. whome
to I auswered, that I was a Priest. and that I had
receuued vnction, and consecration from A
Bishope.

After these words Luther rehearseth all the
arqumets which Sathan did bring fourth to prooue that the Masse was Idolatrie, which arguméts
of Sathans the Protestants (as yet) peruse to day
againft Catholique Romains to prooue after the
Imitation of Sathan that the Masse is no thing els
but plaine Idolatrie. And as Sathan did firft calk
the Masse Idolatrie, so the Protestants and puritans as his difciples call the Masse Idolatrie as M.
Roberte Bruce doth also but wee Catholique
Romains esteeme the Masse to be the much more
holy, and diuine seruice of God, that Sathan doth
abhorre the same, as he doth all other holy things
Profitable to mans saluation as the cheefe author
of all Idolatrie, and heresie to purchase the dam-
naoion of mans presently as he did In ages all before wee will let the Protestants followe after Sathan In this behalse as they doe in manie other
things, considering that no friendlie admonition
can moue them to acknowelege their fault, and
correcte

Corroꝛe the same for their owen saluatioꝛ.

Zuinglus the patriach of the Puritans writeth the historie of him selfe, in his booke intltuled the helpe or soccour of the Eucharist. saying that a spirit came in the night and did teach him that Christ bodie was not with in the Euchoist or holy Sacrement really. but only tyepically or figuratiuely, as the thing signified as in the signe. he writteth also that he did not knowe whether this spirit which did teach him his lesson, was blacke or white.

Considering now that M. Robert Bruce doth followe the doctrine of Luther and Zuinglius in calling the Masse Idolattrie as Sathan and Luther did before him, and in denying Christ Bodie and Blood to be realy within the compasse of the holy Sacrment as Zuingliue familiare spirit did teach him, what should wee surmise of M. Robberts familiara spirii, but to he of that same kind that Luthere and Zuinglius spirits were before night Doctours of darknesse, and of the black Gospell, which leadeth sillie soules to euident perpition.

when M. Robert vanteth of him selfe that he sawe the Triuitie and Preache the same publickly to the people, wee should beliue S. Ihon the Euangelist rether then a fauce glorioons lying heretique. for S. Ihon thus wreteth. *deū nemo vidi ꝯnquam.* No man hath scene God at any tyme. this

he

e fpeaketh of mortall men Liuing in this world.

when it is writen that Moifes did fpeaxe face or face with God as the frind with his frind, it is ot to be vnderftood that he fawe God or yet aake with God perfonally at that time. therefore is faid that he fpeaxe with God face, for face ecaufe the Angel of God fpeaxe to him as an mbaffadour in the perfon of God. for the Lawe vas giuen toMoyfes by the Minifterie of Angeals S. Luke writteth in acts of the Apoftles. And S. oul thelike to the Falatiens. bal. 3. 19. And whan loyfes defyred to fee the face of God, his diuine Hence or God in his glorie, God did anfwer to loyfes, or reather the angell of God as his Embaf-dowr in his perfon. *Non Poteris videre faciem meam, n enim vedebit me homo et vyvet.*

That is: thou canft not fee my face. for no ortall man may fee me and liue, that is abiding this mortall life, he can not fee me. than holly l. R. Bruce did the Trunnie in this mortall life ad yf M. Robert will fay that he wes Rauished vp the third Heaue, as S. Paul was, becaufe he hath fcriptur for proefeof the Rau iffing, wee will liue him no mor thanwee doe a lying heretique.

OF M. *Ihon Chalmer* Minifter of keith

CHAP. XLVIII.

M After Ihon Chalmer Minifter of Keith being a ftudent in Aberine did declare a arefull vifion which he did fee to an other Stud-

                                                            ent

Student called M. Georg Spence, which is no
Miniſter at the Church of S. Trule, the yeere o
God 1611. which viſion was that he did ſee
certen broad band going about from his Neck
on ſyde to the ocheſter hole on the other on th
which band was written. This is thy Condemna
tion. After this time he was made Maſter Regent
and ſince Subprencidall in the Colledge of ol
Aberdine, and laſtly Miniſter of Keith, at whic
time he was ſo tempted with Sathan to beraue hi
of his life, that he could nowiſe reſiſt the vehem
enciee of Sathans tentations, thereafter declar
ring his miſterie to M George Chalmor his Bro
her M. George did conuoy him from Keih t
Aberdine and the did deſire the Brethern to prai
God for M. Ihon, but beholding that all thei
praiers were in vaine his frinds did conuoy ho
from Aberdine to Cullen (where his good Fath
did remaie to ſee yf there he migh be fredde fro
Sathans tenations by his good Fathers praier
but as ti was reporteth Sathan did vexe him the
more thtn before, and taken out of his bedde fro
his wife did ſo trouble him in his Chalmer th
he could gette no reſt at all, nor his wife thereaft
wold neuer conſent to bedde with him again
Laſtly he did retire to the Church a Kinth again
and after he hade married tow peroncs, with gre
vexation of Sathan in his Pulpite, he deſired h
hoſtage to haue his dinner in reddineſſe within

letle time. and in the mean feafon he wold goe
into his Chalmer to performe fome quyet bufinef-
the hade to doe, hes hoft beholding that he did
remeinne to long in his Chalmer from cōmining
this dinner, he did knocke at the doore to defire
M. Ihon to come and take his refection: but the
good man of the houfe confidring that M. Ihon
did make no anfwer at all, he and fome of his Ni-
bours did breach vp the Doore of the Chalmer
wherin M Ihon did remaine, which thing being
done at their firft entriffe they did fee the Floore
ouer runne with blood, and M. Ihon Chalmer
lying ouer a Chift on his breft his head hanging
downe and the blood gufhing out at his throate.
which was cutted with his owen hand by the
perfuafion of Sathan; Thefe men confidering the
miferable fpertackle of their Paftour did fuddenly
take him vp and fowe the cotted Srinnes of his
throate together, the gufhing of his blood being
ftayed, they did afke at him why he wold not
open the doore, who anfwered and faid, that
Sathan wold not premit him to doe the fame vntill
the time he did cutte his owen throate with the
fharpeft knyfe he hede, and that Sathan was fo
great a Fhilofher, that he did find out more Reafons that he should cutte his throat then M.
Ihon could find for the fauetie of his life.
Likewife an honorable Gentlman worthie of
credence with a great multitud of Inhabitants of
the

the Towne did thts speake vnto him.

M. Ihon wee that are all affifting hire ha
taken a great occafion of flaunder at fuch a crue
fact as you haue vfed in putting violent hands in
to your felfe confidering that you which profe
your felfe to be a Spirituall Paftour and Guider
mens fouls to Heauen, take the contrarie way
your felfe to doe aginft the Commandement of Go
by perfuafion of Satdan, therefore wee will defi
you for the loue of God to tell vs the troth whe
her your calling to Preach the word of God an
adminifter the Sacraments be lawfull or no, at
take no feare to tell vs the troth in this behalf
becaufe your life is loofed in this world witho
any hope of Releefe.

M. Ihon anfwered and faid, allace our callin
is neiiher lawfull nor good nor any wife appr
oued by God, Then the Gentlman replyed & fa
M. Ihon why did you abufe the people to le
their foules to Euident damnation out of the tr
way of Saluation. M. Ihon anfwered and f
allace Sir the difordained loue of the world
mooue me fo to doe.

The Miniftes hiaring that M. Ihon hade deny
& his Religiō in this fashion before the Gentlm
his Parishoners they were much fcandalzed
this fact, and therefore to repaire the honno
which they did loofe by the denyell of their Rel
ion. who wos one of the moft learned men am
amon

iongſt them all, incontinently they did bring
e artickles of their Faith vnto him and cauſed
. Ihon to Sweare and ſubſcribe them againſt
: conſcience ſaying vnto him what is this you
: doing will you ſhame vs your Bretheren and
e whole Religion profeſſed in this Countrie.

He confeſſeth likewiſe that all his Preaching
s for pride, vaine Gloire, hypocriſie, and out
ting of him ſelfe, and not for the Gloirie of
hriſt and Saluation of mens ſouls, as the M.
Valter Smyth reporteth.

He likewiſe confeſſeth that he often times did
mite bougrie and the ſinne of Soeomie, and
ien he did confeſſe ſuch things his Bretheren
dnipe him to ſtay him from confeſſing of his
nes, ſaying quyely will you ſhame vs all, M.
on did anſwere to them ſaying: This is my caſe
w but it wilbe yours nixe as you ſhall feele by
: perieace herafter.

VVhen. 14. or. 15. Miniſters were ſtanding
ths Chalmer and Sathan in the mideſt of them,
. Ihon did requeſt all his Bretheren to chaſte
ay Sathan out of his ſight, whoſe preſence did
ich affray him, but Sathan for none of their
jueſts and prayers wold goe away. becauſe they
le no power to cōmand him.

Laſtly Sathán did kindle ſuch an fire wiehin
bowells that he did requeſt Earneſtly the Aſ-
antes to cutte a ſlite in hisſide & to powre in a
barroll

M

Barroll of cold watter to quench that in fernabl site, which did torment him.

VVhen George Dowglas Minister of Culler and M. Pattike Dargue Minister of Fordyce di come to conforte M. Ihon Chalmer in his Ar guish and distresse, Sathan did so trouble and to ament them, that they appeared to manie to b alfe truly posseled and vexed with Sathan as M Ihon was before, neuer the lesse with lapps of tim their feare and great trouble did some whi decay.

Conclufion of this purpose. First good Readi you shall vnderstand and marke sundrie things : M. Ihon Chalmers former life.

First that he was one of the most leacned Sche lers amongst them all, & so konwgainst his ow cofcience.

Secondly that he was a proud vaine glorio man, an hypocrite, and bougrare.

Thridly that he and the Ministers hau n power to chaffe away the Deuill fom them felu and that none of them hath power to helpe other.

Fourthly that he did cutte his owen throate, Iudas did hing him felfe at Sathans Instigatio And not wthhitaning all tbefe abhominab'e sim and codditions, the Ministers doe openly pra in their Pulpits, without all shame, that he is of Gods Elect, but you must vnderstand him suc! an Elect as Iudas was before him.

Lastly to hide their Slauerie and subiection to athan their vsuall custome is to say, that Sathan accustomed to tempt the most Godlie men that e and therfore no man should be scandal zed ith such at tentation as it befell M. Ihon Chal-er. But in that behalfe they shawe their great alice to deceiue Ignorant people whan they ake no distinction betweene a Godly Christian, hich ouerthroweth Satban in his tentation, and a vngodly Minister, which is ouerthrowen to e dead by Sathans tentetons, for Sathan did mpt Christ Iob, S. Paul, S. Anthon, S. Bernard nd many other Godly men, which did tread han and his tentations vnder their feete: But ontrariwise Sathan doth tread vngodly Minis-rs vnder his feete by his dayly tentations as is uidently prooued throgh all the discourse of ur booke.

OF Maister Ihon Straetoun, Minister of Forese

CHAP. XLIX.

M. Allexand douglasse & M. Ihon Streatoun contending on against on othere for the ishoprie of Mourray, M. Allexander Douglasse the last by moyen of friends did preuaile against l. Ihon Streatoun, who seeing him selfe disapo-ted of his Intent, being loftie minded, was seased ith such a deep displeasure, and sadnesse of art, that lastlie he did fall in a deadly disease & dispair

diſbaire of this mortall life. he conſidering hi
ſelfe in ſuch a diſperat plight, and no remaide
be found for the ſauetie of his life, then he d
declaire openly that ſecret which long agoe w
lurking in his ſorofull mind, and confeſſe open
that all things, which he did preach to the popl
were but decefull liee, and ſtrong deluſions, wh
ch forme of lyfe he did peruſe againſt his conſci
nce for loue of riches and preeminence in the ey
of mortall men as M. Ihon Chalmer which d
cute his owen throt did confeſſe before him at t
howr of death, his wife likewiſe a bold chiddi
ſcould, who with her bitier taunts, did ofen tym
wex and torment him his continuall ſong therfo
wos, woe be to me that is thus troubled by a
euill wife and an falſe Religion. his conſien
did of ſtrongly cheche him at that tyme for l
leing hipocriſie in tymes bypaſt, that he did di
aire of Gods mercie for prei hing of his hereſi
and deeeauing of Ignoront ſouls, when frien
exhorted him to crye for mercie frome God abo
he anſwered and ſaid that God hade no mercie
g ue him.

VVhen the Miniſter of Nairne called Ro
came to ſee his Brother, and to confort him inl
anguiſe and diſtreſſe, ſo ſoone as he ſawe M. Ih
in ſuch a diſperat plight, he was ſurpriſed w
ſuch a horcible feare that his face did touren d
ectly to his ſhoulder, not all together in his ne

is Sir Ihon Knox face did when he was preaching
n S. Geels Church of Edinburgh, a Noble Baron
whose name of sete purpose I conceill, said when
e sawe the Ministers face of Nairne so tourned
way from his right seate, that it was the most
ugly feareull sight that euer he did see or behold
with his eyes, when M. Robert Bruce did com to
onfort M. Ihon in his miserie, his wife said to
im Sir you knowe not who is here come to visie
ou. who is that saietd M. Ihon? his wife answered
& said, it is M. Robert Bruce your good friend.
M. Ihon answered and said, he is the first begot-
en of the Diuill away with him.

This is the friendship which is amongst here-
ques and all other vngodly men, when they are
n dispaire of Gods mercie, with a certrine pers-
asion of there owen condmation they hate most
hese who were their greatest friends in this world
s a licherous man hateth to the extremitie that
rompet at the howre of death which with her
iring words and gratious entertenement did
old him continually in deacly sinne, curse and
maledectione of God, and so with her decetfull
easurs lead him pleantly to his eternall damnat-
n. so the greater there friendship hath beene in
e world with the offence of God, so the greater
all there hatred be in Hell, becaufe that each on
f them with there worldly counsell was caufe
ich one to othere of their owen Damnation.

*Hovv the Ministers did consult vvith Sathan in an
assemblie at Elgine a Murray.*

CHAP. L.

M. Alexander Rason Persone of Spyne
being in an assemblie with the rest of the
Ministers at Elgine his wife called Boniman hauing receeued a Missiue letter directed to the perso-
one, she went to the councell house to deliuer the
letter vnto him, but the rest of the Ministers wol
not permit him to goe out to her, nor yet she to
enter vnto him, wherefore she satte daune in the
Church vntill the time they should come out o
the Councell house, at last when they come foor
td together she saw *Sath* an amongst them, whicl
sight did stricke such a feare vnto her heart tha
Incontinently she become, madde & bestraugh
in mind and within ten dayes did loose her li
thus you see how they consult with Saihan t
learne their lessone from him both in secreet
Studies and publique assemblies.

The Deuills Preaching in the Church of North Berrique.

CHAP. LI.

IT is Euidnt to all notabe men which were liu
ing about Edinbrugh in the dayes of Chance
ler Maitland how Sathan did Preach to an assem
blie of witches in the Church of Northberiqu
where the Reader of Tranent was Clarqu
Register which companie of witches were a lit
after execute by publique Iustice.

Whe

VVhen the Euill Spirite did Preach vnto them,
is apparell was conforme to the Ministers array-
ment when they goe to Preach, First Sathan was
inuestd with a long blacke Gowne standing in the
pulpite in the shape of a Minister and since did
beginne his Preaching to the witches as the Min-
isrs are accustomed to doe in theis or such like
ashion.

The last time wee did occupie this place (deare
bretheren and sisters) our texte was of such a
airte of our Gospell whereof our Giosse was in
ome measure to your Edification which thing
id mooue Chancler Maitland to laugh when so
euer he did beholde the Ministers begine his prea-
hing as Sathan did, after the declaration of the
witches.

Thus each one may see how Sathan did Preach
in the Ministere Church in a Mininsters arraym-
nt, in a Ministers Puolpite, in a Ninisters forme
o shewe to all men, what conformitie, anologie
nd proportion is betweene Sathan and Ministers
in the vttering of their false Gospell.

Manie oculare witnesse there were which haue
ene Sathan preach in the shape of a Minister as
recited aboue but no man can be found which
ath seene him celebrate the Massee in the form
f a Priest in a Catholique Chruch at one Catholi-
ue Alter for somuch as Sathan darre not seoffe
t Iest, at the holy sacrifice of Masse, which is the

dinien .

diuine feruice of God as he doth at the Minifters
Preaching, which is a delightfull fporte & mock-
ing ftocke vnto him: but contratiwife, he perfua-
deth Luther by his fophifticall reafons to abolish
the holy Sacrifice of the Maffe as contrarie to his
attempts, which Sathan wold neuer haue done yi
the Maffe hade beene Idolatrie, as the Minifters
Impioufly call it, which Idolatrie is proper feruice
to Sathat.

Of the Raging tempefts vvhich Sathan ftirreth
vp in the Aire during the time of Minifter
Freaching and affembli

CHAP. LII.

Dominous *Nider Inquifitor* of the faith writteth in
his booka Intituled de maleffais CHAP. 4
that a witchman did confeffe before the Iudge
accufsd in Iuftice that when they wold defire aur
Tempeeft to be ftired vp in the Aire they Incalled
the Prince of Deuills by expreffe words reqneftij
him to fend fome of his Inferiours to Execute
their defire. & to obtaine their demand of Sathar
they did kill a blacke foule. and caft it vp in th
Aire in a Sacrifice to the Euill fpirit. which bein
done, then the Euell fpirit ftirreth vp in the Air
fome time fuch Boifterous winds as might pu
vp great Trese by the Roots, and oner throwe th
tops of houfes, fome times fuch ligheings and fe
refull shotts of thundar that they did kill bot
men and beafts, fome times fuch ftormes of hai
an

id aboundance of showres that they did diſtroy
great pairt of the ſuits of the Earth and wracke
ie world with famine.

    VVherefore when all men doe ſee ſuch
aging têpſts in the Arre in the time the Miniſ-
rs doe hold their aſſemblies wee can conie-
ure no other thing but that ſuch Effects should
roceede from the like cauſes, that is when the
liniſters in their aſſembles Incall Sathan, hôno-
r reuerence, and offer vp ſome Sacrifice vnto
im to the end they learne from him in their
ublique conference ſuch things as they deſire to
now of him both preſnt and to come, and in the
iean time to confirme their bloodie decrees of
ieſe Impious aſſemblies ſette out aganiſt perſec-
ted Catholiques Sathan giueth a demonſtration
f his conſent by ſudden ſtormds of haile & great
laſts of wind, which weaſt and doſtroy away the
uits of the Earth.

All men doe ſee theſe thing by dayly Experience
/hen the Mindſters doe holde their aſſemblies &
ouentions, for the deſtueion of Catholques and
ibuerſion of Chriſts true Religion, which our
iodly predicſſours did profeſſe before vs.

Hovv the Doctrine of the Miniſters is the Doctrine of
Sathan becauſe the Deuill doeth teach ſuch things
to the vvitches as they doe to their Auditors.

CHAP. LIII

THeſe which were Inquiſit ors the faith write
  in their booke Intituled marlleus maleficarã
                     the

that when the witches professe them selues to b
Sathans seruants, Sathan giueth thm sundrie pre
cepts to be kept agianst the Catholique Religio
amongst the which he forebiddeth the witches t
make the signe of the Crosse vpon them, but t
strampe on the same when they gette occasion.

Secondly he comandeth them to fast on Sur
dayes, and to make their banquets on freddaye

Thirdly he forebiddeth them to make an
Sacramentall confession of the their sinnes and
Incace they make their confession he comander
them to conceill their gaert sinnes, & to confe
only some litle fatlts.

Fourthly he forebiddeth them to worshipe
adore the holy Sacrament, but at the time
the Eleuation to wincke with their Eyes and nc
to looke to it, or then to looke doune and spit
vpon the Earth & like wise to centemne Chee
and reprotch it with Iniuries and despight of t
holy Sacrament he comanded a witch to faine h
selfe to take the holy Sacrament, and to keepe
quyetly, and since for to dishonour the ho
Sacrament, he comanded to Enclose the same
a potte with a wenemous Toad, which Deuilli
Sacriledge being discloed, this Malitious and a
homiinable witch was punished as she deserue

After that aman witch of that kind call
Sagittaoius hade shote by the comandement
Sathan at the Image of Christ, which wis in forn

a Crucifixe and pearced the same with an Arrowe out of the which miraculous Blooe did Issue, is miserable man by the vertue of God was so immooueably fixed that he could not remoue it of the place a man passing by did speare at m the cause of his Imobilitie the miserabll wih shaking his head and his hands in the which shotte his Arrow, trembleng with all his bodie uld answere nothing, the passinger beholding uond adout him did at the last spy the Arrowe ed in the Crucifixe with blood flowing frō the ne, which after he hade related all things, this serable wttch was taken by the publique Iustice, d after confession made of his Sacreegious fact, d loose his life by such a death as deserueth.

This you may clearely see how the doctrine of e Protestants is the doctrine of Sathan, because th doctrine is taught by them to their auditors Sathan doth teach to the witches, that is the spising of the holy Crosse the contempt of holy ages, the depight they haue against the worsng and adoring of Christs blessed body in the y Sacrament, and banqueting vpon fredday, ing vpon sunday, forebidding of auriculare nfession, & yf Incace they mae their consesto conceill their great sinnes and to confesse ir small sinnes.

ovv the Prsteflants and Puntans for conclusion of our ormerdiscourse are not true Chrisians, but Infidells Idolaters and vvorshiprs of the Deuill.

CHAP. LIIII

FOr better Intelligence of this matter wee mu[
vnderstand that the greatest sinne that ma[
can cōmite against God, is the sinne of Idolatri[
which when a man giueth the soueraigne hōnou[
which is only due vnto God to anie of his Cretu[
res as wtitteth S. Thomas. the Reason is becaul[
is reason that when anie man Giueth the souerigr[
hōnour, which is only due to God to anie of h[
creatures, and chiefly to Sathan which is Ennem[
to God, he pulleth the true God of heauen (;[
farre as lyeth in his power) out of the Soueraigr[
chaire and Throne of gloirie & placeth the Crea[
ture of God, or than Sathan his Ennemie in th[
Soueraigne Throne of Maiestie, and giueth to[
false God the reerence hōnour and worshipe wh[
ch is only due to the God of heauen.

Now that our Protestants and Puritans cōm[
such an horrible cryme you shall vnderstand b[
these reasons which Ensue here after.

First when the Protestants and Puritans Inc[
either tacitly or Expresly, offer Sacrifice vn[
him or consult with him, to learne from hi[
Either things present or to come (as wee ha[
shewen in the liues of Luther, Zuinglius, & man[
Ministers of Scotland as much in their priu[
Chalmers as in their oppen assemblies) they gi[
by such ritts and cermonies that Soueraigne hō[
our vnto Sathan which is only due to the true C[

ſeauen becauſe that Sacrifice is an point of Soue-
uihne hónour whether it be offred vp to God by
n ſecrete actioc of the heart or Externall action
f the bodie, it is forebidden that ſuch hónour
ſould be giuen to anie creature that is but only
ſ God alone, Exod. 22. 20. this is the Reaſon
ſherefore the Catholique Church offerth no
ſcrificee at all, nether to the Virgine Marie,
ſngells and Saintes of heauen but only to God
ſone, wherefor when the witchs Necromancers,
roteſtants and Puritans conſulters with Sathan
ſfer vp aniewiſe Sacrifice vnto him, either to
ſarne from him things preſent or to come, or yet
ſ obtanina anie wordly comoditie by his helpe,
ſey worſhip him as God & Giue the Soueraigne
ſnour which is only due to God to the condem-
ſd Deuill of hell.

Secondly when' the witches, Neeromances
roteſtonts and Puritans, Incall Sathan to learne
om him ſuch things as they deſire to konwe, or
ſaue his helpe in in any worldly matter eithr
ſmodios to them ſelues, or Iniurious to their
ighbours.

his Inuocation of Sathan is an action of falſe
eligion, which is Idolatrie, for ſo much as by
ch prayer and Inuocation, they hónour Sathan
bmitting them ſelues vnto his power, proteſ-
ſg likewiſe by the ſame Inuocation that they
ſue neede of his helpe, as of the Prince & authot
of

of ſnch good things as they craue from him. ſee S
Thomas 2. 2. quaſt. 83 art. 3.

Yſ they accuſe the Catholiqes of Idolarite fo
the Inuoction of the Angells and Sainćts of Hea
uen, much more may wee accuſe them of Idolat.
rie for the Inuocation of Sainćts (which are th
true ſeruants of God) is with an relation to Go
which is Prince aboue them, therefore it can no
be calleć Idolatrie, but becauſe the Inuocation o
Sathan is without any relation vnto God, there
fore it is true Idolatrie for ſo much as the Inuoc
ation finiſheth in Sathan it ſelfe, and not in Go
author of all good things.

For better Intelligence of this matter wee muſ
vnderſtand that Inuocation may by made. 3. wa
yes, firſt abſolutly to God as to the author of al
good things ſecondly to the ſeruants aſ God witl
an Relation to their Lord. thridly to Satha
which is Ennemie to God,

VVhen our Inuocation or praieris directed t
the ſeruants of God that is to the Angells an
Sainćts of Heauen that prayer is their Lord: tha
is wee deſiſe the holie men yet liuind in this mor
tall life, with the Angells and Sainćts of Heauei
to concurre with vs in our prayers, to the eni
that by their concurrance and worthineſſe Go
may be the more mooued to Graunt vs our requ
eſt, & oſ this kind of Inuocation wee haue mani
Examples in holy Scripture as Geneſ. 20. 7. Nui

.7. Iob. 42 8 Rom. 15, 20. Epheſ. 6. :9. but
niefly when Dauid Pſal. 110. 7. ſayeth: *Leuaui*
:uulos meos in montes. vnde veniat Auxilium mihi,
'uxtlium meum a Domino quiſecit cælum et terram. That
: I lifte vp mine Eyes to the Montaines from
hence helpe might come to me, my helpe is frō
od which made Heauen and Eaath the Angells
itriarchs, Prophets and Apoſtles are called by
e Spirit of Prophecie Montaines.

Therefore in an other place ſpeaking of the
ndation of the Church pſal. 86. ſayeth fundam-
ta Eius in Montibus ſantis. the fundamentall
ones of the Church are the holy Montaines,
triarchs, Prophets and Apoſtles, which are
nineniet and high aboue all mortall men, in
nnour digitre and perfection, as loftie Monta-
:s doe tranſcend in altitude litle hills & hillocks

And in an other place ſpeaking of the Angells
d Paſtours whereby God doth gouernē his
urch plai 124. 2. *Montes Incircuitu Eius et Domi-*
in circuitu Populie ſui. that is as yf he wold ſay:
ielicall Montaines doe guard the Church of
d round about, and not withſtanding him ſelfe
in the circuit of his people. and in another
ceth he ſayeth pſal. 90. 11. *Augeles ſuis Manda-*
dete vt cuſtodiant te in Omnibus viis tuis. that is the
rd hath giuen charge vnto his Angells to keepe
in all they wayes.

You ſee in all theſe places how God doth helpe
and

and keepe his people by the Miniſtrie of his holy
Angells and Sanincts of Heauen. and althought
the Prophete did craue helpe from the holy Ang
ells, who did keepe him in all all his wayes by
God, ordinance, yet he acknowlegeth that ſuch
helpe as he did receiue by the Miniſtrie of Angell
was from God, when he ſayeth *Auecilium meum*
Domino qui feeit cœlum et terrā. my helpe is from Go
which hath creted Heauen and Earth.

But whe the Inuoction or prayer is made vnt
Sathan (as it done by the witches, Necromacer
Proteſtante and Puritas, in is done by Soueraigt
honnour giuen vnto him without any relatio
made to God, Becauſe that the Inuocation
praier directed vnto Sathan finiſheth in him
in the principall authot of ſuch good things,
witches, Necrornancers and Miniſters doe cra
from him in their aſſemblies.

For the prayer and Inocation made to Sath
can not be done with any reſpect or relation vn
God (as when wee offer vp our prayers vnto G
) by the Miniſtrie of his Angells or Saincts)
cauſe Sathan is neither friend Seruant or yet En
aſſadour vnto God to beare anie ambaſſage b
weene God and mortall men as the holy Ang
and Saincts are pſal. 9. 11. Tob. 12. 13. hec. 1.
Apoc. 8. 3, In which places the holy Angells
Sainets are a pointed to rule vs to helpe vs in
our affaires, wherefore wee may Iuſtly craue
h

helpe as a meane apointed for our Saluation.

Thridly when the Protestants and Puritans inquire from Sathan the knowlege of future things which are to come and cheefly of man, of such things as depend from the freely which is not limited or determined to one thing, but Indifferent to manie things opposite they worshipe Sanhan with soueraigne hónour as a od for so much as they ascribe to Sathan that iuine prerogatiue to foretell things to come which belongeth only to God by the naturall erfction of his Deite, and to his frinds and ser- ants only by participation and Reuelation. ther ore the prophete Esay sayed. 41. 23. Denounce vs what thing are come, & wee shall know that ou are Gods, but to Inquire the truth of future identell things from Sathan, as from the seruant d frind of God no man can doe the same with- t Great Iniurie done to God as is said, because than is no friend to God, but his Deadly Enne- ie as it is written, psal. 73. 23. *Superbia Eorum qui Odernnt ascendit sumper.* The pride of these which ate the doth alwise ascend from them vnto God. ourthly when they make a couéant with Sathan ither manifest or secreets they forcsaike the eedshipe of God and preferre the prince of dar- ıcsfte vnto the creator of all thing, as the prop- te Esay writteth. 28. 15. *Percussimus faedus cum rte, et cum Inferno fecimus pactum that is quia posuemas ndacium spem nostram.* that is wee haue made a uenant with Death and agreement with hell,

O

becufe wee haue fette our hepe vpon a lye, which
is as much to fay by a couenant made with Sathar
Prince of Hell, wee forefaixe the true frendhipe
of God, & put our truft and confideuce in Sathan,
which is the Father of lyes for a man can not feru
tow Mafters contrarie to othors in all things a
God and the Dcuill are. Math. 6. 24.

Eyftly yf fome of the Proteftants and puritan
will fay that they neuer did fee Sathan nor ye
fpeake with him, and therefore that fuch crime
of Infidelitie & Apoftafie can not be laid to thei
Charge as it may be done to Lnther, Zuinglius &
other heretiques aboue mentioned.

VVee anfwere that althought they haue no
made a band or couenant with Sathan by word
Expreffe (as others haue done) yet wee fay tha
haue a quyet and fecrete band made with Sathar
when they approoue the open couenant and agre
ment with Zuinglius & Luther made with Satha
in points and heads of Religion.

For Luther him felfe confeffeth in his boot
Intituled *De Maffa priuata et vnction Sacerdotum*, tha
he did abolifhe the Maffe at Sathans perfufion, &
likwife that Sathan gaue him the title of his boot
wherein he did abolish the Maffe, which title
de Abroganda Mifta, which band and agreemer
betweene Luthea and Sathan. the Proteftants an
Puritans doe all approoue vnto this day, when
fore they are als guiltie in this Cryme as Luth
which did abolish the Maffe by his couenant ma
wit

with Sathan.

Luther confeſſeth in manie pairts of his workes, that he did know the Deuill and was ſo well aequainted with him that did eat a meaſure of ſalt in his fellowſhipe & companie, aganinſt that which is written. 1. cor. 10. 20. *Nolo autem vos ſocios fieri Demoniorum,* I will not that you be companios vnto Deuills. ſee the like deut. 18. 20. where it is forebiden to couſult with Deuills or yet witches or Necomancer or with anie other which foretell things to come by the the ſpirit of Sathan or to obſeure vaine Dreames.

Alſo the Puritans and Sacramentares can not Excuſe them ſelues to haue no ſocietie or ſeecreete couenat with Sathen when they Approoue the band and agreement which Zuingius made with Sathan Inſtruction which did teach him in the Night that Chirſts bodie was no otherwiſe in the Sacrament then Mropically that is by only ſigne and repreſntation, aud non really ſubſtantially as the Catholiques beleeue. This is Zuinglius owen confeſſion in lib. de ſubſidion Euchariſtiae ſurius in his hiſtorie *Año.* 1524. *Genebrard lib. I. Chronogr. ano. eodem.* who deſyretd to ſee more of ſuch matters couenants and bonds made with Sathan let him Read S. Thomas. 2. 2: *quæſt.* 95. *Art.* 4. *et Malleu. Malleſicar. Tom.* I. *Part. ſt. quæſt.* 2. *etz. Tom.* 2. *pag.* 493. *et Sequentibus.*

Laſtly the ſpirit of God is not contrarie to it ſelfe as S. Paul wriiteth, 1. car. 14. 32, but Luther
and

Zninglius with their spirit are contradictoriou̅ one to an other in the Misteries of Religion i̅ calling Ech one an other hertiqoee and seuere̅d from the Church of God.

For thus Luther writeeth in defens. *verboru̅ cane pag.* 381. *Serio censemus* zs wee Earnestly desc̅ erne all Zuinglians Sacra̅entaries to be heritiqdue̅ & seuere Seuered from tbe Church of God, whicl deny the bodie and blood of Christ to be reciue̅d with a corprall mouth the venerable Eucharist

Thus you see how Luther calleth Zuinglu̅ with all other Sacramentaes heretiques seuere̅d from the Church of Zuinflius adorneth Luthe̅ with such like titles of hōnour Tom. 2. *responf. ai confeß Luterif al.* 450. thus writting Lutherus *summ̅ aft blasphemous is* Luther is blaspheeus in the highes̅ degre, a shamelesse kailleer a furious man bestr̅ ught in mind possessed with a Deuill, ablockehe̅ aded fellowe a foule loathsome swyne Inuadin̅ the Glorie omnipotent power, pure vertiie and diuine Essence of God, by manifest furie and Extreame blasphemie, on heretque Incorrihlte a false Imposture & dceiuer of the world, a grea̅ deale worse then Marcion the haretque which di̅ diny that Christ hade a true naturall bodie.

This is the concord which is betweene Luthe̅ and Zuinglius, who were taught in the Night b̅ two Spirits, which as you may Easill see were to̅ Deuills stirring vp these tow pillars of this new̅ Reiigion to contranous heresies.

THE LV: Chapter shevveth hovv their liues and morall
Doctrins teacheth the heresie of the lebertens hovv no man
is bound in Conscience to keepe the lavve of God or yet
of men (because they) that they are made free from
all lavves by their faith in Christ and libertre of
their Gospell and consequently that sinne is but
an false Imagination of man and echone may
doe vvhat he lisleth vviehout sffence of God
and nothing may Condemne the man
but only Infidelitie.

CHAP. LV.

NOw behold Protestant what Edification
thou mayest find in the liues of Luther,
inglius, caluin, Beza, Bucerus, oc co Lampad-
, Knox, and others such like which were acco-
ed to be the Pillars and foundatours of this
r Church, yf thou wist niligently viwe their
ne of life thou shaft nothing worthie of praise
to be Imitated by vs, but contrariwise thou
t find manis thing abhominable, and to be
asted and abhomrred by all good Christians.
t please you to viewe Luthers life you shall fid
ich of Vowes made to God abhominable pol-
n in a Sacrilegious bedd betweene an apostata
r and Apostatesse Nunne, a Monstrous coni-
tion of tow abhominable persons againist the
e of God and man and how he could no more
aine him selfe from venus Game then he
d doe from spitting, how he did resist his coe-
ce the space of ten yeeres to Embrace his errours

errours, and Giue councell to others to doe tl
like, how he did abrogate the Masse at Satha
persuasion, and so choise the enémie of God ar
man to be his Master, so that you may know tl
holynesse of this blacke Gospell by his pestifero
Doctrous which did teach him his lessone.

Yf you please to behold his doctrine you sh
see how he relsaleth the raines of the concupissi
to all abhominable crimes of the world, witho
all pricke of conscience seare of God or shame
the world.

For this he writteth in his booke Intituled
Captiuitate Babilonia cap. baptismo. thou se
how riche the Christion man is who willingly c
not loose his Saluation vnlesse he will not beler
forno sinne can condéne him but only Infidelit

Againe in his booke de liberate Christti
writteth that on good workes doe make a go
man nor Euill workes an Euill man.

So after this sentenee of Luthea you may c
what you list, for a man is no better for go
workes, nor worse for Euill, according to t
doctrine.

Againe he writteth in that same booke of C
istian libertie, that on Euill works may make
man Euill or worthie of damnation, but c
Infidelitie.

Ahaine in Sermon, doe nouo Testasten to l
eth thus: *Caueamus a peccato sed multo magis a b
Operibus, tantum attendamus dei promissionem et sic*
                                                    tl

hat is to say let vs take heede hrom sinne, but
uch more from lawes and good workes, and
tend only to the promise of God and to faith.

Againe he writteth in cap. 2. *ad Galat.* that only
ith is necessarie to make vs Iust all other thnihs
e fre and Indifferent neither Cómanded or yet
rebiden *Ibidem* he writteth: yf thy conscience
cuse the that thou haft sinned, answere I haue
ied then God will punish and condemne thee
i, but the lawe affirmeth the same. but I haue no
ing to doe with the lawe, where fore? because I
i made free from the same by Christian libertie.

Againe in his booke of Christian libertie writ-
h: that *Nullo opare. nullolege homini Christiano opus est*
m pea sidem fit liber ab Omni lege. the Christian man
th no neede of any worke or lawes, because he
made free from all lawes by faith.

As Luther maketh all men free from all lawes
God. and not bound in conscience to keepe the
ne, to Establish his Iustification by only haith,
doth he affirme that no man is dedfull in Con-
ence to keepe the lawes of temporall princes,
:ause sayetd he that each man is made free from
:keeping of all lawes by their Christian liberte
d faith in Christ.

For thus Luther writtetd lib. de cap *tiuii Babi-*
ta cap. de Baptisme. hy what Righi doth the Pope
lrine lawes vpon vs, who gaue him power to
uft vs in Captiuitie, the libeitie which si giuen
is by Baptisme. Neither the Pope, Bishope or
                                              any

any other mortall man hath power to bind an
Christian with the lawe of a sillabe, vnlesse, it b
the mans owen consent.

Thus you see how Luther affirmeth that n
Christian man is bound in conscinc to keep
the lawe of God, or man that is of Spirituaall an
temporall Princes.

Hovv Caluins life and Doctriue carie avvay
Iu conflant foules to plaine Infidciltie.

CHAP. LVI

CAlvin auoucheth the same doctuine wit
Luther. for first. lib. 2. Inst. cap. 7. sect. 1.
he writitteth thus of the lawe of God, that is th
ten Cömandements *Nunc Ergo quoneam.* Now the
efor because the lawe hath an power towards th
faitfull not such an power as may bind their con
cience with any accurse (Infra) or to make the
astrayed confounding their consciences condem
or destroy the aranfgeffours thereof.

And againe. lib. 3. Inst. cap. 19. sut. 2. wri
tetd that the lawe hath no power in the conscinc
of the faithfull to accuse them before the tribun
Seate of God (Ibidem) sith the lawe leaueth o
man Iust or Righteous before God, either wee
Excludede from all hope of Iustification or th
wee must be made free and loosed from all law
and so that there is no reguard of good work
thus mueh concerning the law of God.

As concerning the lawe of man Caluin bib.
Inst. 19. sect. 14. writteth thus after long diputi

Christian libertie fam vero cum is no wee there-
e sith faithfull consciences hauing receiued
h prerogatiues of libertie, as wee haue aboue
e foorth, wee conclude that they are Exempt
m all power of men (Infra) paul declareth
t Christ is destroyed vnesse our conscience
nd fast in their libertie, which verily they haue
t yf they will at the well of man be snared with
bondes of lawes and ordinances.

Melanch then in confess. Augustana and his
ologie for the same, the rigorus Lutherans of
conie in confess. Altem bergensi doe Subscribe
same with Luther. and Caluin.

Thus Protestant thou mayest see Euidently
w Luther & Caluin with their broad doe sette
de the lawe of God & man with all good workes
Establish their Iustification by only faith sith
man is bound in conscience to keepe the lawe
God (according to this doctrne) to what pur-
e should any man paine hime selfe to worke
d workes seing that he is not bound in consc-
ce to doe the same, or yet can he hope for any
uenly rewarde at Gods hands for such things.
Moreouer yf no man be bound in conscience
keepe the lawe of God (according to this doc-
e) no man shalbe boūd in conscience, to wor-
pe honour and serue God, as is cōmandēd in
first Table.

kewise no man shall offend God when he lyeth
h his Nighbours wyfe when he taketh away his

Nig

P

Nighbours goods whom he betrayeth his Mas[ter]
when he forsweareth him-selfe for anie worl[dly]
comoditie, when he slayeth his Nighbour to s[a]
sie his wrath or comitteth any other cryme agai[nst]
the lawe of God or man, because he is not bou[nd]
in conscience to keepe such lawes and worke go[od]
workes as wee haue shewen aboue, according [to]
the doctrine of Luther and Caluin, but all m[en]
shalbe free to doe what they please by Chris[t]
libertie without the controllin of any lawe: Hi[s]
diuine or humaine, at yet of any conscience.

Thus thou seest that these Newe Gospellers [doe]
open the Gatte of mischiefe, release the raines
enchpiffance to all horrible crimes by the libe[rtie]
of their Gospell,

Besides these things this doctrine of our her[e]-
ques taketh cleane away all sinnes, because [the]
sinne is no thing Else but a transgression, su[ar]-
ing or declyning from the lawe (as the Gr[eeke]
word o Vomix Imporieth) 1 Ihon. 3. 4 w[here]
there is no lawe which bindeth the conscience [of]
men, there is no transgression of the lawe, t[here]
is consequently no sinne at all, as S. Paul wit[nes]-
seth. Rom. 4. 15. which is the very heresie of [the]
libertins, Children Engendred in the snox[e of]
Luthers and Caluins heresies abaue mention[ed]

So thou mayest Euidently see how the Doct[rine]
of the Protestants and Puritans doth lead [mens]
soules vnawares to the enter of atheisme & [Gulfe]
of Infidelitie.

V

VVhen Mr. welsshe in the second, pairt of his,
ly obiesth to vs that manie popes did lead an,
godly life, wee answere and confesse that in the
urch of God there be white and chaffe, mat. 3.
good and badde fishes. Mat. 13, 48. some
dde with the wedding Garniemt others not
dde with the same, Mat. 22. 12, some the-,
goats Mat. 25. 32. foolish Virgins, some wise
th. 25. 2. some Veshells. of honnour some of
tumelie. 2. Tim. 2, 20. some Reprobate Mat.
14. augast. *Tract 45. in Ihoannem, at lib. cont. cres-*
um cresconium cap. 34. and amonigst the rest a
ditor Inddas amongst the Apostles Mat. 26.
wherefore as the faithfull Apostles should not
onemned for the Prodition of Iudas; Right
he holy Apostles & docours, the holy Martires
virgins of the Catholique Romaine Church
ld not be condemned for the leud leucs of
ers.

lbeit some of the Popes in their owen proper
ons haue ouerseene them seules in their dutie,
ther mortall men doe, yet they haue not com-
ed such crymes as welsche affirme them lyn-
o haue done.

Ind because it belongeth not to my purpose at
time, to Examine seurall all welsches, forged
& Malitious detractions in this behalfe, I will
sette doune tow Examples for all the rest,
reby the Indiffernt Reader may by the Euid-
lyes sette doune in these two Examples by
welsche.

welsche coniectuae his forged lyes and malitio
detractions in the rest of the Popes liues detract
by him malitiously.

As concerning the first Example it is of Po
(Iane) which welsche alleadgeth to haue dece
fully cropen in the Apostaicall seate and likew
in her Papall dignitie to haue conceiued a
borne an Childe.

To knewe this to be a forged lye and Euid
fable, let the Reader Read Cardinall Bellarm
lib. 3. deponti; Rom. cap 24 where he proou
this truth as I ascerten it to be,

The. 2. Example is of Pope Grehorie the
where welsche bringeth in a false Schismati
called Bennoto accuse the holy Pope Malie
(as the Iewes brought in a false witnesse to acc
Christ our Sauiour) and to see the light of
purpose Read Cardianall Bellarmine lib. 4
Pontif. Rom. cap: 7. and you shall find all thi
in this behalfe as I ascerfaine them to be & well
likewise a malitiouse detractour and forger of
But wee haue that aduatage of the Protestant
Puritahs that the Doctrine and liues of the
Pastours and Doctours, Martires and Virgin
the Catholique Romaine Church were conn
by diuine Miracles which is the Infallible tes
onse of God, and their festuall dayes celebr
yeerely for the same respect by the Catholi
Romaine Church for a testimonie of the Re
ous honour due to their holinesse, as to the faith

Instrum

Instruments of the holy Ghost true seruants and friends of God.

But when our Protestants & Puritas wold haue confirmed their false doctrine by false Miracles (and thus to make as much as lay in their powere, God an false God, and false witnesse) God did tourne their attempt to their owen shame and reproch, when Luther did Endeuour him selfe to cast the Deuill out of a possessed persone, the Deuill did chasse him away. Staphil. apolog. 2. Genebrard lib. 2. Chonogr. anon. 1545.

VVhen Caluin did attempt fainedly to raise a man from death to life for confirmation of his false doctrine he did kill a quicke men by his hypocrisie according to the Iust Iudgment of God, Bolsecus in vita Caluine.

Likewise knox the chiefe minister of Scotland Preaching in S. Gills Church in Edinbrughe did suffer such a publique sham before the people that his face did tourne in his Necke as such that did see that Monstrous sight did aelate the hame vnto my selfe.

Thus as Erasmus sayeth since time they did beginne their new Religion they could nuer cure in lame Horse of his disease.

And concerning their liues yea the patriarchs prophets and Pillars of this now Religion, which laue them seluer out for the to reformers of the world. and as faithfull guids to Heauen, were of such abhominable & detastable liues that no man halbe able to find out more malitious treasons,

Cruell seditions horrible slaughter of Church
men, perturbations of Realmes, such practise of
Necromancie and forcerie, adulterie, simonie, &
spoling of Church men, and Catholique Roaines
of their goods and Guere then was done by Luther, Zuinglisus Caluin, Beza, Knox King Henry
the Eight in England and by suchlike others which did defend them in their Malitious deeds, as
you may see in the historie of Surius. *Genebrard, lib.*
2, Chronogr. Bolsecus in vita Caluene et Bazæ, Stephilus
in his Apologie, Doctor Sanderus in *sellise mate*
Anglicano, Stanislcans, Rescus polonus. lib 2. de atheismis
et phalarismis Euangelicorum, M. Nicol Burne in his
Disputation Against the Ministers of Scotland, and
others which haue written the histories of our
dayes.

For not their abhominable libes aboue mentioned
but also the spirit of contradiction which is amongst them silues in grunds of Saluation, doe Euidently shewe vnto vs that they are send from
Sathan, author of all discord and dissention, and
not from God which is only cheefe Prince of
peace and concord in doctrine of Saluation, but
also the conseruer of the same in his Church by
the perpetuall assistance of the holy spirit Ihon. 14
16, 2 12 and continuall succession of Pastours &
Doctours, which keepi the flocks of Christs she-
epefolde in vnitie of faith from circumuention
of Erruaur as S. Paul writteth Ephes. 4. 2 yf it
please the thou mayest see the these things plenti-
fullij

fulby prooued in our booke Intitled the hunting
of the Foxe,

Befides thefe things they haue not only made
men free, as much from obfrnaton of the lawe of
God, as of the lawe of man by the pretended libe-
ftie of their gofepll & Iuftificatiō by ōly faith, but
alfo they Endeuoure them felues (as much as lyeth
in their power.) to aboliish and difanull the lawe
of nature or light of Reafon, which iscalled confcience, that thus by degree & degree defcending
more and more to Hellish Pitte profound, they
may carie away the foules of men more craftelie
hy the hellish lure of crrnall libertie, from the true
feruice of God, and open the broad gatte & large
way to all delidght of finne ane mifchiefe which leadeth to perdition, as Chrift did forewarne
vs in his Eungell.

For better Intelligence of this purpofe wee muft
declare the qualities and conditits as much of a
found as of a wounded confcience to the end wee
may know how a good men of a good treafure
lord bring out good things and how an Euill man
out of an Euill treafare doth bring out euill things
The wife man fayeth that the confcience is a
ight which shewth vs the way of life where wee
houuld goe & liewife the way of perdition, from
vhich with all diligence wee shoud declion, becaufe, and all the lawes of the world are but ftreaes
which flowe from the fountarn of Reafn, and
leemes which deiue from the light of confcience,
which

which is the Eye of the soule, yf wee make our
seules free from the obseruatin of all lawes, wee
must also forersaise to followe the light of vpright
Reason, which is the mistresse, and Queene of all
ciuill lawes approoued amongst the sonnes of men

The ten morall Comandements of God are nothing els but a declaration of the lawe of nature
which is the light of Reason when the Prophett
Dauid phieeteth to himselfe who shewe vs good
& Euill he answereth againe that the light of God
rountenacc (that is a prihticipatio of Gods Eternall wisdome) is printed and Engraphed in our
vnderstading, which light sheweth vs these good
things, which are to be done, and what Euill
things are to be eschewed.

Becausc as Cicero sayeth Magna est vis conse-
iencię in vtramque partem, great is the force o
Conscience both the partes, that is both i
good and Euill, wee must shewe what actions th
conscienceof man (which is the lawe of nature
hath both in good and illuill.

The first is, it sheweth vs the good that wi
should doe. psal. 4. 7. Rom, 12. 15.

Secondly when we doe will it defendeth
against the detestation of Euill, villars 1. cor. 4,
13. 4

Thirdly it is a constant wituesse of our fidelit
Rom. 9. 1.

Fourtly it rewardeth vs with loy and com-
mentatio wee haue done well prouerb. 15.

2. cor

Fyſtly it Engndreth much hope and confidence
God 1. Ihon. 3 21.

But in all Euill things hath contrarie actins.

First it sheweth the good things which wee
ould doe and likewise Euill thinge from which
ce should decline, and binnetd vs by her power
id authoritie to doe good, and decliue from
uill. pſal. 4. 7. Rom. 2. 15.

Secondly when the man doth against her lawe
id direction she accuseth him of diſſobedience
cclef. 7. 23. Rom 6. 16.

Thridly she condemneth him of guilte cryme
p. 17. 11 tit. 3. 10.

Fourtdly she punisheth him for his misdeed like
jnawing worme without any reſt. Eſay. 51. 8.

Fyſtly she bringeth Euill men to diſpaire of
eat crymes as it is meniſeſt in Caine. Geneſ. 3°
. and Iudas. mat. 27. 8.

Thus you see how conscience is a pedagogue &
jole maſter, which God did gue to teach vs our
tie. hold vs in awe, and trreſie vs faom the del-
it of ſinne, eun then when Secrecie promiſeth
curitie to defend and reioyce vs whn wee doe
ll, and to accuse and condemne vs when wee
e Euill.

VVherefore yf men and weemen be perſuaded
their consciences that no man hath freewill in
: Inward action of the soule to eſchue ſinne and
ie Election of vertue, but that all humaine
ſions are deſigned aud deſtinated to an end by
Cod

O

Gods Secreote direction or that the coōmanden
ents of God are Impossible and farre beyond th
reach of mans power, or that all Christians a
made free from the obseruaition of all lawes,
much diuine as haumaine, as all Protestants an
Puritans teach by the libertie of their Cospell.

Then when soeuer a Gentlewoman is tempte
with the the lust of flesh, a man with reunge,
seruat with couetofnesse of his Maiters goods,
Merchant with deceite in buying & felling a fal
witnesse with periūie, lawe to Iudge wrangousl
she for bryberie, they shal haue no more scruple
conscince to cōmitehomicide, thifte, adulteri
periurie, treason, with all such horrible crime
when they may Eschue the penalities of Prinies
rullers then Beasts haue to drinke watter, and ea
their meate when they are vrged by hungare at
thrist.

You see now how the doctrine of our Prott
tants and Puritans is altogether sauourable for t
aduancement of sinne and vice, with the abolis
ing and destruction of vertue, likewise how
leadeth away sillie soules from the true seruice
God to the center of atheisme & gulfe of Insidei

Hovv the Iustification of Protestants by only faith stand
vvith all Deadly sinnes of the vvorld, except
only Incredulitie.

CHAP. LVII.

LVther libe de captiuit. Bibilonicæ cap.
Baptismo thus writteth: thou seesihow i

ie man Christian is that Euen willingly he cañ
ot loose his saluation how great soeuer his sinne
t vnlesse he will not beleeue for no sinne can con-
emne him but only Incredulitie.

Here you see that their faith in Christ wherebe
iey are Iustisied standeth with all the sinnes that
ian can comite in this world as homicide, thise,
luluerie peoiurie sacriledger treason, deceit,
ioleie oppressioo, scisme, hypocrisie, detraction
f their Nighbours good same, dissobedience of
iildren to their parents, of subicts to their Frin-
s, of seruants to their Masters pride, Enuy, des
ight, Malice, couetousnes of their Nighours gods, seruants or other things suchlike, so that
ie cómtting of such sinnes can not condemne
ie Baptised christian which beleeueth in Christ,
it only Insidelitie.

VVherefore it is that these sinnes can not
ondemne them, because (say they) that the Ius-
ce of Christ, which they apprehend by faith
ydeth all these sinnes, so that God will not Imp-
te them to such as comite them.

Caluin subscribeth with Luther this same doct-
ne. lib. 3. Inst. cap. 14 sect. 12. thus writtings
ir corruption & vncleanesse being couered with
ie puritie of Christ are not Imputed to vs, but
:ing so luied and hidde they shall not come to
ie Iudgment of God to aecuse vs.

Caluin sheweth by this opinion, as Luther did
:fore him, that their sines being hidde & couered

by

by the Iustce and puritie of Christ apprehended
by their faith shall ont appeare in the Iudgmen
of God to accuse or condemne them. likewise h
teacheth that the abhominable filth & vncleanes
of sinne. (which maketh the man reseauble vnt
Sathan) doth still remaine within their soules, &
only hidde by the Externall Iustice of Christ, a
yf you wold couer an blacke Ethiopian with
white garment External y, you see than what
malitious spouse full of corrupt stinch, the Prote
tant soule is to Christ, the beutifull some of th
liuing God, which is an abhominable thing to b
hard.

Caluin in anitidoto concile Triden tmisess. c
can 18. writteth: that some seede of the true liuel
faith remaineth still amongst great deadly sinne

Yf their true liuely faith abideth amongst gre
deadly sinnes, then they may doe what they li
because their faith will Iustfie them in the midde
of their great deadly sinnes by the apprehensi
of Christs Iustice which hid then sinnes that th
come not to the Iudgmen of God for to accu
them. Is not that a pleasane libertie they take
selues to comite all sinnes without scruple of con
cience or any other repelhension.

Caluin algane lib 3. Inst. cap. 2. sect. 3. sayet
beholding that Christ doth Iustifie vs not by a
probation of our proper Innocencie but by Im
uation of Christs Iustice wee are Esteemed to
Iust in Christ, who are Iniust in our selues.

y

You fee finne and Iniquitie doc ftill remaine, n the Proteftants foules, Euen when they are ultied by the Imputatioa of Chrifts Iuftice whih they aprehend by faith. fo you may behold hat all kind of finne, Impietie, Malce, hypocrifie nd fniftice may ftand with their Iuftification by nly faith in Chrift, a faith forefuith very meete o Nurish theeues adulteaers, homieids, Travters, hypocrits, falfefiers of their faith, becufe they 6mite all thefe finnes with many others without eprehen finne in the Iudgment o God or good, onfciences according to the former Doctrines f Luther and Caluin.

Hovv Iuftification by only faith doih contemne all good vvorkes vvithout all ferre of God to comite Euill vvorkes, vvhich are pleafant to the finner.

CHAP. LVIII.

FOr probation of this point Luther. lib. de libert. Chriftiano thus writteth: good workes make not the man good, nor Euill workes the man Euill. fo according to Luthers doctring good vorkes and Euill are both Indifferent, becaufe hey can neather make the man good or Euill, elpe or harme him therefore the man needeth euer to paine him felfe to doe anie good workes, r likewife feare to doe any Euill workes, becaufe hey can not make him worfe then he is, but to oe anie thing which liketh him beeft, whether it e good or Euill, for it is his only faith Chrift vhich maketh him Iuft and acceprable vnto God

or

or Euill, for it is his only faith in Chrift which
maketh him Iuft and acceptable vnto God & not
his good workes, for as his good workes con not
helpe him, fo his Euill workes cannot hinder his
faith to Iuft fie him, wherefore a man may do
what he lifteth without hurt of his Iuftificatior
by only faith, this is the libertie of their carnal
Gofpell.

Caluin taketh Luther by the hand in this matter. lib. 3. Inft. cap. 19. fect. 2 thus writting for
fith the lawe leaueth no man Iuft or righteous
aither wee are Excluded from all hope of Iuftific
ation or wee muft be made free and loofed from
the lawe, and fo that there be no regarde at al
of God workes.

Thus you fee to Eftabish his Iuftificaton by onl
faith, he affirmeth that no man should haue reg
airde of good workes, but to haue recourfe onl
to his faith, which Iuftifieth him by the apprehe
nfion of Chrifts Iuftice without Regaird of goo
workee.

Luther againe in fermone de nouo Teftam éo
fiue de miffa thus writteth: caeuamus a peccat
fed dmulto magis a *legilus, et operibus, bonis tantu*
atteedamu Dei promiffionem et fidem; That is let vs tak
heede the keepe our felues from finne, but muc
more from the lawes and good workes let vs onl
haue the Eye of faith and our mind fixed vpon th
promife of God. fo Luther will haue the man t
haue no regaird of good or Euill workes, but on

o considder the promise of God by his grace in
Luther againe in sermone eodem, sie deus dilexit
nundum, this writeth: because the way is straite
which leadeth to heauen thou must be made slen-
ler and then, yf thou woldest enter thereby (and
litle aftre) yf thou wilt come charged with sacks
ull of good workes thou must lay them doune oth-
w.see thou canst not enter in at the stratite way.

Luthers Disciples in Colloquio Altembergnsin
ffirme that wee should praie to prseuere in faith
o the end without all good workes.

Caluin lib. 3. Inst. cap. 19 sect. 2. 4. 7. wrtteth
hat where there is any assurance of Iustification
here should be no regaird of lawes or good wor-
es, and that all externall workes are Indifferent
o their Iustification, for they can neither helpe
r Impaire the same so you see how their Iustifi
atian bv faith destroyeth all good workes as not
eedefull to the same.

*Hovv the faith of the Protestants is an abbominable faith
and sinkefull of all mischiefe, corrupt fountain' vvhence
manie venimous springs runne out a naughtie ore
bearing fruits full of poyson and abbominateon.*

CHAP. LVIIII.

THis assertion of ours is manifest by their
owen Doctrine before all things you must
nderstand that there is no thing so odious and
bhominable before the Eyes of God as sinne ",
r sinne was cause that God did expell the
bellious Angells out of Heauen, sinne was cause

to

to banish Adam with his Posteritie out of parad
ice, sinne is the cause of all the pouertie, sicknesse
trouble and miserie, when by men are wexec
tossed and tormoilled in this mortall life. beside
these things it is cause of damnation of mani
millions of soules. so that the most perrillons an
dangerous thing which is in this world, is tha
thing whence doth proccede because that sinne
is cause of all mischiefe which doth fall vpon mai

Now to shewe that these Iustifing faith is the
naughtie tre, as wee haue recited aboue & Deadl
sinnes the venemous frits thereof it is thus pro
oued by their owen doctriae.

Luther Patriarch to all the heretiques of of ou
age in Assert. omnium aat. suor. art. 51. 52 (
afferrmeth boldly that omrria opera Insto
ruim sunt peccata mortalia. that is all the worke
of Iust men are but deadly sinnes.

So all the workes which Issie or spring out fro
their Iust men Iustified by their Iustifing faith a
no bettea fruits then poysoned deadly sinnes
that when the best and Iustest Preestant that
amongst them Goeth to the Church to heare t
Preaching to praie God to Reuerence and ob
his Minister to receue the comuion to than
God there after for the same giue almes to
poore ate the Church or by the way syde dotd
other thing but worke deadly sinnes wherefore
were better to him to sitte Idly at home then
prine him selfe to worke deadly sinns.

As concerning Caluins opinion in this matter
he is altogether with Luther. lib. 3 Inst. cap. 12.
sect. 4. thus writting: but they that shall Earnestly
as it were in the sight of God Enquire of the true
rule of righteousnesse, shall certenly find that all
the workes of men, yf they be Iudged by their
owen worthinesse are no thing els but vncleanesse
& filthinesse, that which amongst common people
is accounted righteousnesse is before God meere
wickednesse, that which is Iudged puritie is vncleannesse, that which is reckned Glorie is but
shame.

You se here according to Caluins doctrine that,
which is Esteemed by men righteousnesse is before
God meere wickednesse, so that all their praiere,
preachings to men & receiuing of the communion,
which appeare before men to be the seruicee of
God, and righteous workes of religion, are nothing else but meere wickednesse which is the pesti-
ous fruits of their Iustifsiinh satth.

Caluin againe lib. 3. Inst. cap 14 sect, 9. writeth in this fashion. thus wee haue shewen that
there cometh not so much as one good worke out
of holy men, which yf it be Iudged in it selfe deserueth not a Iust rewarde of shame. so the best
workes of Religion and best fruits of their Iustifsing faith deserueth no rewarde but shame and
reprotch. therefore they they should not find
fault with Citholiques which reprotch the acts of
their Religion and fruits of their Iustifsing faith

R
a5

as worthie open shame and reprotch.

Caluin. againe in Antidots concili. Ttident,
Seſſ. 6. thus writteth: they are not ſo much to be
reprotched who ſaid all good workes yf they be
Iudged by exact rigour to the extremitie are
rather worthie of Eternall damnation then any
rewarde of life.

So you ſee how the beſt workes of their Relig
ion are more worthie of Eternall damnation the
anie rewarde of life, yf ſo be what difference pu
they betweene the ſinne of Lucifer, wherefore h
was condmned Eternally, and their good worke
which deſerued Eternall damnation with Sathar
wee are conſtrained to ſay that faith, whic
yeeldeth ſuch damnable fruits muſt be an vnha
pie faith, which bringeth to man rather Eterna
damnation by her naughtie fruits then a
rewarde of life.

Caluin againe lib. 3. Inſt. cap. 5. Sect. 19. th
writteth. let this ſtand as a ſure foundation vn
vs, which can not be ſhaken by anie Engine, th
the mind of man is ſo alienate and aſtringed fro
the Iuſtice of God that it can not conceiue Ent
priſe or deſire any thing but that, which is Imp
us warſted, or crooked. The heart of man is
Infected and defiled with the poyſon of ſinne t
it can breth out no other thing but a corr
ſtinch. and althought men ſome time apeare
outward ſhewe to doe ſome good workes, Neu
theleſſe the mind is full of hypocriſie, and

obliquitie and also wrapped and Intangled with rowardnesse aud malitiousnesse of nature.

Beholee here good Reaeer the true descnption of a Protestant sette doune by Ihon Caluin their chiefe Doctour, which is althought the Protestant apeare some time in outward shewe to doe some good worxes, Neuerthelesse his mind is full of hypocrisie and false obliquitie, & also wrapped nd Intangled with malitiousnesse of neture, his ieart likewis so defiled with the poyson of sinne hat he can breath nut no other but corrupt stinch

Then when the Minister or protestant apereth o men outwardly to doe some good worxes in reaching his new Gospell to his audetours, or in iuing the comunion to anie man, and in the ieane time (as Caluin affirmeth) his mind is ill of hipocrisie false obliquitie and wrapped in Malice, wherefor should wee giue eare to his Preeding or beleeue him, beholding that with such eceitfull hypocrisie and malititious mind, he can reath out no other thing but corrupt stinch. of eresie.

Therefore wee can say no thing more Iustly to he Minister then that which Christ said to an iuill seruant: I Iudge the by the words of thyne wne mouth o naughtie seruant. because the linister or Protestant doth confesse his owen ialece and hypocrisie where with his mind is in-cted, euen when he appeareth outwardly before ien to doe some Good worxes, according to
the

the doctrine of Caluin, which cõmandeth all Ministers and Protestants to hold this vndobted truth as a sure foundation of Religion, which can not be shaken by the Engine of man.

You see here most truly how their Iustifiing faith is but an abhominable sinke of all Mischeete, which can breathout no other thing but corrupt stinch of heresie philipe Melanchthon Luthers faithfull achates confirmeth this doctrine of Luter and Caluins whin he writteth in locir ano 1501. Tit. de peceat. saying: Stfolsoreth therfore that all the workes of men as much worthie of praise as you please are nothing Cztse but sinnes as worthie of death otherwise deadly sinnes.

So wee will conclude wiuh that sentce of Christ, which sayeth; the good tre is knowen by the good fruits and the Euill tree by the Fruits Mat. 7. 17. considering than that all the fruits and workes of their Iustifiing faith, are but fillanesse, vnclánesse false obliquitie, deadly sinnes aud malitiousnesse of mind which can braith out no other thing but corrupt stinch, you may easily Gather that such a Iustifiing faith is no thing else but an abhominable sincKe of all mischiefe a corrupt so untaine full of poysoned springs, a naughtie tree whose venemous fruits doe Euidently shewe the pestilence of the soule from whenec they doe deriue.

Hovv the protestants haue no true Religion of God but of Sathan: because that all the fruits and good vvorkes of their Iustofiing faith are nohting else but deadly sinnes

45

An abhominable sincze
as vvee haue prooued in the former Chpter (according to
their ovvne docrints) in vvhich consisteth the seruice of
Sathano & not the seruice of the true God of heauen

CHAP. LX.

BEcause God is the Creator collator and conseruatour of all good things, soueraigne Monarch of heauen & Earth soueraigne honour, seruice and obedience is Iustly due to his heauenly Maiestie therefore he comandeth vs to adore and seruice and obedince. Deut. 6 1. 13. Mat. 4. 10. Tit. 1. 17. heb. 5. 9. so Religion is a vertue wheby wee serue God, according to the rules sette dune by him in the olde and New Testament.

That this seruice consieth in good workes actable vnto God, & not in deadlly sinnes which be hated by God it is thus prooued by many examples of Godly men let doune in the holy Scripture.

VVhen Abell did offer vp Sacrifice vnto God the Sripture sayeth that God did approoue the Sacrifice of Abell as acceptable vnto him, and did despise the Sacrifice of Caine as vngratefull vnto him, It is Euident that God doth not approoue deadly sinnes, but doth reprooue and punish men for the same, as it is manifest in the fall of the Angells, fall of Adam destruction of the whole World by, the deludge consumptio of the Townes Sodome & Gomer by the bolts of fire send downe from heauen. so it is supperssuous to bring in Innumerable passages of the holy Scripture for

probation

probation of this purpose.

Likewise the Sacrifice offred vp to God by no
after the generall deludg was so pleasant befor
the Eyes of God that the Scripture sayeth, tha
God was repliinisheed and Reioyced with th
Sweete sauour and odriferous smelling of the sam
and likewise that God Incontinently did promi
neuer to curese the earth againe. as he did by th
generall deludge for the sinnes of men who wi
say that God did delightin deadly sinne and w
replinished with the sweeie Sauour & odoriferou
smelling of the same, beholing that he hatte
sinne as a thing abhominable and detestable vnt
him.

VVhen Abraham did offer vp his sonne Isa
vuto God as God did cōmand hime his obedien
in this respect was so acceptable seruice to Go
that he did say to him: I shall blesse the & mul
plie thy seede as the starres of the heauen and t
Sands in the Sea shore, & in thy Seede all natio
of the Earth shalbe blessed, because thou did
obey my voice.

You see here how the Seruice of God consiste
in good workes acceptble vnto God and not
deadly siinnes This Sacrfice of Abraham was
acceptable and gratefull to God, as S. Iames wr
teth 2. 21. that he was Iustified before God in o
ing the same, it is ceren that deadly sinne can i
Iustisie a man, but rather make him Impious,
curst, Iust, and abhominable before God as

Sc

ripture witnesseth.

Iobe likewise was so perfect before God in offring
is Sacrifice keeping his Innocencie in his mind
d heart that God said him selfe to Sathan, doost
ou not considder my seruant Iob, that there is
ot the like of him vpon the Eartd, simple rig-
eous sereing God and keeping his Innocencie
d Integritie. and againe the Scripture sayeth:
his great tribulatron in all these things
ob did not sinne nor speake any fuolish word be-
re God.

You see here how the seruice of Cod consisteth
good worxes acceptabe to God, as the Sacrifice
f Iob was, and not in deadly sinnes which is the
ruice of Sathan.

VVhen S. Ihon Baptist Praached the word of
od to the Iewes. Mat. 3 2. & Baplttist thē in the
ood of Iordan Marc. 1. 4 did weare a garment
ade of Camells haire, vilde hony to his re-
ction, leae an austeere life in the wildernesse, all
e acts and worxes of the holy mon were so accptable seruice to God that Christ (as a faithfull
inesse) of his holynesse and Godly life) did
ffirme that there was no man borne amongst the
nnes of men greater or moro excellent then S.
hon Baptitist. Mat. 2. 2.

Yf his acts and worxes were no otherthing but
eadly sinnes, Christ wold not haue cōmended
im so, but rather reprotched him as he did the
ewes for their vngodly liues.

When

VVhen S. Peter did glorifie Chriſt and conſeſ
him openly to be the ſonne of the liuing Go
Mat. 16. that confeſſion of faith was ſo gratefu
ſeruics to Chriſt that he gaue the Keyes of th
Kingdome of Heauen after his reſurrection whe
he made him ordinare Paſtour of his Sheepefold
as a man worthie of that office.

VVhen Marie Madalen anoilled Chriſts fee
as it is written Mat. 26. 7. that ſcruis was ſo a
ceptable vnto him that he cõmended her for th
ſame, aſcertaining that she hade done a goo
worke vnto him, it is moſt certen that Chri
wold not haue cõmended a deadly ſinne as a goo
worke accaptable vnto him; Therefore goo
workes wher in conſiſſeth the ſeruice of God ca
not be deadly ſinnes, nar yet Iufected with deadl
ſinnes, as almes deeds giuen by hypocriſie.

Laſtly S Paul ſpeaking of the holy fathers
the olde Teſtament ſayeth that they ouer com
Kingdomes, wrought, Iuſtice, obtained the pro
miſes, ſtopped the mouths of Lyons.

Here the Seripture reſtfieth that the holy fath
ers of the Olde Teſtament, wrought Iuſtice obt
aine the promiſes, ſtopped the mouths of Lyon
it is certen that the holy Scripture wold not ca
deadly ſinnes the works of Inſtice, not yet Go
wold not giue theſe things, which he prmiſed
reward deadly ſinnes. works acceptable vnto hi
by Miracles in ſtopping the mouths of Lyons an
ouerthrowing of theſe cruell beaſts by ſampſon
Daui

Dauid and Daniell the Prophet.

what shall I say the time wold faile me yf I wold ring out all the Examples of good workes where-1 consisteeh the seruice of God set doune in the oly Scripture then fore wee shall content our lues as this time of these Exampler recited abaue y vs.

As Sathan is Enemie to God in all things so is he ontrarie vnto him in this point, & as God wilbe rued with good workes acceptable vnto him, so athan wilbe serued with Euill wokes and deadly nnes, which are gratefull vnto him. This ts the iuse wherefore he stirreth vp the hearts of men deadly sinnes and when they obey him in this spet they are called the seruants of Sathan which ath dominion ouer their soules and ringeth in eir hearteby deadly sinne.

So as the seruice and Religion of God doth onsist in good workes accptable vnto him Right-the seruice and Religion of Sathan doth consist Euill workes and deadly sinnes which are gra-ull vnto him, and because all the best workes of e Protestants are but meere wickednesse and eadly sinnes before God, all their seruice and eligion must be the seruice of the Deuill, & not e seruice of God, therefore S. Ihon in hiscaoicall pistle sayeth 3. 8. he that sinneth is of the Deuill. hrist likewise Ihon. 8. 44. you are of your father e Deuill and the desires of your fether you doe. Here you see that these which comite sinne and
performe

S

the deſeres of Sathan are acconnted by Chriſt and his Apoſtlss to be the ſeruants of the Deuill, and ſonnes of Sathan & conſequently all their ſeruice and Religion is the ſeruice and Religion of the Deuill from the which I praie God to preſerue & and defend vs Amen.

Hovv the Proteſtants doe much Iniurie to Chriſt vvhen they take avvay the fruits of Chriſts paſſion to Eſtabſiſh theïr Iuſtiſicætion by only foïth.

CHAP. LXI.

CHRIST did come in this world and diẽ ſuffer death vpon the croſſe firſt to deliuer vs from the Slauerie of ſinne Ihon, 8. 36. from the power of the Deuill colleſſ. 1. 1g. from gilt of Eternall dãmation. Rom. 8. 1. theſe thrie things arꝛ vnseparable one from an other, for man by ſinne maketh him ſelfe Enuemie to God obeying Sathan 1. Ihon. 3. 8. and worthie of Eternall damnation mat. 25.

Secondly Chriſt did ariſe agine from death for our Iuſtification, and the Apoſtle writteth: that thus by his mercy he might purchaſſe vs grace i this world to cure the diſaſesof our ſouls. luc. 1 30. and ſo maꝛe vs to Ariſe from deadly ſinne t newneſſe of life according to the example of h reſurrection.

VVherefore as he that ariſeth from deadly ſin by the grace of God to newneſſe of life is partaꝛ of Chriſt paſſion, ſo he that abideth ſtill in dead ſinnes as the proteſtants dœ, are nowiſe paꝛ

ipa

participant of Chrifts paſſion, becauſe in deede by
their doctrine, they deny the cheefe fruits of the
ſame, which is to deliuer vs from the ſlauerie of
ſinne, Tyrranie of Sathan, & gilt of Eternall damnation as is aboue reeited.

Now that the Proteſtant abide ſtill in deadly
ſinne, and cnnſequently in the power of Sathan,
and gilt of Eternall damnation (for the rewarde
of ſinne is Death, Rom. 6. 23) it is thus prooued
by their owen doctrine.

Luther ſpeaking of Baptiſme in tſſert art. 2.
thus writteth: I know (ſayeth Luther) what they
will obiect to me that is, all ſuch as are ſaid will
prooue that no ſinne is left in vs after Baptiſme
but only a defect or Infirmitie (Infra) but I can
nowiſe aſſent to them which call it an defect, and
paine of ſinne and not the culpe of ſinne it ſeife
(Infra) in the meane time the fauour of God
reciueth and holdeth vs vp in not Imputing to the
death, the reſt of ſinne which is in vs althought it
be truely ſinne and may be Imputed to vs.

Thus you ſee that the ſinnes of man (after
Baptiſme) abide ſtill in them according to Luther
loctrine, and nowiſe taken away by the grace
and meritr of Chrifts paſſion, according to that
entence of S. Ihon. 1. 29. Behold the larnbe of
God which takerh away the ſinnes of the world,
but only hide them in not Imputinh the ſinnes of
men vnto them, as yf God should winke at their
ſinns aud not behold or punish them.

philipe

Phiſipe Melanchthon princ to the Lutheran
confeſſioniſti in locis cōmuni. Tit. de peccate
originaly Embraceth this doctrine with hi
Maſter Luther.

Petrus Martyre in comet in cap. 5. ad Rom
writteth: wherefore yf it wilbe asked of vs yf it b
ſinne which remineth in the regederared afte
Baptiſme? wee anſwere that it is ſinne. ſee Cardin
all Bellarmine lib. 5. de Amiſſione gratiæ. cap 5

Philipe Melanehtoon in Apoloogir art. 2. con
feſſ. Auguſt. thus writteth lyiugly of S. Auguſtii
ſaying: Auſtine ſayet: thas ſinne in Baptiſme i
renitted, not that it is not, but that it is Impute
to man. This is an Euident lye which Melancht
hon Fathereth vpou S. Auguſtine as Luther hi
Maſter did before him. ſee Bellarmine bib. 1. d
Baptiſmo cap. 13.

Caluin. lib. 4. Inſt. cap. 15. ſect. 12. thus witteth
Baptiſme Indeede promiſeth vs that our phaoi
prowned with the mortificat on t ſinne, yet no
ſo that it is no more no may ro mane trouble v
(Infra) let no man ſlatter himſelſe in his owei
Euill, when he heareth that ſinne alway duelleth
in vs.

Caluin agine lib. 3. Inſt. cap. 14. ſect. 12. writ
teth: our filthineſſe & vncleanneſſe being couere
with the puritie of Chriſt are not Imputed vnt
vs but are hidden, as yf they were buried that the
come not to the the Iudgment of of God to accu
or condempe vs.

Remark

Remarke that the finnes are not taken away out of the Proteſtants foule, but only hidde by an Externall Clocke of Chriſts puritie. fo deadly finnes abide perpetuall in their foules, and confequently they remaine in the Tirranie of Sathan, gilt of Eternall damnetion.

Caluin angaine in antidoto Concil. Trident. eſſ. 5. writteth; finne remaineth truly in vs and is not Extinguished by Baptiſme Incontinenly but ecaufe the abligation of paine is taken away, the finne is accounted nothing by not Imputation of he fame.

Here Caluin oppofeth him felfe to the vniuerfall Councell of Trent which teacheth vs that finne is taken away by the Sacrament of Baptiſme, accoring to the fentence of S. Ihon Baptiſt Ihon. 1. 26. tholde the Lambe of God which taketh away ie finnes of the world. but Luther & Caluin will ot grant, that finne is taken away out of the roteſtats foules by the grace merit of Chriſt, but ily hidde & couered by Chriſts Externall Iuſtice. Caluin againe lib. 3. Inſt. cap, 3. fect. 10 writ-th thus againſt S. Auguſtine and all the Ancietn thers, of the habite of concupiſſance and her uolntarie acts, but wee eſteeme that to be finne ien a men is tioxled by his concupiſſance againſt : lawe of God yea the concupiſſance it felfe ich Enguder fuch defires wee aſtiime it to be ne.

Caluin in thefe words againſt the doctrine the

whole

whole antiquitie affirmeth that not only the ac
concupissance is sinne, whether the will of mar
consent or resist vnto the same but also the natu
rall habite it selfe is vnseparable from the soule o
man during the the time of this mortall life.

Now good Reader you see how sinne neue
taken away out of the Protestants soule, by th
grace and merits of Chrifts passion, but only hide
and couered by an Externall Clocke, according
to their owen doctrine.

As it is dishonour to the Chirurgiane which ca
not cure the wonds of a mans bodis with his salu
but only hide them: so the Protestants dishonou
Chrifts passion as not Effectuall to cur the disese
the soule, and take away sinne, hellish Inferna
sting cleane out of the same, but only to hide th
wounds of our soule with an Externall salue whic
can noe cure them.

So you see how they deny the efficacie of Chrif
passion, meries and grace, as Insufficent to tas
away the Infernall darte of sinne whereby th
Soule of man is deadly wounded, but let the sam
remaine still within the soule of man without ar
cure or sauctie from the same.

This is the Miserable Estate of the Protestan
soule to be continually wounded to the death wi
the darti of deadly sinne, which is hells Inferna
sting, and neuer to taken away out of their sou
by any vertue merite or grace of Chrifts passio
but only doth still remaine within that miserab

ſoule wiehout remeede during the time of this mortall life.

As Chriſt is much:dishenoured by the Doctrine of the Proteſtants, which ſay that the Infernall king is neuer taken out of the wouoded ſoule by the grace and merits of Chriſts paſſion, but only ſtirme all with one conſent (is wee haue reciteh aboue) that the Proteſtants ſoules is ſo Infected with the peſtilent poyſon of deadly ſiinne that no race of Chriſt can cure the ſoule and free her from the ſame.

So Chriſt is much honoured by the doctrine of the Catholique Church teocheth vs this Chriſt the true ſamaritan did power in oyle of holy grace in the wounded ſoule to cure the ſame, after the man coming downe from Hieruſalem to Iericho was Robbed of his Spirituall Garment & deepely wounded by Infernall Theeues, which depairted from him leauing him halfe dead, as it is written Euangell of S. luke. 10 30.

So the proteſtant wold haue the ſillie ſoule to remaine ſtill halfe dead as it was wounded by Satan, and neuer to be cured with the grace of Chriſt againe, the true phiſition of the ſoule, which is great dishonour to Chriſt, and his grace, & great great hurt (I ſay) to the Proteſtants ſoule, but not to the ſoule of a true catholique and Godly Chriſtian, which is cured by the Inherent grace of Chriſt, from the peſtslent poyſon of deadly ſinne and nſed from the power of Sathan.

thus

Thus the Proteſtaants make Sathan more powe-rfull to hurt the ſoule by malice, then Chriſt by grace to cure and heale the ſame, which is a great blaſphemie aginſt omnipotent power of God, & an Euident lye againſt the holy ſcripture when S. Paule ſayeth Rom. 5. 20 where ſinne did abound, grace did more abound then ſinne, than muſt ye-elde place to grace, as darkneſſ to the light, for ſinne and grace can no more ſtand together, then light, and darkneſſe, life and death & becauſe the Proteſtants affirme, ſinne to be vnſeparable from their ſoules (as they giue Example of the concu piſſance recited aboue) they muſt haue continu ally in their ſoule ſpirituall death and darkneſſ which diriuie from deadly ſinnes and want ſpirit uall life and light which flow from the Inheren grace of Iuſtification, as the beames of light do flow from the ſunne.

For as the ſoule liueth by the grace of Iuſtifica ion Rom. 8. 10 ſo it dieth by deadly ſinne Rom 1. 15. and as ſinne fillethe ſoule full of darkne Ihon. 3. 19 ſo the grace of Iuſtifiction bringe ſpirituall light to the ſame Epheſ, 5. 8. ſo the Pr teſtants ſoule is continually poſſeſſed wtih dead ſinne and is alſo ſpiritually dead and full of ſpi tuall darkneſſe. that is the miſerable Eſtate ther vnhappie ſoules

An other probation howv the proteſtants deny the vertu and Efficacie of Chriſts baſſion to Eſtablesh their Inſti fication. by only faith.

S. Paul writteth. heb. 13. 12. Iesus suffered without the gate that he might, sanctifie the people
with his owen blood, and likewise eleanse his
Church from all spotte of sinne by the the lauer of
regeneration Ephes. 5. 26. that thus his Chosen
children may be sanctified tauth & not by a vaine
imputation of Externall sanctification as Christ
did praie his Father for the same. and was heard
of his Father for his reuerence. Hebr. 5. 7.

Therfore yf the the Chosen Childoen of God were
only sanctified by an Externall veale of Iustee &
not in truth and Effect by Inherent Iustice and
sanctifiction in the soule in cureng it from the
pestilnt poyson of deadly sinne really, and Indeede
then the cheefe fruits of Christ passion should be
taktn away by the doctrine of the Protestants, because cheife fruits of Christs passiō in this morttll
e ar to take away the sinnes of the world Ihon 1.
1. deliuer the soules of men from captluitie of
sathan collossen. 1. 13. cure the wounds of the
soule cōtracted by the fall of Adam by the oyle of
inherent grace luc. 10. 34 reconcile men to God
by grace, which were Enemies to him by sinne,
rom. 5. 10. Cleanse his Church and sanctifie it
from all spote of sinne and lastty deliuer it from
then the gilt of Eiernall damnaio. Rom.

So yf deadly sinne remaineth still within the
soule of man (as the Protestants will hau to doe)
and his Malrce and Impietie being only couered
with

with an Externall veale of Iuſtice he shall by ſuch
deadly ſinne, be ſonne & ſlaue to Sathan as Chriſt
ſayeth Ihon. 8. 44. and likewiſe abide ſtill in the
eurſe and malediction of God pſal. 118. and gil
of Eternall damnaton. Math. 25. 41. and conſe
quently with out any partciption of the fruits o
Chriſts paſſion, or then wee muſt ſay (as the
teach in deede) that the paſſion of Chriſt wa
not Effectuall and ſuffioient to deleuer the ma
Indeede from ſuch miſeries as are recited abou
but only to couer them with an Externall veale
Iuſtice and ſanctified in truth and Indeede.

So as the couering of a blacke Ethiopian with
white garment taketh not away the blackneſſe
the Ethiopian to Maxe her white Indeede: ſo th
Externall veale of Chriſts Iuſtice taketh not aw
the hypocriſie, Impietie Iniuſtice which are reall
Inherent in the Proteſtans ſoules to ſanctifie an
Iuſtifie the ſoules in truth and Indeede but on
by an Externall ſhewe and Apparance.

Therefore as the Ethiopian, not with ſtandir
the white Garment remaineh ſtill aſilhie ſtinchin
blacke Ethiopian in truth and Indeede ſo the Pr
teſtats ſoule, not withſtanding the Extecnall vea
of Chriſts Iuſtice biddeth ſtill full of by pocriſ
Iniquitie and whollie Infeeted with the peſtie
poyſon of deadly ſinne in truth and Indeed.

So the Paoteſtaants ſanctfication & Iuſtiſieati
by only faith. is not that ſanctifieation and Iuſt
ication which Chriſt did obtaine by his praier ſ

h

Father to sanctifie his Chosen Children Ihon 17. 17. whose praier was hard for his reuerne heb. 5. 7. but a false Imagination and vaine Imputation of an Externall veale of Iustice, which neither can Iustifie not sanctifie them in truth and Indeede, as the grace of Christ Inherent in the soule doth sanetifie and Iustifie his Chosen Children in truth and Indeede Ihon. 17. 17.

Likewise yf there by no grace at all to cure the soule of man woundeds by the Infernall dart of deadly sinne then the Miserable soule must ly still in that woefull Estate with that Infernall sting still in the soule without any hope to be resueued from the seme or his wounde to be cured in this mortall life. beholde the miserable Estate of the Protestants soule,

But Luther in assertion onmium artic suorm art, 1. Caluin lib. 4. Inst. cap. 15. sect. 12. answera: althought deadly sinne remane still within their soules (as the concupissance which is vnseparable rom the same) Neuertelesse God, for the respect of their faith in Christ, will not Impute their sines nto them, or punish them for their misdeeds how reat so euer they be because (sayeth Luther) where faith is, no sinne can hurt the man in ermone sic deus dietit mundum.

VVee answere, first guinh and not grating such manifest vutruth that although God wold winke t their sinnes against the rule of his Eternall Iustice, & behold the Protestäts in perpetall adulterie
with

with the Deuill cōmtting continually deadly sinne with him, as S. Ihon sayeth 3. 8. who sinneth is of the Deuill will and desires. Ihon. 8. 44. an, not to punish aud correct such a villan, strumpe(and adulterous sppouse, becaufe she beleeueth in Chrift, then they shall make Chrift not a taker away the sinnes of the world, but a furtherer and mantainer of sinne (which should be a Medicine to cur wounded soule from the pestient poysor of sinne) a veale to couer their Malice, a elocke to hide their Impietie and Iniustice, and a shielde to saue them from all punition of theer misdeeds, & detestable crymes eōmitted against God and their Nighbour. is not that a pleasant Religion for the flesh, an Rnauish libertie they take to them selue to doe all things what they list, since make the pai fion of Chrift a Bucklare & sheelde tō defen then from all punition desrued for their malitiou crymes and mesdeeds

As that man is truly accounted to be man mise rable Estate, which by the persuasion of his Enne mie stricketh him self in the bodie with an sharp dagger, and so leauing it sticking in the woun albeit his Prince punish him not or such a faul Right so the Protestants soule is truely Iudged be in a woefull plihht, which by the tentation Sathan wounded him selfe in the soule by theIn ernall darte of deedly sinne without any remee to drawe the same out of the wounded soule agin albeit God wold wincke at his offencs, and n

punis

punish him for such a deadly sinne, to kill him
elfe euen to the spirituall death of the soule again
ost the comademete of God & leaue the Infernall
darte of deadly sinne sticking in the soule,

For the Protestants graunt the them selues that
albeit, God take away the paine and punition of
sinne, for their faith (as they alleadge in Christ)
which paine and punition is both Iust and holy &
of God, althought it be Dolorous to such as suffer
he same, Neuerthelesse they confesse that the pes-
ilent poyson of deadly sinne it selfe, that hellish
sting and Infernall darte doe neuer depart out of
heir Miserable wounded soule during the time of
his mortall life.

Wherefore you may Easily see their woesull &
unhappie Estate to beare continully about with
hem the pestilent poyson and Infernall sting of
deadly sinne in their wounded soule, with their
counterfooted Iustifiing faith, which can not
help them to cure these deadly wounds of their
soule but they must alwise abide in that woefull
plight during the dayes of this mortall life with-
ut any remeede at all..

This discourse is most true in the Protestants
according to their owen doctrine, which are
received by a false beleefe and counterfooted faith
in Christ and not truly redeemed by his pretious
blood, nor yet partakers of his passion so long as
that pestiient poyson and Infernall sting of deadly
sinne shall make residence in their wounded soule,
but

But the the truth is not as they say in Godly cat-
holeques, but altogether contrarie to their doctrine, for so muest as the cóming of Chiest in thi?
world and chiefe fruits of his passion, were not to
suffer that pestlient poyson and Infrnall darte of
deadly sinne to remaine within the wounded soule
of man and only to hide that Infernall sting with
the Miserable wounds of the souse by an Externall salue and reale of Iustice, but for many other
fruits and Tffects which Ensue hereafter.

The first fruit and Effect of Chrifts passion is to
toke away the pesthilent poyson of deadly sinne
out of the mans soule. Mat. 1. 22. and Marie shal
bring foori a sonne and thou shall call his Nam
Iesus for he shall saue his peple from their sinne?
Ihon. 1. 29 behold the Lambe of God which tax
eth away the sinne of the world Tit. 2. 14. wh?
gaue him selfe for vs that he might redeeme vs fr?
all Iniquite and purge vs.

You see by these authorities of the holy Scrip?
ture that one of the chiefe fruits and Ewects of
Chrifts passion was to saue vs from our siinn?
Redeeme vs from our Inequiuies, take away th?
sinns of the world, and purge cleane from them
not that Infernall darte remaine within the wou?
nded soule to their liues end, as the Protestants sa?

The second fruit and Effect of Chrift passion?
to cure the wounds of soule by the holy oyle ?
Inherent grace. luc. 10. 34, the Charitie of Go?
is powred in our hearts by the holy Ghost whi?

s giuen vs. heb. 13. 12. Therfore Iefus that he might Sanctifie hes people with his owen blood uffered without the gate Ihon 17. 17. & for their aikes I Sanetifie my felfe that they alfo may be Sanctified in truth Ephef. 5. 16. Chrift gaue him elfe for his Church that he might Sanctifie it and Cleanfe it by the lauer of regeneration in the word You may fee how the wounds of the foule are ured by the oyle of Inherent grace powred in the ame and fo purified from finne and Sanctified in truth.

The thrid Effect and fruits of Chrifts paſsion is to reconcile vs vnto God by grace who were made Encmies to him by finne. Rom. 5. 10. for yf wee were finners when wee were reconoiled vnto God by the death of his fonne, much more being reco-ncilled wee shalbe faue by his life.

Fourthly faith hope and Charitie with all vertue giuen to vs are the fruits and Efſects of Chrifts paſsion with the holy Sacraments.

Thefe are the fruits and Effects of Chrifte paſ-ſion, firft to faue vs and take away finne out of ur foule and Redeeme vs from our Iniquitie fe-ondly to cure the wounds of our hurt foule by he holy oyle of Inherent grace powred in our oules. Thridly to reconale vs with God by grace who were made his Ennemies by finne, Fourthly hat fo taking away the peftilent poyfon of deadly inne by the merite of Chrifts paſsion and curing he viaulent vlcers of our wounded foules by the
holy

holy oyle of Inherent grace the Church of God might be Sanctified in truth & cleansed from all spot of deadly sinne in deede, and so to be made with out blame in the sight of God.

Now you may Easely beholde, what great Iniurety they doe to Christ when thy affirme Iesus Christ the only begotten sonne of God for all the paines and troubles he ded suffer the space of three and thertie yeeres for all his great humitie and obedience to his Father, for his most Dolorous death passion, he could neuer obtaine so much grace and fauors from his Father, as to make our soules free from deadly sinne, & to cure the wounds thereof with the oyle of Inherent grace, and so to make vs the friends of God and Sanctifie vs in truth.

They deny all the fruits of Christs passion by vs recited aboue to Establsh their Iustication by only faith which is a false faith altogether against the word of God, as wee haue prooued in our former discourse by the authoritie of the holy Scripture.

How the Protestants make Christ one of the most deformed Monsters of vvorld to Establishe their Iustification by only fatth,

CHAP. LXIII

FOR better Intelligence of this mattir we must before all things declaire our purpose by a Smiltude like vnto the same.

Yf you wold Imagine a man which haue
beunifull

eutifull head well fashioned Euery where whofe
urling licks were like gliftring threeds of Gold
his Eyes like two bright shining Starres moft ple-
fant to beholde his cheecks adorned with beutifull collours, whit and Read well proportioned
like Rofes and lillies mixed together his lep moft
pleafantly framed of crimfon collour, his teeth
well fette in ordour round about like beutifull
pearls in his cheeke bones, the breath of his mouth
fweete and odoriferouis, like the fweet smelling
fauour of conall and odorifooouis flowres, his
neeke pleafantly shapen, & whinte like geancing
oyrie, and fince a blacke ftinching bodie to be
oyned to this beutifull head full of virulent vlcers
Peftiferous byles, the Members, leggs, and armes
thereof full loothfome Scabbes and venemous
oiches, from whence doth flow a filthie matter,
with a corrupt ftinch defilling the aire round a-
out, wold you not thinke such a man to be one
f the moft deformed Coeatures that can be Ima-
ined in this world.

Truly this is the pleafant forme and shape which
hey Proteftants giue to the fonne of God when
hey make him head of their Church which isall
foamed and more blacke then an Morian or
Ethiopian full of corrupt ftinch by the peftilint
oyfon of deadly finne, which neuer depairteth
ut of their foules, as wee haue prouuen aboue by
heir owen doctring, for they take away all Inhe-
ent grace, (which nurgeth the foule from all
deadly

V.

deadly ſinnee, and maketh it holy beutifull an
Iuſt before God) to Eſtablish the their Iuſtifica
tion by only faith whereby the apprehend Chr
iſts Iuſtice to hide ther filthineſſe, Imundictiti
and corrupt ſtinch of deadly ſinnes, which defil
thier ſouls.

In this Monſtrous paterne ſette doune abou
tow things are to be conſidere, the beutifullne
of the head, and deformite & vncleauneſſe of t
bodie, the beutifullneſſe of the head beloneth t
Chriſt the ſonne of Gode wheme they alleadge t
be the head of their deformed Church. The bla
kneſſe, vncleanneſſe, and corrupt ſtinch of th
bodie pertuinie to the Church of the Proteſtan
which they alleadge to be the Miſticall bodie
Chriſt becauſe S, paul. colloſſ. 1. 18 writteth th
Chriſt is head to the bodie of the Church.

As concerning the beutifullneſſe of the he
which is the ſonne of God, which they alleadge
be head of their Monſtrous and poluted Chu
ther is no queſtion thereof, becauſe he is more
utifull then all the ſonnes of men, pſal. 42. full
grace and cruth Ihon. 1, 14 without all blamish
ſpote of ſinne Ihon. 8. 46. 1. pet. 2. 22. by th
alſo he is the brightneſſe of his fathers glo
heb. 1. 3.

As concerining the Monſtroues of frome of th
deformed Church it is Eaſely prooued by th
owen doctrine. and beeauſe they affirme (as
haue prooued aboue) that all their good wo

re deadly sinnes, and that deadly sinne doth me
er depairt aut of their soules, wee must declare
whar damnable fruits & Effects fleow from deadly
sinnes, and then you shall see Euidently what a
Moustrous thing it is to Ioyne such a pestiferous
Church as theirs is, to be a Misticall bodie to Ies-
s Chist the beutifull sonne of the liuing God.

Before all things is maketh the man Ennemie to
God. plal. 9:. 10 Thy Enemies o Lord shall pirsh,
nd all these that wire Imiqiutie shalbe destroyed
say. And I shall ease my selfe of my adueresaris
nd auinge me of my Enemies.

Secodly dead sinne maketh the man to Incurre
he curse and Mulediction of God. psal. 118.
1. they are accursed which transgresse the comã-
dement Mat. 25. 41. Depairte from me you that
re accursed vnto Euerlasting fire for I was hung-
ie and you gaue me nor to eate ca.

Thridly it maketh the man slaue and & naught
he Childe of Sathat. Ihon. 8. 44. you are of yonr
ather the Deuill and the desires of your Father
ou dee i. Ihon 3. 8. who worketh sinne is of the
Deuill.

Fouruhly deadly sinne as hells Infernall dart
oundeth the soule most cruelly luc. 10. 30. a
rten man full amongst theeues & they Robbeth
m of his rayment, & wounded him & depairted
auing him galfe dead.

The Deuills are the Theeues which did spoile the
ule of Inhererent grace, the spirituall Garment
of

of the foufe of all his merits and good worke
and likewife did wound him deepely in the foule
with deadly finne which is hells Infernall darte.

Efay writteth to this purpefe. 5 faying. wherefore fhould you be fmitten aty more, for you fal
away more and more, the whole head is ficke, &
the whole heart is Heaune, from the fole of th
foote to the head ther is no thing whole their in
but wounds and fwelling and fores full of cornip
tion, they haue not beene wrapped and bound v
nor Molified with oyle.

Behold the Infernall wounds of deadly finne
which is hellish dart, & manie fores full of ftinc
and corruption, Perptually refident in the Pro-
eftants, foules which are not bound vp and curd
be the holie oyle of Inherent grace but only coue
red with an Externall veale of Imputiue Iuftice

Fyftly deadly finne maketh the foule more black
in the fight of God, then an foule blacke ftinchin
Ethopian or Morian, is in the fight of man lame
ntations of Iermie 4 8. Now their face and vifah
is blacker then a coale they can not know them i
the ftreets their skine is withered like a ftock

The foule of man by deadly finne is made
backe as the face of man berayed with Inke an
vls dead as a withered brach vpon a tree whic
beare no fruit at all to the fight of God fixtly de
dly finne maketh the foule full of corrupt ftinc
in the Noife of God & abominable vnto him. pfa
83. 1. They are corrupt and abhominable in the
worke

workes plal. 5. 11. Their heart Emptie and full
of folie, their throat is like an open sepulchere:
that is they are full of spirituall stinch, corruptiō
and abhomination.

As a good worke ascendeth vp to God with a
sweete sauour & odorifrous smelling, as the sacrifice of noe did smell sweetly before God, so the
worke which is adioynid with deadly sinne is like
corruat stinch and abhomination before God,
prouerb. 15. 8. The Sacrifice of the wicked is
abhominable vnto the Lord but the praier of the
Iust is acceptable vnto him.

You see here how deadly sinne maketh not only
the soule of man, but also his worke is full of corrupt stinch and abhominatian before Cod.

Seuinthy deadly sinne Excludeth the soule from
Entring in the Kingdome of Heauen. Mat. 7. 22.
many will say to me in that day haue wee not by
thy name done manie Great workes & Miracles
and then I will professe to them I neuer know you
depairt from me you that worke Iniqitie.

This was a true faith in Christ wherby they did
cast out Deuills and worke great Miracles, and
preach in the name of Christ, Neuerthelesse bo-
cause they did worke deadly sinnes, which are
workes of Iniquitie their faith in Christ could not
aue them but were most Iustly excluded from the
Kingdome of Heauen.

S. Paul likewise. 1. cor. 6. 9. thus writteth: know
you not that the Iuinst shall not possesse the
Kingdom

Kingdom of God, doe not Erre, neither fornicators, nor seruere of Idolls. nor adulterers, nor the Effeminate, no bugrers, nor Theeues shall possesse the Kingome of God.

Thele corinthians whome to S. Paul writteth were Christians and beleuers in Christ, yet their faith in Christ, with such sinnes as are recited aboue could not Iustifie and saue them as Luther sayeth in Sermone *sic Deus dilevit mundum,* where faith is, no sinne can harme the man.

Eightly deadly sinne maketh the foule of man a nest of Infernall corpions. a denne of dragons a Dungeon of Deuills Esay. 13. 21. and Beasts shall lodge and make their habiation there, their houses shalbe full of dragons, shall dwell there and the hoaie sayres shall daunce thee howlets shall cry in their palices, and the sirens in their Temples of pleasours.

The Deulls ar called Beasts becau se they stirre vp the heartiof men to beastly desires. actions and manerse The Deuill also hath the cōnone Namea of som Beasts, by Reason of some harticulare conformltie he hath to these Beasts in causing men to sinne.

The Deuill is called a dragon, because he Infecthe foule with the pestilent poyson of sinne as the Dragon doth the aire round about him with a venemous qualitie which Issueth out of him.

The Deuill is called and ostriche for so much as the ostriche consumeth the hard yron by a natu-

naturall

naturall qualitie which is in him. ſo the Eeuill ſpoileth the ſoule of man, by deadly ſinne of all grace, merits and good workes before God.

The deuill is calld an howlate, beuſe that as ſuch a foule worketh all her cheeſe workes in the Night ſo the Deuill maketh feeble Inconſtant men by his tentations to ſeeke priuie places, darke corners & lureing holes to performe the Deuills deſires in cōmitting deadly ſinnes. Therefore Chriſt ſayeth: he that doth Euill hatteth the light that is for feare of reprehnſion.

The Deuill is ſaid to be Satire becauſe he ſhall aocuſe vs bettely beſore the Iudgment of God of all offences and ſindes cōmitted, which are not blotted away by true penitence.

He is called a ſvrene, becauſe as ſome writte that ſuch a Monſter Marine (which is a women from the waſt vp, and an fish from the waſt doune) ſitting on a Rocke in Sea, by her ſweete ſongs did alure paſſingers to come to her and ſince did kill them: Right ſo the Deuill doth allure men by his ſweete aentatians to deadly ſinnes, that thus he may kill them by Eternall damnation.

S. Gregorie in the ſirſt books of the Kings in cap 7 writteth: that alſe manie Deuills aelident in the hearts of men, as there be filthie & vncleäe deſires

Therefore S. luke writteth that ſeauen Deuills did goe out Marie Magdalen when our Lord Ieſue did deliuer her ſoule from the peſtlent poyſon of deadly ſinnes which Deuills did lodge within her
body,

body, during the time she was defiled with the seauen deadly sinnes

Here you may see that the Protestants are continuallie possessed with Deuills. by an spirituall & Inuisible possession, because that their sinnes doe neuer depairte out of their soules, as they writte them selues and where so euer deadly sinnes are there the Deuill doth make his habitation, as it is Euident by these former authorities of the holy Scripture.

Nyntly deadly sinne maketh the man quiltie of Eternall damnation. Mat. 25. 41. Depairt from me you cursed to Euerlasting fire, for I was hungred you gaue me not to Eate, I was thristed and you gaue me not to drinke.

Yf such be damned vnto hells fire which gaue not meate and drinke vnto the poorem the tide of necessitie, how much more shall they be dānee vnto hells fire, which cōmite thifte homicide adulterie, sacriledge, periurie, and other such lixe hynous crymes which are fore bidden by the com mar de nint of God.

Now to make a colleetion of all these thing re cited aboue which accomdainie deadly sinnes we shll douclude most truly, that because the Protes tants soules (according to their owen doctrine ars alwise possessed with deadly sinne, they mu haue also these propper qualities and condition in their soules, which are vnsearable from deadli sinne, that is to be Enemie to God to be accurse of God, to be the Naughtie slaue and Child of th

Deuill, to be deepely wounded in the soule by deadly sinne which is hells Infernall darte, to be spoiled of all grace and merits, to haue the soule blacke before the Eyes of God, as an black Echiopian is before men, to be withered like a drie stocke without any sope of grace or deuotion, to be full of corrupt stinch and abhomination before God, to be Excluded from the Kingdome of Heuen, to be a nest of Deulls and & denne Infernall Dragós to be compaimons to hellish spiritss and guiltie of Eternall damnation, what thing in this world can be more accurst, miserable, & vnhapie then the soule of the Protestants which abide perpetually in deadly sinne, & consequently all these former miseries, which are vnsparable fró deadly sinne.

Bnt they will say to me that they will couer all their Imundicities, vncleanesse, abhominations, curses, corrupt stinches, virulent vlcer, pestiferous oiches, venemous byles. Infernall scabes, contacted by the banne of deadly sinne in their soules with the Iustice of Christ apprehended by their faith, which shall cause God to wirke at all their sinnes, & abhominations, and so not purish them as Caluin writteth. lib. 3. Inst. cap. 14 sect. 12. our filthinesse and vncleanesse being cuered with the puritie of Christ are not Inouted vnto vs, but the hiddee, as yf they were buried, that they may not come to the Iudgment of God.

VVee answee first that they doe great Iniurie Christ the sonne of God, who ar the true phisi-

X

phisitiõ of the world come to take away the Infernall darte of deadly sinne out of the soules of
men, wounded by Infernall theeues, and to cure
their woundes with the oyle of Inherent grace
powred in their woundes, as it is written Iue 10.
33. when they teach tacitly by their doctrine that
he could not merite or deserue so much grace at
his fathers hande, by his obddience death and pas-
siõn as maigt takee away the Infernall darte of
deadly sinne out of the Protestants soule, and eure
their wounds in truth, with the holy oyle of Inherent grace powred really in their wounded soules,
but was constrained by the Insufticiencie of his
merits, death & passion, to let the Infernall darte
of deadly sinne, remaine still within the wounde
soules of the protstants and couer only thei
virulãt vlcers, pestifrous boiches, venemous byle
and corrupt stinch of their Infernall scabe cont
racted by the pestilent poyson of deadly sinne with
an Exteeranll veale of his owen pure Iustice an
let them ly still vnder such a wourded th
death luc. 10. 34. o miserable estate of Protestant
soules to ly halfe dead wouuded an continuall
pyned by Innumerable soires without any remee
at all.

Godly Catholiques are deliuerd frõ such miseri
becaufs our Loud Iesus by the mirits of his dea
and passion hath taken out of their soules th
Infernall sting of deadly sinne and curéd the
wounds with the oyle of Inhrent graeepowred
their wounded soule luc. 10. 34.

Secondly wee answere that they dod much shame
to them selues when they confesse tacitly that as a
black stinching Ethiopian is couered with a white
shirte, a corrupt sepulchre and filthie Iackes with
white lyme a stinching dunghill with whire snows
ight so the Imundieitie, corrupt stinck, Infernell
blaewnesse, virulent vlcers, pestiferous byles, and
enemous boiches contracted in their soules by
deadly sinne. hells banne and Infernall poyson
are only couered and hidde by an Externall veale
of Iustice, which is as farre distant from their sil-
hie soules as the heauen is from the Earth.

VVherefor such an abhominable Church which
is full of Imundicties like a ofithie Iacks & stinch-
ig dunghill is no wise worthie oryet deceet to be
called the holy Church and beutifull spouse of our
Lord Iesus the beutifull spouse of Christ, who
hath sanctified his spouse and Church with his
preeious blood, heb. 13. 12. & Elcansed from that
infernall spotte of deadly sinne and hath made
er holie to him selfe without blame. Ephes. 3. 12.
to the end then might be some decent proportion
etweene him selfe & his spouse in the honorable
and of Marriage, which is made by Iudgment
iustice faith and Mercie ose. 2. 19.

Therefore it must be the holie Catholique Romaine Church whose faith is much comended by
the holy Apostle Rom. 1, 8. which is the only true
ouse of out Lord Iesue Christ, most beutifull
fore God, cleansed from the Infernall spote of
adly sinne, apoc. 1. 5. in her holiest Members

from whence she taketh her Domination- as th
ſóne of God witneſſeth when he ſayeth cani 4.
my loue thou arte beutifull and no ſpotte is in th

S. paul. Rom 8. 3. wrireth to this purpoſe tha
God hath ſent his ſonne in the ſimiliade of ſi
neſull fleſh, and for ſinne condemned ſinne th
the Iuſtification of the lawe might be fulleſille
in vs.

You ſee here that the ſóne o God did condemr
ſinne in the fleſh (that is in the ſacrifice of h
fleshy offred vp to God his father vpon the cro
ſe. that ſo the Iuſtificaton of the lawe might be ſu
lſilled in vs. Thus Ieſus is not only Iuſt in hi
ſelſe, but the holy Membeas of his Church are all
Iuſt in them ſelues by the Influence of grac
which thy doe teceiue from Chriſt their head, ſ
ſuch Iuſtics and perſicetion as the lawe did requi
of thm, it was ſullfilled in them by that gra
which Chriſt did purchaſſe for them vpon tl
Croſſe, by his holy death and paſſion that the
might be ſome decent proprtion betweene tl
bridgroome and his ſpouſe in the band of Ma
riage, the head and the Members by Miſtcall vɪ
on o grace, for otherwiſe yf the holy Membe
of his Church were not ho y and Iuſt in the
ſelues by the Influence of grace flowing from t
head. the holy Scripture could not be true wh
it ſayeth, that the Iuſtification of the lawe w
fulſfilled not in Chriſt only, but alſo in vs alth
ught mor perfectly in the ſonnc of God then in

The Iuſtication of the lawe can not be fullfill

in the Proteſtants which walke after the fleſh becauſe all their beſt worke ſelues, are deadly ſinnes
as they confeſſe them ſelues, but in Godly Catho-
lipues which walke after the ſpirit, becauſe all
their good workes, are workes of Iuſtice according to the lawe and acceptable ſeruice vnto God,
as the Prophet Malachias foretolde. 3. 5. ſaying:
hey ſhall offer vp Stcrifice in Iuſtice and the Sa-
trifice of Iuda, ſhlbe acceptable vnto God.

Tbridly wee anſwere that they diſhonnour them
ſelues when they compare them ſelues to withered
brăches which bring out no other ſtuits but deadly
ſinne, which fruits are gratefull to Sathan Ihon.
8. 44. for ſo doing they ſullfill his deſires, they are
alſo hatefull to God, as the Impious and his Imp-
pitie areſap. 14 9. therefore the proteſtants can
not be liuely branches reſident in Ieſus Chriſt,
which is the trie oflife, becouſe ſuch boughes as
bring not out good fruits pleaſant to God are
cutte away from Ieſus Chriſt the true trie of life,
to be burnee (as ſite ſuell) in hells fire Eternally,
as S· Ihon witneſſth. 15, 16. as Chriſt is glorified
when the branches beareth good fruits: ſo he as
diſhónoured when tbe branches beareth Euill
fruits as the Proteſtants doe.

So Godly Catholiques muſt be theſe branches
graffed in Chriſt the trie of life by the Inſtuence
of he grace, which beare good ſruits acceptable
vnto Cod, as the Proteſtants are withered brăches
which are acceptable fruits vnto Sathan. Ihon 8.
44. whőe to the fire of hell is preparee, & likewiſe

to all withered branches which beare no good fruits vcceptable vnto God, as the Paotestants are yf they amend not both in life and Religion.

Fourthly S. Paul writteth Rom. 8 29. that God hath predstinated all his Flect to be made like the Image of sone that he might be the first borne amongst manie brettheren.

As concerning the Protestants which bearie continvallie deadly finnes in their souses, they are rather conforme to tbe Image and similitude of Sathan then to the the Image & similitude of God becaufe that as the Inherent grace of God in the soule of a Godly catholique maxeth such a catholique like vnto Christ, which is full of grace, and truth Ihon. 1. 14. so the Infernall spotte of deadly finne in the Protestants soule cheefe caufe and author of sinne, that Christ calleth Satban their father, for so much as the Protestant conittinng deadly finne continallie performeth so doing Sathans desires will and gartfull seruice.

whrefore it restaeth that the Godly Catholques, which are Iustified by Inberent grace resident in the soules. should be called the Elected bretheren of Christ, becaufe they are like vnto the Image of Christ by the brightnesse of Inherent grace which is resident in thcir soules, and not the Protestants. which by deadly finne resident in their soules are made like vnto Sathan, chiefe author of sinne, for which caùse Christ calleth him their father Ihon 8. 44.

Likewise as a mulitude of blacke Morians or

Ethiopians can not be truly called the bretheren
if such a on as most faire and beutifull. so the
Protestants whose soules are like be called brethe-
en like vnto the beutifull sonne of God, because
they are more resernbland to Sathan by the blacke
infernall spotte of deadly sinne, then to Christ by
nie brightnesse or beutifllnesse of Inherent grace,
s Godly Catholiques are.

As these which are Endued with Inherent grace
are parteipant of Chrifts beutie and gratefull vnto
God. so these which are filed with the Infernall
pote of participant of his Infernall blackenesse
and alse gratefull vnto him as they are odious vnto
God. sap. 14. 9. Now to conclude this Chapter
according to these authoities of the holy Scripture recited aboue which declare to vs the proper
conditions whinh are vnseparable from deadly
sinne, yf a spouse which were Enemie to God,
strumpet & harlote to Sathan, deepely wounded
in the soule by deadly sinne, hells Infernall dart,
spoiled of all Inheret hrace mertis & good workes
blacke before God, as a foule Morits or Ethiopian is before man, withred like a drie stocke. without ali sope of Grace aeuotion, full coreupt stinch
and abhomination before God full of corruption
like a Rotten sepulcher or stinching dunghill full
of spirituall & virolent vlcers, pestilent boitches,
venemous bylles, Inferntll scabbes contracted by
deadly sinnes in the soule, excluded from the fellowshipe of all holy pirits and citzens of heauen,
a nest of **Deuills** denne of **Infernall Dragonse** a

Partaker of hellish damned ipirits guiltie of Eternall damnation yf such a spouse which is disfigured and deform:d by all these former abhomrnable qualities & conditions, which followe foote for foote the pestilen poyson of deadly sinnes, were Ioyned Either as spotse, ar yet as a misticall bodie to the beutifull sonne of liuing God as head to the same, which is the brightnesse of his fathers glorie full of grace and truth, wold not that coniunction of such a moustrous bodie, that noble & beutifull head, appeare to be the most monstrous coniunction that can be Imagined by the Enmine of man there is no man Indued with his naturall witts which can deny the same.

Truly deadly sinne which is alwise resident in the soules of Protestants and likewise in all their workes (as is taught by them selues) disgrceth, ciffigureth so their mistiall and vnhappie Chrach with such abhominable qualities as ane recite aboue, that it can nowse be called the Imaculaate spouse or Misticall body of Christ, the beutifull sonne of God, wherefore it resteth that the Catholique Romaine Church, much cómendedby the holy Apstle *S.* Paul. Rom. 1 8 should be truly Esteemed the vnspotted spousce of Christ as she is termed by the holy Ghost. cant. 4, 7. Thou ar whole beutifull my Ioue and no spote is in the.

Althought that good & badde fish be in Christ net Mat. 13. 47. good corne and Cockle in his fielde (Ibipem) wise and foollish virgns in his Kingdome Mat. 25. 1, Sheepe and Goats his

sheepefold Ibidem. 32 his Church is call holy &
vnspotted from the Iust and holie, and not from
the wicked and vngodly, for there be manie Iust
& wisemen in the Church of God, & their workes
in hand of God Eccles. 9. 1. as the holy Scripture
witnesseth in diuers places, as of Abell, Noe. Iob,
Zacharias Elisabeth, S. Ihon Baptist, and others
suchlike Genes. 6. Iob. 2. 5. luc 1. luc. 16 7 Ihon,
17. 12. 1. cor. 6. 11. 2. pet. 2. 7.

Hovv the Protestants, deny Christ to be Redempter of the
vvorld to Estableshe their Iustification by only faeth.

CHAP LXIIII.

FOR so much as the Protestants will Acknew-
ledge no graes or Inherent Iustics by the gift of
God to be in the soule of a true Christian where by
he may be truly called Iust before God, they haue
recourse to the Iustice of Christ, to the end they
being cloathed Externally by his Iustice apprehe-
ded by their faith, and likewise their malice,
impictie, Iniustice, hypocrisie, & all other deadly
sinne resident in their soules, hidde & buried by
the same Iustice they may appeare Iust before God
who are truly Impious and Iniust in them selues.

Luther therefore in his cōmentarie in the 2.
chap. to the Galatians thus writteth: Ergo fide
apprehensus Christus Therefore Christ apprehended by faith, is the Christian Iustics whereby God
esteemed vs Iust, and giueth vs Euerlasting life,

Caluin lib. 3. Inst. cap. 11. sec. 2. thus writteth
contrariwise he shalbe Iustified by faith, who set-
ing a side all workes of Iustice apprehendeth

Y

Chrifts Iuftice by faith, being couered he shall
apeare not as a finner, but ar Iuft man in the fight
of God.

Caluin againe lib. 3. Inft. cap. 2. fect. 5. Chrift
doth Iuftifie vs not by our proper Innocencie, but
by the Imputation of Chrifts Iuftes & Interceffior
that wee may be Efteemed Iuft in Chrift who are
in our felues Iniuft.

The reft of Lutherane agree with this doctrine
of Luther and Caluins. fee bellarmine lib. 2. de
Iuft. cap. 2.

This doctrine appeareth to make much fo
Chrifts glorie in Externall apparance, but wher
it is founded to the deepe it shallbe found muc
Iniurious to Iefus Chrift and full of Infidelitie, b
menie reafons grounded in the holy Scripture, be
caufe the Proteftants can not defend fuch doct
ine vnleffe they deny Iefus Chrift to be the Re
demptour of the word.

The firft Reafon is taken from the thefe auth
rities of the holy feripture, where it is written th
Iefus shall faue & Redeeme his people from the
finnes and Iniquities. Mat. 1. 21. and Marie sha
bring feorth a fonne and thou shall call his Nan
Iefus, for he shall faue his people from thir finne
Tit. 2. 14. who gaue him felfe for vs that he mig
Redame vs from all Iniquitie.

For Chrift fayeth verely verely I fay vnto y
that who fo euer cõmitteth finne he is feruant v
to finne, and the feruant abideth not in the hot
for Euer, but the fonne abideth for euer yf t

sonne' therefore shall make you free you shallbe free Indeede Ihon 8. 34.

Yf the Protestants cōmittting sinne as Christ sayeth ar ye seruats to Sathhan how are they made free Imdeede, for so long as they abide in sinne, cōmit sinne, and are sllaues to sinne they are not saued from sinne & Iniquiitie, nor Christ llxiwise can not be called a Redeemes and saueour men from sinne so long as sinne remaineth, in them, & they slaues and seruants to sinne, as a Phisition can not be said to haue cured a man dieased so lond as the disease a bidetd within his bodie.

The seconnd Reason is taken from the victorie of Christ which he hath obtained against Sathan Colloss. 2. 13. and he hath spoiled the peralities powers, & hath triumphed thē in this same Crosse

This victorie and triumphe of our Lord Iesus Christ against Sathan can not consist in no other hing but in that wherein Sathan resisteth vnto God, which is no other thing but sinre for as all goods are of God, so all Impietie, malice, Imquitie Inustice, are cheefely from Sathan, who by his Malitious crafte did deceiue our fivst parents, & raw them with all their Posteritie by originall sinne from the obedience of God vnto his owen subiection. 2. cor· 2. 3. wherefore our Lord calieth im the the prince of this world Ihon. 12 13 by reason of the soueraigne power & Dominion he obtained ouer men in making them to disobey God and serue him by sinne.

VVherefore yf our Lord Iesus hade not taken

away which is the obedince and ſeruics of Sathan
whreby he obtaineth power and Dominion ouer
the ſoules of men, he can nowiſe be ſaid to haue
triumphed ouer Sathan nor ſpoiled him of the
ſoules which he did poſſeſſe by deadly ſinne nor
God likewiſ can not be Eſteemed to haue deliuered men from the pewer of darkneſſe & tranſlated
them to the Kingdome of his deaire ſonne as S.
Paul writteth colloſſ. 1. 13. yf deadly ſinne abideth ſtill in the ſoules of men, by the which men are
detainend captiue in the the power & Domininon
of Sathan.

You ſee then that yf deadly ſinne abidoth ſtill
in the ſoules of men, and only couered by an Externall veale of of Iuſtics (as the Proteſtants wil
haue it to be) that our Lord can not be though
to haue triumphed truly ouer Sathan & ſpoiled
him truly of the Soules, of men, which he did poſſeſſe by deadly ſinne, becauſe the Externall veale
of Iuſtics, Imagined by the Proteſtants taketh no
away the Kingdome and dominion of Sathha
with his ſeruics and obedience, which he hath i
the ſoues of men by deadly ſinne, ſo long as deadl
ſinne (which is the ſeruice of Sathan) abideth ſti
in their ſoules.

As concerning the guilte or deſerte of panie wh
cih followeth the ſinner it dependeth from th
erdinance of God which maketh his lawe wit
ſuch ondition that whoſoeuer ſhould tranſgreſ
his lawe ſhould be worthie of punition.

The punition of ſinne is likewiſe from the Iuſti

of God, which punisheth each sinner according to his misdeeds.

but sinne it selfe is properly from Sathan & such as obey him against the cōmandement of God wherefore Christ triumphed against Sathan must properly consist in taking away deadly sinne it selfe out of the soules of men, wherfore Sathan hath obtained dominnon ouer them, for otherwise Christ can not triumph ouer Sathan, or destroy his Kingdome or dominion, which he hath obtained ouer the soule of men by deadly sinne, vnlesse he take away deadly sinne (wherein consisteth the seruice of Sathan) cleane fourth of the soules of men by the Infusion of his Garce, as the sunne Chaceth away the darkenesse of the night by the cōmunicution of his light dispersed through the Aire.

Thus you see how the Protestants deny flatly victorie ane Triumph of the sonne of God against Sathan, when they affirme that deadly sinne (in the which consisteth the Kinghom and pominion of Sathan) abideth still within the souler of men and only cuered and hidde by an Externall vcule of Iustice Imagined by them.

The thrid Reason (not vnlixe to the scond) is that the cōming of the sonne, of God in this word was to destroy sinne, which is the worke of Sathā as S. Ihon writteth. 1. Ihon. 3 8. he that sinneth. is of the Deuill, for this purpose the sonne of God vos manifest that he might disolue or driue away the workes of the Deuill

VVherefore yf deadly sinne abidoth still in the soules of true Christians and all their workes likewise deadly sinnes worthie of damnation (as is is taughe by the Protestants) then consequently they must confess that the cōming of Christ in the world was to no purpose, and him selfe disputed of his principall intent considering that he could neuer by all his merits, & suffuoring, disolue deadly sinne, and deirue it clane away out of the soules of true Christians, and make their workes meritorious and acceptuaby vnto God.

Thus you see how the Protestants deny they Redemprion of man from sinne & Iniquitie with the destruction of deadly sinnes in the soules of Christians, which are Sathans workes which destruction of sinne should haue beene the chiefe fruit of Chrsts passion, consequently they must deuy Christ to be Redempton of the world because all men are detairied in captiuie of Sathan by deadly sinne, vnseparable frō the soules of men (as the Protestant write of the concupiance by other deadly sinnes in the which Sathans Kingdome & dominion ouer men doe properly consist

The fourth Reason is that the cōming of Iesus Christ in this world was to make the sonnes of Sathan the sonnes of Gode and haires of his Kingdome, as S. Paul writteth to Titus his disciple of 4. but when the bountifulluesse and humanitie 3. our saueour God did appeare onr by workes of Iustce which wce hade done, but according to his mercies he saued vs by the lauer of Regenerarion and Innotion of the holy Ghoſt which he hath powred vpon vs aboundantly through Iesus Chriſt our fauⱺour, that wee being Iuſtified by his grace wee should be maide hairs according to hope of life Euerlaſting.

S. Paul sheweth by theſe words that the chiefe cauſe wheoerefore the ſonne of God did appeare to vs by his Incarnation & paſſion, was to ſaue vs and Iuſtiſie vs from our ſinnes and Iniquities and make vs the ſonne of God & heirs of Eternall life, by the ſacrament of baptiſme or louer of Regon-eraton.

VVherefore yf all deadly ſinnes and Imqities Remaine ſtill within the ſoules of men. & all their workes deadly ſinnes alſo (as is taught bv the Proteſtauts) they are not ſaued & Iuſtiſied from thei ſinnes, and Iniquities by the merits of Chriſts paſſion, and conſequently they are not made the ſonnes of God, and heires of his Kindome by the Sacrament of Baptiſme or lauer of Regeneration. and ſo Chriſts Incarnation and paſſion are vnproſitable to them to make them the ſonnes of God and heires of his Kinhdome.

For ſo long as deadly ſinne remaineth within the ſoules of men, & them ſelues worKers of Iniquirie they muſt be ſonnes of Sathan and not of God as Chriſt him ſelfe ſayeth. Ihon. 8. 44. ſpeaking of vngodly men: you are of your father the Deuill & the deſires of your father you will doe. againe. 1. Ihon. 3. 8. who cõmitteth ſinne he is of the Deuill, which things are true in the Proteſtants but not in Godly Catholiques.

Thus yf deadly sinne maketh the man sonne to the Deuill, as the holy Scripture auoucheth, is Impossible that he be also sone to God, & likiwise brother to Iesus Christ, who is the first borne amongest many bretheren. Rom. 8. 29. for sundrie Reasuns.

First because no man (as our Lord sayeth) Mat. 6. 24 can serue tow Maisters the one contrarie to the other (as God & the Deuill are) consdering then that deadly sinne maketh the man seruant and sonne to God, seruant and sonne to the Deuill bouh together.

Secondly because such an assertion carith with it selfe an Euident contraction, for as God & the Deuill ate contrurtie on to an other in wiil and Effection, so their children and seruants must be contraie in all points.

Thridly because deadly sinne maketh the man sonne & seruant to the Deuill, as is procced aboue, he can not be called the brother of Iesus Christ, vnlesse you style our Lord Iesus with that most horrsble title to be sonne and seruant to Sathan & his bretherene are, which thing is most horrible & blasphéous to be hard, for they can not be called brerherene of Christ as sonnes of God, but only of Sathan by deadly sinne, therefore the most be called (as they are Indeed) the sones of the Deuill

Thus you see how the doctrine of Instificatior by only faith, & deadly sinne abiding in the soule driueth the Protestants to shamelesse absurdibt

and horrible blafphemimies aginft the hônour of
our Lord Iefus Chrift.

But they will fay that our Lord Iefus Chrift
couereth their Impietie, Iniuftice, Mallce hypocnfie and all other deadly finnes refident in their
foules with his Iuftice apprehended by their faith
as wee haue recited aboue.

wee anfwere that their affertion in this behalfe
is both falfe and blafphemous, becaufe they make
Chrift (man) Iniurious vnto God, and kindly
friend to Sathan, when they make him to mantaine and protect with an Externall veale & Imputation of his Iuftice, the hônour and feruice done
to Sathan, by homicids, Theeeues, adulterers,
deceitfull Traitors and other malitious finnes.

Lilkewie they make our Lord by fuch beleefe in
him not to feeke the hônour and feruice of God,
which is the ouerthrowe of Sathan & deftauction
of deadly finnes, but to defend and hide Sathan
poffeffing the foules of the proteftants be deadly
finne & Sathan are alwife Ioyned together, which
ftirreth vp togethere. and Endeuonreth him felfe
to concurre with them to offend God in all humaine actions is not that a God office the afcribe to
Chrift to couer and hide with the Imputtation of
his Iuftice apprehended be their faith all horrible
Crymes and Mifdeeds of cruell Murtherers deceifullT raytours, cômon theeues wilde ftrumpets,
falfe hyjpocrits, shamelesse prriinrers, and all blafphematours of the name of God.

VVhat greates frindfhipe can Chrift shewe vn-

Z

Vnto Sathan, then to maintaine and defend him and all his seruants in their crymes and misdeeds, with an Externall veale of his Iustice Imputed to them, & to saue Sathans seruants, that they come not to the Iudgment of God to be accused and to be punished for their sinnes & misdeeds is not that gratefull seruice made to Sathan and fortification of his Kinghome against the aduancment of the Kingdome of God, which consisteth in the Expelling of Sathan, & all deadly sinnes out of the soules of men (when Christ did cast seauen Deuills out of Marie magdalen, when he did purge her soule from deadly sinne, as S. luke reporteh in his Euangell. 8. 2.) to the end that as Sathan did Raigne and domine in their soules as their Prince & King by deadly sinnes so God should thereafter Raigne in their soules as Lord & Prince by Inherent grace whereby men doe seure & obey him, & so men are translared from the power of Sathan to the Kingdome of his deare sonne.

Therefore Christ cnme not in this worldd to hide Sathan & his workes in the soules of men by an Externall veale & Imputation of his Iustice but Rather to Eypell Sathan out of the soules of men, as he sayeth him selfe Ihon. 12. 31. now the prince of the world is cast out, and likwise to destroy his workes which are deadly sinnes, as of the Deuill, for this purpose the sonne of God was made manifest, that he might dsolue & driue away the workis of the Deuill.

VVherefore yf our Lord Iesus did come in this

world to diſolue and driue away the workes of the
Deuill out of the ſoules of men, which truly bele-
elue in him, & ſerue him aiter his cōmandement,
then it muſt be a graet blaſphemie to ſay (as the
Proteſtants aſſirme) that Chriſt did appeare in
our humanitie to hide & couer deadly ſiñe Sathans
workes in the ſoules of men by an Externall veale
and Inpuerent grace, can no more abide together
in the ſoule of man, then death and life, light and
darkneſſe, which are in comparable together.

The ſiite Reaſon is that the ſonne of God did
ſuffer death to the end that the Iuſtification of the
lawe might be fullfilled in vs and not in Chriſt
only as the Proteſtants aſſirme.

S. Paul thus writteth. Rom 8 3. for (that was
Impoſſible to the lawe in as much as it is weake
becauſe of to fleſh) God ſeding his owen ſonne in
the ſimilitude of ſinneſull fleſh, and by ſinne condemned ſinne that the Iuſtification of the lawe
might be fullfilled in vs, which walke not after the
fleſh but after the ſpirit.

You may ſee by theſe words of the apoſtls that
God did ſend his ſonne to condemne ſinne by the
Sacrifice of his fleſh offred vpon the Croſſe to the
end that the Iuſtification of the lawe might be
fullfilled in vs.

VVherefore yf ſuch Iuſtice as the lawe of God
doth require of vs be not found in a true Chriſtian
by the grace of Chriſt, then God is diſapeinted of
his Intent, which ſend his ſonne to offer him ſeiſe
in a Sacrifice to purge vs frō our ſiñes & Iniquities,

that the Iustification which the lawe of God did require of vs should be ulfilled in vs by the grace of Christ, and likewise Christs passion should be fruittesse, and vnprofitable vnto vs that could not daserue or merie as much grace at Gods hands as might truly purge vs from our sinnes, adorne our soules, with as much Iustice of Inherent grace as the fullnesse of Gods lawe might require of vs.

To say that God is di apointed of his Intet and Christt passion fruittesse in this respect, are tow open blasphemies, the one against the power of God, the other against the merits of Chrifts passion? which is the doctrine of the Protestants who affrime that the Iustification of the lawe is only fulfilled in Christ by Inherent end actuell Iustice & not in the true Members of his Misticall bodie, which is Expresly against the holy Scripture aboue recited.

As withered branches dishonour much the tree so doformed & filthie Members disgrace the beutifull head: Contrariewise as beutifuill branches and fruitfull boughs doe much adorne the tree: so beutifull Members in the Misticall bodie of Christ belong to the honor and beuitie of the head as S. Gregorie auocheth & Reason it selfe confirmeth.

Now to conclude this purpose beholding that deadly sinne abiceth still in the Protestants soules and that all their workes also are deadly sinnes worthie of dammnation, yf they be Iudged according to their worthinesse in the Iudgment of God as it taught by them selues, it followeth conseque-

consequently that Iesus Christ hath not redeemed them frō their sinnes & Iniquitie that he hath not obtained victorie against Sathan in distroying his workee in them which are deadly sinnes, & Expelling Sathã him selfe with deadly sinne out of their soules, & that he hath not obtained by his death & pass õ so much grace as might purge their soules of deadly sinne, that the Iustification of the lawe might be fullfilled in vs, wherefore Christ can not be a Redeemer of the Protestants from their sines & Iniquities, not yet from (he captiuitie of Sathã, whose power & dominion ouer them consisteth in deadly sinnes as they teach of the concupissance by manie other deadly sines not likewse they can not be redeemed from the gilte of eternall damnation which vnsparable from deadly sinne as wee haue prooued aboue.

Thus you see how Christ is no Redeemer of the Protestants from the sinnes & Iniquities, Tyrrnie of Sathan & gilte of eternall damnation, according to former doctrine because the cheefe fruits of mans Ridemption consist in thefe things recited aboue, which things they deny as much against thefe holy Scriptures recited aboue, as to their owen confusion and Euident damnation.

It is not so with Godly Catholiques because he hath saued & Redeemed them from their sines & Iniquities, deliuered them from the Tirrarnie oƒ Sathan, which he obtained ouer them by deadly sinne, and translated them in his Kingdome, and likewse hath purchassed as much grace by his death and paſſion from God father, as might purifie and cleanſe their Soules from all ſpote of deadly ſinne, that ſo the Iuſtification which the lawe of God did require of them, might be fullfilled in them, likewiſe being formally Iuſtified by the grace of Chriſt Inherent in the their ſoules they might be made the ſonnes of God by adoption and hires of the Kingdome of heauen.

Hovv the Proteſtants muke God falſe iu his promiſe to Eſtabliſh their Iuſtificatiou by only faith

CHAP. LXV.

GOD promiſed in the olde Tſtäenr to purifie the hearts of Godly Chriſtians from ſinnes & Iniquities & to write his lawe in their hearts, & not in Tables of ſtone as he did before, when he gaue the lawe ſo written vnto Moyſes, Exod. 31. 18. ſo that the Iuſtice which the lawe of God did require in the oide Teſtament as it written in the hearts of true Chriſtians by the ſprit of grace, which is to loue God with all their hearts and their Nihhbour as them ſoule. Rom. 13. 2. therfore the Proteſtants to Eſtabliſh their Iuſtification bv only faith, and not by the lawe of God written in the hearts of true Chriſtians by the Inherent grace of Chriſt, are conſtrained to make God falſe in his promiſe, as is prooued by the authoritie of the holie Scripture which Enſue heareafter,

Moyſes Deut. 30. 6. thus writteth: Lord God ſhall circumciſe thy heart & the heart of thy ſeede to the end thou loue they Lord thy God with all thy heart with all thy mind.

VVherefore yf no man can be found that loueth God with all his heart & mind (as the Protestants firme) God must be esteemed false in promise.

The Prophet Ezechiell. 36. 27. I shall put my sprit in the midest of you and I shall make you walke and keepe my Iudgments.

VVherefore yf no man con be found which kepeth the Iudgments of God and walketh in his comandements, as the Protestants auouch, they shalbe constrained to make God false in his promise The prophete Iermie writteth also to this purpose Ierenie. 31. 31. behold the dayes shall com sayeth the Lord) & I shall consumare vpon the house of Israell, & vpon the house of Iuda a New Iastament, not according to the Testament which I leite to their fathers in the day that I tooke their to bring thē out of the land of Egipt, because they did not continue in my Testament & I neglected them (sayetd our Lord) but this is my Testament which I will dispose the house of Israell after these dayes (sayeth our Lord) giuing my lawes in their mind, & in their hearts I shall write them.

In these sentnce of the holy Scrpture God hath promised their things to be Exactly acconplishid and performed in th New Testament.

First that he should circumcise & purge them that beleeue truly in him all spote of deadly sinnes, that so being purified from their sinnes. they may loue the Lord God with all their heart and mind.

Secondly that he should write his lawes & graffe

them in the hearts of true beleeuers by the grace
of Christ, which is powred in the hearts of the
faithull by the holy Ghost which is guen them a
the Apostle writteth Rom. 5. 5.

Thridly that he should powre his spirite vpon
faithfull in such abondance that he should make
them to walke in his cōmadements & keepe hi
Iudgments.

Now I will aske at the Protestants whether Go
hath perormed his promise or no? yf they wi
say that God hath performed his promise in th
behalfe then they must grant that the saitfull ar
not only Iustified by faith but also by the lawe o
God written in their hearts, & mind, as the hol
Scripture aboue mentined sheweth most Euiden
tlsi in Exprisse words. Deut. 30. 6. Iermie. e1. 3
& likewise by walking in the cōmandementes o
God, & keeping his Iudgments. Ezechiell. 36. 2

Yf they will say that God hath not performe
his promise in this qehalse, to saue their Iustifica
tion by only faith then they must maxe him to b
false in his promise & consequently to be a lye
when they maxe his word & his deede not to go
soundly together qut contraie one to an othh
which is a manifest blasphemie. for so much
God, which is the first, & Eternall truth, can n
wise lye mor be false in his promise as the Apost
writteth. Tit. 1. 2. hepr. 6. 18.

But Luther in visitatio. Saxonice Melanch th
in locis vltio edntis titul. de lib. arbirt de peceat
Kemnitius in Examen concil. Prident grant

that men may Kep the comandements Externally,
that is not to kill not comire theefte or adulterie,
or other such like thigs which Luther called ciuill
Iustiee or Iustics of the flesh, but they deny that
men may kcepe the Interiour acton of the soule
from sinne and Imundicities, so that these Morall
workes in keeping the comandements Externally
are Iust before men but Iniust before God, because
that the Inwarde action of the soule is not corres-
pondent in Iustuce to the outward action of the
bodie and in this selfe (accondring to their doct-
ine) God hath prforrmed his promise, therefore
Calun affirmieth with Luiher, Melanch then and
Kemnitius that workes, which amongst the com-
on people is accouted Righteousnesse is before
God mcere wickenesse.

VVee answere that yf it be true as Protestant
teach they giue much honour to God in the per-
forming of his promise, to make an hypocrite for
a true Christan, which worketh good workes
Externally before men and in the meane seasou
remaineth still vnclane, Impious and Iniust in
the Inward action of the soule in the presence
of God.

Thuse you see good Reader how their blasphemous doctrine of Iustification can not stand with
the promise of God, and truth of the holy Scripture, because that Eitablish their doctrine of Ius-
tificrtion they ar constrained to make God a lyer
and the holy Scripture false as wee haue prooued

A

aboue in confronting their doctrings with the promiſes of God, and Sentence of the holy Scripture.

But it is not ſo as they ſav in Godly Catholiques that worke, which is Iuſt before men is meere wickedneſſe befor God, for ſomuch as the lawe of God written & graffed in their hearts by the grace of Chriſt powred in their ſouies, as is prooued aboue maketh the in ward action of the bodie both Iuſt before God and acceptable vnto him for otherwiſe the lawe of God can not be ſaide to be written in their hearts, by the vertue and power of God, vnleſſe they be called from ally luſt by that ſame Iuſt lawe, which is formally reſident, and the Inherent in their ſoules, and the actions alſo Iuſt, which deriue from the ſame.

For as the Moone and Starres are full of brightneſſe by the light which reſident in them althought the light which is with in them, begiuen to them by the ſunne and the Aire likeiſe bright by the light which Inſſue out of them: Right ſo the ſoule is full of Iuſtice where of the lawe of Iuſtice is graffed in the power of God and grace of Chriſt and all the actions of bodie alſo Iuſt before God which ſpring out from that lawe of Iuſtice giuen bv God reſidedt in the ſouſe.

Hovy the Proteſtants aboliſh aud vuull that ordiuance of God vvherby vve sre cōmended to praie for grace and Remiſſion of ſinnes to Eſtabliſh their fals, Religion and Iuſtification by only faith.

Chap. LXVI.

THE Proteſtants teach all that the **grace of Iuſtificaꝝ**
tion vvhereby the man is formally iuſt, is no giſte of
grace reſident in the ſoule of man, but only the Iuſtice of
Chriſt Apprehended by their faith (as they alleadge in
Chriſt) as vve haue ſhevven elſe vvhere before.

They teach alſo that the Eſſicient cauſe of their Iuſtification putteth nothing really vvith in the man, but is only
an action reſident in God vvhereby he accepteth them in
his ſauoura and friendſhipe for the only reſpect of theiꝝ
faith in Chriſt,

Thridly they teach that no man is to be Eſteemed to be
one of the faithfull, but ſuch as beleeue vndoubtedly that
theey are receiued in the ſauour of God vvith remiſſion
of ſinnes for their faith in Chriſt,

Fourthly it is taught by them that they are als certen of
their Iuſtification and ſaluation, as they are certen that
Chriſt is the ſonne of God, and that ſuch as vvill not
beleeue his ovven Iuſtification and ſaluation as he beleeueth
Chriſt to be the ſonne of God, not to be Eſteemed as a
faithfull Chriſtian bnt an Infidell, and likevviſe that faith
is the only true Iuſtifing faith, vvhereby they beleeue
themſelues, as certenly to be Iuſtified (that is to be receiued in the ſauour and grace of God vvith remiſſion of
their ſinne of God.

For probation of this point Martiuus Bucerus a Domi-
ean frier (Maſter to Ihon Caluin, as Caluin vauntetr him
ſelfe) in Colloquio Ratisboneſi vvritteth that his faith
maKeeth him as certen of his Iuſtification and ſaluation
as it maKetb him cert n that Chriſt is God or the ſonne of
God, and that ſuch as beleeue not the one as cerrenly as
the other, is not to be Eſteemed one of the faithull.

Caluin his Diſcple lib. 3. Inſt cap. 2. ſeci, 19. thus vvritth
to the ſame porpoſe ſaying vere fidelis non eſt no mam is
to be accounded truiy faitfull, but ſuch as are truly perſuaded that God is both a mercifull and bounuiſnll Father vnto him, and that the benignititie of God and likevviſe haue

such a confidence in the promises of Gods benevolence that he may account himselfe most certen of an Infallible Expectation of Saluation.

Kemnitius in Examen, concil. Tridant. Sesse 6. cap. 11. reprobeteth the vniuersall councell of Trent, because the said councell teacheth vs that no man can be certen of his Iustification and saluation, vvithout an speciall Reuelation of God, vvhere h. holdeth the contrarie, that ech faithfull Christian should hold himselfe certen of his Iustification and saluation.

Petrus Martire in his coment in the 8. to the Romaines doth Auoch the same.

Luther also in assert. Art. 10. 1. 11. Melanch then his Disciple in Tit. de fide et in Apoleg confess. August. Art. 4. et d 9. doe all affirme this doctrine, of the Certaintie of Iustincation and Saluaton, because the Puritant affirme this doctrine of the certaintie of Iustification and saluation more boldly then the Protestants I haue put the Puritans in RancKe before the Protestants.

Novv considering that these Puritans and Protestants are alse certen of their Iustification and Saluation by their Iustifising faith as they are certen that Christ is God or the sonne of God. I vvold a ke at them vvhefore they praie God more for the the Remission of their sinnes, then they doe praie him to send his sonne for the Redemption of the vvorld, beholding also that they beleeue their sinnes to be as truly remitted vnto them, as they beleeue Christ alreadie to be send for the Redemption of the vvorld.

They haue no more Reason to praie for the Remission of their sinnes (vvhich are alreadie remitted by only faith) then they haue to praie God for the Redemption of the vvorld: because he is alreadie send by God the father for this some respect.

Therefore as it is a Blasphemie to praie God to send his Sonne for the Redemption of the vvorld, because God the Father hath send him alreadie for the same respect, as

The holy Scripture and Articles of our faith doe so Euidently declare vnto vs, as so it must be Ablasphemie and point of Infidelitie to them to praie God for the remission of their sinne, vvhich they haue alreadie obtained by their faith in Christ, becanse their sinnes are alreadie remitt,d by the blood of Christ, as it maKeth them certen that God the Father hath send his Sonne for the Redemption of the vvorld.

Thus you see good Reader hovv the Puritans can vor praie God for the Remission of sinnes vnlasse they blaspheme God, according to their orven doctrine, yf it be troe vohich they affirme by their common doctriue reciteh aboue that their faith maKeth them als cerien that their sinnes are remitted, as they are certen that Christ is the Sonne of God, and alreadie send for the Redemption of the vvorld.

Scondly praier is a Godlie vvorke and painefull Action of the bodie, as vvhen the Prophete Dauid said, my throaie is become heare vvhilst I did cray to o Lord all the day long ssal. and as vvhen our Lord did vvatch the vvhole night long.

Therefore vvhen any man obtaineth grace and Remission of sinns by humble and puinefull praier as the publicane did luc 10 10 14 they must confesse that a man is Iustified by good vvorkes, and not by only faith yf they vvill say (as they doe in deede) that all such as are Iustified, obtaine grace and Remission of sinnes by only faith in the blood of Iesus Christ, and nou by any painefull vvorKe of praier, then they must confesse that all praiers offred vp to God for grace and Remission of sinnes are spent in vaine, because that men doe neuer obtaine grace, and Remission of sinnes by praeer offred vp to God, but only by faith in the blood of Christ, so they must liKivvise confesse that Christ the Sonne of God hath commanded vs to praie for the Remission of sinnes in vaine, vvhen he teacheth vs to praie in this fashion, for giue vs our trespasses as vvee foregiue them hat trespasse against vs Mat. 6. 12.

... you see hovv their faith and Religion can not stand
vvith the ordinance of God vvhereby vvee are comanded
to praie for grace and Remission of sinnes, but either they
must say that their Iustifiing faith, is a lying faith, vvhen
they affirme that men doe obtaine grace and Remission of
sinnes by it only, or then that the ordinance of God, vvhereby vvee are comanded to praie for the Remission of sines,
is vaine and to no purpose: because men (as they say doe
neuer obtaine remission of sinnes by prayer offred vp to
God, but by faith only.

vvherefore to say that the ordinance of God vvhereby
vvee are comanded to pray God for grace and Remiss en of
sinnes is in vaine and to no purpose, is an open blasphemie
against the vvisdome of God, vvho can neither doe or com-
and any thing in vaine, but all to seme purpose, therefore
vvee must say that the only Iustifiing faith of the Protes-
tans is a false lyinh faith, and directly against the holy
Scripture and ordinance of God, vvee are comanded to
praie for grace and Remission of sinnes vvhich things are
obtained from God, not only by true faith in Christ, but
also by humble prayer the feare of God penitence and other
suchlike vertues, and not by only faith.

Thirdly to praie God to doe the thing vvhich he hath
alreadie done, as yf man vvold praie God to bring him saue
and sound not of his mothers vvombe, after he is alreadie
borne, is no vvorrhipe of God, but Iesting and Scoffing of
his diuine Maister.

So vvhen the Protestant desireth God by his prayer Iustifie hims remite his sinnes and make him his Childe by the
grace of adoption, vvhich things God sath in Christ, according to his ovven doctrin vvhat can such praier be but Iust-
ing and Scoffing of God to craue againe from him that thing
in his praier, vvhich God hath alreadie giuen to him before
for the respect of his faith.

Yf a poore man after that he hath receiued an hundreth
Crovvnes from a Prince deliuered to him in his Right

hand, vvold hold out his left hand againne, and request
Prince to giue him that same hundreth Crovvnes in his left
hand, vvhich he hade receiued before in his Right hand,
vvold not the Prince haue iust occasion to say to such a one?
vvhat meaneth your Impudencie to hold out your lefte
hand and Craue from me the 100. Crovvnes vvhich I did
deleeuer vnto you in your Right hand vvhen you did beleeue
me to be a liberall Prince before? So God may Iustly say vnto the Protestants vvhen the praier God for grace and Remission of sinnes vvhat misbeleefe and Infidelitie is this in
yon to craue grace and Remission of sinnes from me in your
praiere: considering that yeu houe alread obtained these
things from me before, for the respect of yonr faith in the
blood of Christ vvhich vvas shedde for the Remission of
your sinnes.

Yf you be Certen that your sinnes are remitted by fyith
vvhy Craue you then Remission of them by praier? yf you
thinke to obtaine Remission of them by praier then you
must beleeue they are not remittaed by only faith in Christ.

So their Iustification by only faith and praying for
Remission of sinnes can not stand together.

Considering then that Iustification by only faith and praying for Remission of sinnes can not stand together, vvee
must foresaike the Iustification by only faith, vvhich is the
doctrine of Protestants, and Embrace the praying fo. Remission of sinnes, vvhich is the ordinance of God and doctrine of Christ as a true meane to obtaine grace and Remission of sinnes.

FINIS.

APPROBATION.

Ibrum hunc Anglica Sermone conscriptum
nihil continere quod alienu sit à fide Catholica
testimonio doctrinum prorumque hominum
eiusdem nationis accesermur. Dactum Rotho-
magi. Februarij 1615.

Signé,   GVYION, Vicarij Generalis.

NINIAN WINZET
Certane Tractatis
1562

Certane tractatis for

Reformatioun of Doctryne and maneris, set
furth at the desyre, ad in ye name of ý afflictit Catholikis, of inferiour ordour of Clergie, and layit men in Scotland, be
Niniane Winzet, ane Catholike Preist
borne in Renfrew.

☞ (✳) ☜

⟨ Quhilkis be name this leif turnit sall schaw.

Murus aheneus, sana conscientia.

Edinburgi. 21. Maij,
1562.

☞ THE FIRST

ANE Exhortatioun to the maist excellent and gracius Souerane, Marie Quene of Scottis. &c. To the Bischoipes, and vtheris Pastores, and to al thaim of the nobilitie within this hir graces Realme : For vnfenzeit reformation of doctrine and maneris, and for obtening of licence, to propone in wryt to the Precheours of the Protestantis, certane Artyculis tweching doctrine, ordour, and maneris approuin be thame.

THE SECVND.

THRE Questionis, tweching the lauchful vocatiō of Johne Knox, & his brether Precheours to the Protestantis, in Scotlande : quhilks ar in noumbre the xxiii. xxxiiii. ād xxxv. of the four score thre questionis proponit to thaim be the saidis Catholickis, togidder with thre wryttingis deliuerit to ye said Johne : quhairin is replyit aganis his ansueris maid to ane part of ye said thre questiōis.

THE THRID.

ANe declamatioun to the honorable Prouest Baillies, and Counsell of Edinburgh, for the obseruatioun of the glaid solemniteis off the blyssit Natiuitie, Circūcisioun, Epiphanie, Resurrectioun, and Ascensioun of our Saluiodnr, with the feist of Witsonday : haistelie maid one Pasche twisday. Anno. 1562. Quhē thair apperit ane daingerous seditioun in Edinburgh, throw calking of the durris on euery syde : as efter sall follow.

Dominus mihi adiutor, non timebo, quid faciat mihi homo.

ℭ The first Tractat to the Quenes Ma-
iestie, Pastouris, and Nobililitie.

FTER that we thy graces humill Subditis, Marie maist excellent and gracius
Quene, be our small Jugement hes con-
siderit the statt of this thy Realme, at this
present, twiching religion (quhair vpo the weil-
air thairof is onely groundit) can esteme it, to
a thing mair lyke, thã to ane schip in ane dede-
ly storme, enforsed be contrarius wyndis, betuix
maist daingerus sanddy beddis on ye rycht hãd,
and terrible rolkis presenting deth alrady on the
eft. Quhilk gydit thir mony zeris be sleuthfull
Marinaris, and sleipand sterismen (we mein of
Pastores of the kirk, & in that part of thair p-
noueris) is euyl crasit on the schaldis. Quhair-
at sũ effrayit, and almaist desperat of thair awin
and vtheris lyues in the sampn schip, hes pullit
the rudder and gouernmēt fra the formare rewlaris, maist vnworthy yir mony zeris of that name : and be our Jugement fleing fra the sanddy
beddis, speidis baith with airis and erect salis,
to brek in splederis the schip on the feirful rokis.
For the quhilk peril, we now mair effrayit, than
we and thay wes for the vther, may not contene
vs for na feir of man, sen ÿ mater standis in dainger of our bodeis ãd saulis, bot exhort the latter Marinaris, albeit impatient other of reproif,
or aduertisment, to lat down ane gret dele, thair

To the que-
nes maies.

Our ressonis collectit as ȝanis thee last reularis intent.

ble saillis, and hald to wyndwart, returning thair
course set by the first sett compasse, and direct t
to sū mair sure harbery place, than thay first in
tendit to. To that end we haue collectit, as w
mycht for schortnes of tyme, our apperand reso
sonis, that the passage and dew course is partlie
tyll vs knawin: Exhorting thaim to assent to ou
counsell, or to schaw mair plaine demonstratiou
of strenthiar reasonis for thair interpryse: or tob
tugeit wylfull and led be sum phrenesie, & thair
for not to be hard. Zit sen the godlye wysedom
of thi Maies. hes be ane edict inhibit ony questi
oun or controuersie to be mouit in this action fo
a tyme, to the end that seditioun be eschewit: w
differ to present our said aduertisment and resso
ning to the craibit rewlaris foresaidis, quhill thy
gracious licence be had thairto: quhilk we hop
to obtene, our ressonable despyts being knawin
alrady preset in wryt, as we for schortnes mych
collect to that effect: hoipand ȝ thay sall answe
W mair expedition & circūspect aduisemēt to pe sa
myn (quhilk thing we maist ernestlie despyre) fra
thay psaue our ressonis to be knawin to thy ma

To the bischoppis ād vtheris pastoris.

ies. And also war not ye vrgēt schortnes of tyme
ād iminēt dainger of deth afore our eis, thun
deris in our earis to hald ād defend vs but dela
fra the rolkis of errour, heresie, & manifest sedi
tioun in this thy Realme, manassing alrady des
tructioun, of ȝour reuling misreulit ād misgydi
gouermēt, Fatheris Bischoipis ād vtheris Pas
toris, we wald lamētafore god, & cry for remeid
afore the warld: Suppose vtherwayis for hono
ur of ȝour offices we dar not cōtemne ȝour selfis
And albeit ȝ time be schort, suithing of ȝour prais

mã we speik. Bot quhidder sal we begin ȝour cõ=
mēdatioñ & louing at ȝour haly lyfes, oʒ at ȝoure Off thare
commenda=
tioun.
ȝelthful doctrine, we at douish: Sē ȝour godly
euing garnisit w chastitie, fasting, pʒayer, & so= Off thare
lyues.
bʒitie, be ȝ woʒthi frutis ꝑrof (quhat nedȝ mair)
s patēt to al mã. Zour ī̃chãdʒice, ȝour symonie,
our gloʒious estait, ȝour solicitude be mariage,
fter to haif bʒocht ȝ baronis to be impis of ȝour
osteritie,& witnessing in all aiges to cum of ȝour
godlines, quhay speikis not of it? Zour libera=
itie to ȝe pure,ȝour magnific Collegeis of godly
earnit i ȝour cũpanie, ȝour nurissing of pure stu=
entis, of ryche igȝnis able efter to reull ȝe kirk
of God, in helthfull teachemēt, all cuntreis and
Collegis dois deploʒe. Zour godly & circũspect
distributiõ of benfices, to ȝour babeis ignoʒãtis
& filthy anis, al Ethink, Turk,& Iow may laugh
at it, ȝ being ȝ special grõnd of al impietie & diui=
siõ ȝis day win ȝe O Scotlãd. Zour wyse, saige
& graue familiar seruãds, void of el vanitie, bo=
delly lustis, & heresie, ar spokin of to ȝour pʒayse,
god wate. Zour dum doctrine in exaltig ceremo=
neis only, wout ony declaratiõ of ȝe samin. And Off thare
doctryne.
fer mair keipig in silence ȝe trew woʒd of god ne=
cessar to al mãnis saluatiõ, & not resisting mani=
fest errours, to ȝe warld is knawin. Quhat pt of
ȝe trew religiõ, be ȝour sleuthful dominiõ & pʒin=
elie estaie is not coʒruptit oʒ obscurit? Hes not
mony thʒowilak of techemēt i mad ignoʒãce mys=
knawi pair deuty quhilk we al aucht to our Loʒd
god, & sua i pair ꝑfite beleif hes fairlye stũmerit?
Wes not ȝe sacramētis of chʒist Iesꝰ ꝑphanit be
ignoʒãtis, & wikit ꝑsones, nother able to ꝑsuade
to godlines be lernig noʒ be leuig? Of ȝ quhilk
nũmer.

we confesse the maist part of vs of the Eclesiast-
call stait to haue bene, in our ignozant and iner-
pert zouthe vnwozthelie be zow admittit to the
ministratioun thairof. Geue thir thingis maiste
speciall thzow ignozance and Auarice be bzocht
fra thair puritie: quhate maruell is it, that materis of les pzyce, as of Ymages, the inuocatio-
nis of sanctis to pzaye foz vs, the pzayar foz the
saulis departit, and mony siclyke thingis in so-
bzietie and learnit simplicitie Iesum, to be at this
tyme cozruptit, and pzophanit fra the mynde of
our auncient Elderis, be the sampn vices? War
ze comandit in vaine of God be the mouthis off
Ezechie.
33.
Actu. 20.
Proue. 27.
Of the dis-
ponyng off
thair ren-
tes.
Actu. 4.
his Pzophetis and Apostolis to walke attentlie
and continualie vpon zour flok, and knaw diligetlie the sampn be face? Oz gaif the Pzinces of
the erth zow zeirly rentis (as the Disciplis in the
beginnyng, sauld thair landis, and gaif the pzy-
ces thairof to the Apostolis) to the end, that euery ane of zow, mot spend the sampn vpon his dame Dallda and bastard bzowis? And albeit it
chance oft to the infirmitie of man, that he fal on
sleip, quhe he suld crast walk, and be geuin to pas-
tyme, quhe he sulde maist diligetlie labour: Bot
zit O mcykful god, quhat deidly sleip is this, that
hes oppzessit zow, that in sa gret vpzote, tumult,
& terrible clamour, ze walkin nocht furth of zour
dzeme? And in sa gret dainger of deth, ze haif na
regard of zour awin lyues noz vtherts? Walke
awalk we say, and put to zour hande stoutlie to
Psal. 120.
Hebre. 4.
saif Petiris schip: Foz he nother sleptis noz slum-
meris, quha beholdis all zour doingis, and seis

ȝoure thochtis: bot sall require the blude oute
of ȝour handis, of the smallaste ane that sall pe-
rise throw ȝour negligêce. Bot the tyme not per-
mitting vs to speik ferder in this mater, occasió Eȝe. 3. and 33.
ȝouokis vs to schaw sũ thing to ȝour honourts, To ȝ noble litie.
O worthy Nobilis, of ilke degre withî this real-
me: and that in hope of reformatioun in ail thee
partis of Godis kirk. The speciall rutis of all
mischeif we suspect nocht ȝour prudent nobilitie
to mysknaw, to be ȝ twa infernal monstris,Pryde Ecclia. 10. I. Timo. 6.
and Auarice: of the quhilkis vnhappelie hes
opsprung the electioun of vnqualiferr bischopis
and vtheris pastores in Scotland: And that la-
tlie, as we cã collect, within thir hundreth ȝeris,
in the gret destructioun of the trew religioun off
christianis, and in prouocation of Godis wraith
contrare vs. For afore thay dayis, na man gentle nor vther for feir of conscience, ãd dout of his
inhabilitie, wald resaue ȝe office of ane pastour,
quhil he wes almaist compellit thairto. Ane witnessing of the samyn may be the ceremonie obser
uit be mony now in hypocrisie, *Nolens volo.* And ȝit
we may nocht dout of the lauchfull ordinatió ãd
auctoritie of al: as we may not of onr lauchful so
uerane be name. For i boutig thairof, quhat ellis
is it, bot to plant but rutis of ordour, ane manifest confusion & vter exterminion of this realme:
setting vp ane peple heidles left of God, as thee Ose. 3. 2. Para. 15
Prophetis speikis, Absq; rege, absq; lege, & absq; sacer
dote: that is witout ane king, without ane law,
and without ane preist? Bot geue ony spote, or
blek be in the lauchfull ordination of our pasto-

The Syno
nie off thee
Nobilis.

4.Reg.5.

Actu.8.

Of the ri-
gour done
to the pure

tores: we maye nawayis of reasone, bot impute
that cryme to the hie reproche of 3our nobilitie.
Call heirfor to remembrance, we beseik 3our humanitie, that 3our seifis on lyue togidder w 3our
Eldaris in the lait aige foresaid, fra the lawaste
to the hieast degree, to haif bene the inuentaris,
nurissaris, and Simoniacall merchandis of the
sampyn mischeif, playand to 3our inferiouris the
part of lippir Giezi in this mater, sayad: Quhat
wyll 3 geue me. And to the kingis of this realme
(bot god impute not that to 3ow and 3our posteritie playande the part of Symon his compan-
3one, sayand, schir, quhat sall we geue the: And
sua 3e nobilis specialie, & 3ouris lait pgenitours
blyndit be carnall effectioun of 3ours babis, brether, or vtheris freindis, or be Auarice, hes destroyit the trew religioun and triumphand kingdome of Christe, safer as 3e mycht: putand in the
place of godly Ministeris, and trew successouris
of the Apostolis, du doggis. Quha for the maist
part in extreme dainger of thair maisteris housse
the kirk of Christe, quhair ennimeis ar without
and within, dar not only nocht barke, bot mais
schamefullie peyit with staff & sting, dar nother
quhrpne nor quhynge. Bot of the rigour to thee
pure done on 3our awin landis, and of the appro-
pryping pe kirk ladis w vtheris dewiteis thairof,
to 3our awin kechingis: of the depaupering thee
tennentis be 3our fewis, augmetationis & vtheris exactionis: or of the schutting of honeste men
fra thair natiue roumes, be tytle off 3oure newe
quhitlie fewis, tyme seruis not to schaw. Heirfo

[s]en be his iustice god punissis oftymes, in ye sa[m]yn thing, quhairin man offendis: That sũ off [y]our houssis hes bene laitlie, aiuterlie destroyit, [a]nd put out of memorie: And the vtheris detec[t]it to pouertie, is not that ye iustice of god? And [t]hat vtheris degenerat fra ye auncient nobilitie [o]f thair Eldaris, be fallin in extreme ignorance [o]f god, and in obstinat stubbirnes to leir sinceir[l]ie his law, or walk thairin ʒforme to yair knaw[l]ege: bot hauãd regarde to ye wrek of this warld [o]r lustis of thair bodyis, leuis as Epicurianis, [w]ut faith or lufe to god or man. And vtheris cõ[t]rarie reioyses tobe callit Gospellaris, and cun[n]ing in Scripture: quha rest vp in hie curiositie [o]f questionis, and (as apperis tyll vs) inmani[f]est errours and presumptioun, makis of the gos[p]ell ane takin craft but ferder practise off godis [l]aw in deid. Quha albeit thay cry out fast vpon Ydolatrie: ʒit thay ar na les thã the vtheris de[-]generat ignorantis abone specifeit, as wikit E[-]thinkis, and bund subditis to ỹ monstrous ydo[-]latrie of Auarice, neuir intendand to clenge yair handis of ye kirk rentis, nor of ye blude ãd sueit of the pure anis, spurrande fast vtheris to refor[-]matioun, bot in deid neuir reformand thaim sel[-]fis fra the ydolatrie of Auarice: neuir change[-]and in this daingerus battel of religioun, thair babis with men, thair ignorantis with learnit: except in ane clokit maner to sustene ane Minis[-]ter, quhare thre hundreth ryche & pure wes sus[-]tenit afore. O Immortall God, quhy persaue ʒe nocht thir thre plaigis tobe the scurge of thee

Sapi. 11. Of ye plagis on thee nobilitie.

duine iustice for zour former impietie, ād deuilis-
che simonie? Sen ze and zour last forefatheris
in the wyldsū way of this daingerous lyfe chesit
zour selfis sa blynd gydis: quhat meruell is it,
that ze sa lang indurat but repentance, be fallin
in the pot of ignorāce errour or vice? Quhy clen-
with idola-
rie, with
ane simple ge ze not zour hart & handis fra Ydolatrie, quha
be toung cōdamnis ydolatrie sa mekle? Sen god
geuis vs libertie efter our vnderstande frelie to
think: sall this zour ydolatricall auarice psuaid
our cōscience (albeit we be ruid of letteris ād iugemēt) that ze intend only to trampe doun ydolatrie, and set vp Christis kingdome? Or thate
zour forbearis quha distributit thair awin iuste
geris and landis to exercise the louing of god, ād
to sustene the pure, to haue bene ignorantis of
god ād ydolatouris: And zow (saifing zour dew
honoris we speik quha rugis, as ze may, fra god
& al godly vse, to zour awi keching) : to be þ trew
Discipulis of Christe? Na na, trewlie: sen ye ve-
Luc.16.
Luc.14. ritie pronunces this : Non potestis deo seruire & mam-
monæ. And againe, Nisi quis renunciauerit omnibus quæ
possidet, non potest meus esse discipulus. Nochtheles we
psaue mony amāgis zow (to god be glore) quha
with humil spirit, wald flee fra al Ydolatrie, su-
perstition and abuse : and siclyke fra errour, heresie, and curious presumptioun w vaine babling : and practissis the law of god, leuing sobir-
lie, godlie, and iustlie. To quhome we committ
I.Cor.10. this regiment : Qui se existimat state uideat, ne cadat:
As we do to the warldly ignorantis abone spe-
Psal.31. cifiit, this vther of the Prophet : Nolite fieri sicut

equus & mulus, in quibus non est intellectus. And as we
haue schawin sum thing, as we may for tyme to
our Pastores, exhortyng thame to reformatión:
swa we suspect nocht zoure gentle humanitie, zee
Noble potêt Lordis, Baronis, & vtheris quhat
sumeuir of the Nobilitie of Scotlande, tobe of=
fendit with vs zour pure anis, bot our Souera=
ne Ladyis fre liegis, to zet in vnfenzetlie the ve=
ray selfis affectionis of oure myndis, as in thee
bosūis of yaim monywayis deirbelufit: se we of
the law sorte ar to gidder with zour excellence, in
the samyn schipe of thee commoun welth of this
realme, participant conforme to oure small part
of all prosperitie and aduersitie thairof.   And
thairfor of nature and of conscience ar mouit to
wys gude to al in the samyn. And zit we attempt
this mair bauldlye, that we ar compellit be ane
part of zour nobilitie and zoure Prechouris, as
we efter sall schaw.

Bot to thy Maiestie maist excellent Soue=
rane we returne, beseikand maist humlie thy G.
and thy nobilis foresaidis, to impute nocht that
tyl vs as a falt, that we speik in ye cause of God
sa frely : desyrande licence that we may but iuste
offence of ony persoun, ppone in wryt to the pre=
chouris of thaim callit the congregatioun, thay
thingis quhairin specialie we ar offêdit, twoche=
ing doctryne, ordour and maneris approuin bee
thaim : to the intent that all errour ād abuse be=
ing cuttit away, we al ō baith sydis mot knaw y
veritie and glaidlye ād vnfezetlie embrace the
samyn, as the deir belouit dochter of God.

To re que=
nes maies

The peti=
tioun to ye
wryttaris.

The quhilkis we set furth for twa causis. The
ane is, that we intending tobe faithfull christia=
nis, and reddy to suffer thy graces lawis for ony
cryme conmittit be vs, ar compellit other to af=
firme in religioun afore man contrare our cons=
cience : or tobe incarcerat or exilit, and haldin be
the warld as Infidelis, Heretykis, apostatis, or
wikit persones vnworthy the companie of chris=
tianis : And i ye mein tyme at sic extreme pouer=
tie all we of the clergye, that we ar almaiste losit
Wout ony mercy of mã. The vther cause is : that
we being of smal learning, and zit laith tobe hy=
pocritis to our cõdemnation, hes lang abydit for
ressoning of the Bischopes, Theologis ãd vthe=
ris weill learnit tyl ane godly reformation rycht
necessare. Quhilk thing not cãde to passe, bot
mait cure had of the keching nor of the queir, we
may nawayis langer contene vs, bot expresse on
al sydis, as we think : referring our iugemẽt to ÿ
haly catholik kirk and that without eloquence or
manly persuasion, of ye quhilk we haue lytle re=
garde in respect of the diuine veritie : knawand
yat lyke as ane beutiful persoun is lustie aneuch
in ane sobir rayment, that sa is the veritie in ane
rud style. Bot sen this controuersie and tumult,
O gracius Souerane, cũis but dout of the for=
mare iniquitie, and contempt of God in vs, and
our forbearis : quha of his gudnes besydis * his
mony maist excellẽt giftis geuin to the amangis
al Princes, hes geuin to thy hienes ane maist ex=
cellẽt of all : in ÿ preseruing to this day thy bew=
tifull body & saule, fra al spot of notorius cryme

in ony of baith : We may not, bot exhort the our
maist excellent Souerane to haue ye gudnes of
thy God in memorie intedyng be his grace to p-
seuere sa to the ende, walkande and panceand in
his lawis day and nycht. Quhilk thing consistis
nocht in the reidyng of mony cheptours (albeit
that be proffetable to ane humill mynde) bot in
haly feir, trew faith wyrkad be charitie : quhair
on dependis sure hope of temperal prosperitie, &
blys eternall. For the kingdome of god is nocht
* in word bot in worke. Bot because gret cōtrouersie is new for the dountraping of Ydolatrie:
to ye outruiting of ye quhilk we beseik thy prin-
celie Maiest. maist effectuslie. for ẏ lufe of Christ
(quhome in word we all professe) to bent vp thy
mynd maist ernestlie : sen that is the falt, quhair
with the maiestie of God is maist greuouslie offendit. For albeit mony in thir dayis hes laborit
to abolise, and pull the samyn mercyles vp be ye
rutis, and erd the leist memoriall thairof oute of
the mynd of man : and in the name of it in thare
greif, hes destroyit mony thingis nawayis ydolatricall : Zit thay left to thy victorious hand a-
mang vtheris mair smal, thre of the gretast ydolis but controuersie vntwechit, verray ydolis in
deid, &c, ẏ rute, top, & body of all vtheris ydolis.
Of the quhilkis ane we haue schawin the monst-
truus Ydoll of Auarice : w the quhilk the Princes of the erd maist cōmonlie cōmittis Fornication. To the end that thy Maies. be neuir thairwith pollutit, nother in Ciuill nor Ecclesiasticall
estatis, euery day we pray war in thy mynde the

The soum
of our chri-
stiane reli-
gioun.
I. Pet. I.
Galat. 5.
I. Timo. 4.
I. Cor. 4.

*

Of ydola-
trie.

Thre ydo-
lis lefte zit
vntwechit

The ydoll
of auarice.

The Idoll
of the dum
Pastores.

Zacha. 11.
the kindis
of pis idol
at pi spret.

historie of Naboth, of Ananias, and Saphira,
praying that wikit persoun quhatsueuir, quhay
wald defyle thy conscience and fame thairwith,
haistelie to returne to oppin repentance: or to haue the reward of wickit Jezabell in exemple and
terrour of vtheris. The secunde idoll is, the wickit dum pastour: of the quhilk we mak thre kyn-
dis. Sum for saying only to our ruid reformcaris: My maisteris Your doctryne plesis vs : hes libertie to
bruke the kirk rentis, and leue als dum in godis
cause, as ony fische in the watter, and in mair licentius lyfe, than euir thay did afore. Ane vthir
forte stattis vpe faithles, euery zeit embraissyng
with gret brak the faith of the starkast pty. And v-
theris for not saying this ane word : My maisteris
vs lufe You and Your doctryne : at deposit of thair offices, denudit of thair rentis : and y appetandlye
be the pmissioun or erar reuenge of god, sen thay
being afflictit, hes na compunctioun nor doleur
of pair former necligence, nor intent to reformatioun, bot only luckis bakwart with the Israelitis
to thee potis of flesche in Egypt : that is to thare
former licentius leuing. Quhilk sort ar les prof-
fitabyll to godis kirk, than wes Lothis wyfe to
him, efter pat scho wes turnit in ane stane of salt.

The thrid Idoll and werst of all is the fals Pre-
cheour sittand in the temple of god schawand him
self (as S. Paule speikis of his maister the An-
tichrist) as he war god : that is exaltit in the con-
sail and consience of man, and estemit to haue that per-
fectioun that he can nocht nor may nocht lie.

Thir thre Idolis be the mycht of thy Maiestie
and bauld assistence of thy nobilis and trew Pas-

toꝛes, being with the speciall grace of god, anis
in ȝis ȝi realme suppꝟit: we dout not bot al Ido=
latrie, quhilk is now in contꝛouersie in religion,
ȝe men of mein learning, amang al peaceble mē,
ſalbe pacifiit be small labouris, to ane godly cō=
coꝛde. We ſpeikād frelie in the cause of our god
to his gloꝛe, ād in feruent zele, efter our small iu=
ʒement, to the weilfair of thy maiestie, nixt efter
god to ᵫs thy trew Subditis maiſt deirbelouit
in erth, ſuspectis na godly persoun tobe offendit
with ᵫs. Foꝛ geue we had kepit langer ſilence,
we ferit baith the offence of our god, and our cō
science tobe ſmotit ᵫ the cryme of leſe maiestie,
foꝛ not aſſiſting to the veritie, in this daingerus
tumult. Farder sen all man hes this woꝛd refoꝛ=
matioun in mothe, willing to refoꝛme ᵫtheris:
that al man haue iuſte occaſioun alſo to refoꝛme
ane, that is him ſelf: We maiſt humelie and er=
neſtlie beſeikis thy Maiestie, maiſt gratious ſo=
uerane foꝛ the suppoꝛte of ᵫtheris, ād euery ane
within this realme quha bnfenȝetlie lufis God,
and ane godly refoꝛmationn, to luke in the mir=
rour ᵫnderwꝛyttin set ᵫp be the finger of God,
ₐ ȝe mouth of his haly Pꝛophet Ezechiel: quhair
in euery stait may see his ſmot, and haue iuſt oc=
caſioun to refoꝛme hym self firſt, and thairefter
be mair able to help his nychtbour oꝛ inferiour.
The spirit of Iesus Chꝛiste our only Saluiour
ₐ mediatour mot conuoye the hert of thy Maieſ.
ₐ al chꝛiſtiane Pꝛinces wꝛour Subditis in eue=
ry degre, to behald attentlie euery day ȝ samyn
mirrour, ₐ to purge ₐ weſche all ſmotis expꝛeſſit
be it.   Amen.

To all Estatis.

THE worde of the Lorde come vnto mee, saying thow Sone of man, the house of Israell is turnit into drosse, or roust. Al thay that suld be tin, Irne, ād led, ar in the fyre becum drosse. *&c. And a lytle efter,* thow art ane vnclene land, quhilk is not raynit vpō in the day of the creuell wraith.

The gredy precheouris

The Prophetis that ar in it ar lyke ane lyone roryng and takand ȝ pray: thay haue deuorit ȝ saulis, thay haif relauit ryches and gloze, ẜ multipliit the wedowis in ye middis of it.

The wikit Preistis.

The preistis of it hes contemnit my lawe, hes defylit my Sanctuarie, betuix the haly, and the vnhaly, thay haue had na difference: and fra my haly dayis thay haue turnit away thair Ein: And I wes vnhallowit in thee middis of thaim.

The princes.

The reularis in the middis of it, ar lyke woulfis rauisching yair pray, to sched blud, to destroy saulis, ẜ gredelie to scarce lucre.

Thee fals prechoures.

Bot the Prophetis of it, spargeouit thaim with vntemperit morter, seing vaniteis, and propheciig leis vnto thaim, sayand: The Lord hes said this, quhen the Lord hes not spokin.

The peple.

The peple of the land vsit wikit extorsioun and rubberie. Thay vexit the pure and nedy and opprest the strainger aganis rycht. I socht of thaim ane mā that wald mak vp the haige, ẜ set hym self in ye slope before me in the landis behaif, that I culd not vterlie destroy it: bot I could fynd name.

The punisment,

Thairfore I haue pourit oute my creuell disple-

sout vpon thaim, in the fyre of my wraith haif I
consumit thaim. Thair awin wayis haif I recom-
pencit vpon thair heidis, sayis the Lord God.

Delyuerit to the Quenes Grace, the **15.**
of Fabruar. **1561.***

THE SECVND TRACTATE.

☞ Geue Johne Knox be lauchful Minister,
the xxxiii. Questioun.

S En we reid that nane suld tak the honour
of Ministratioun of Godis word ād Sacramentis on him, except he be lauchfullie
callit thairto : other be God imediatlie, or be mā
haifand power to pmot hym to that office. And
sen we reid nane callit be god ōlie, except sick as
schew yair power geui to yaim be him, ✷ be power of ye spirit, or in signis & wounderis. Heirfor
giue zow, Johne Knox we say, be callit immedi-
atly be God : quhair ar zour meruellis wrocht be
the haly spirit ? For the meruellis of woltring of
realmes to vngodlie seditioun and discorde, we
adnūber nocht tobe of his gyftis : Bot giue ze be
callit be man : ze moist schaw thaim to haue had
lauchful power thairto : as ȳ Apostolis ordinatit
S. Paule and Barnabas, albeit chosin be God
afore : and thay siclyke vtheris in the xiiii. of the
Actis : and as S. Paule ordinatit Timothe ād
Tite, geuand thaim power & cōmand to ordour
vtheris : quhaim apperis the lauchfull ordinatiō
of Ministeris. ᴣ our lauchful ordination be ane
of thir twa wayis, we desyre zow to schaw : sen ze

α

Rom. 10,
Heb. 5.

✷ Quhate
it menit be
yir wordis
is efter de-
clarit.

Act. 13,
Act. 9.

1. Timo. 4,
2. Timo. 1,
Titum 1,

renunce and estemis that ordinatioun null, or ex
tar wickit, be the quhilk sumtyme ze ware callit
Schir Johne.

Giue Johne Knor be not lauchfull Bischope,
quhow can thay be lauchfull ordinatit be
him the xxxiiii. Quektioun.

Johne kno
nis anlucr
to this wes
I ordinat
naue luper
intendentis
nor minis=
teris.

GIue he can nocht schaw him self ane lauch=
full ordinatit bischope, nocht onlie ane pre
ist or inferiour minister ? quhow can ze Super=
itendentis or vther inferiour prechours ordina=
tit and electit be him not haifand power thairto,
iuge zoure selfis tobe lauchfull ministeris in the
kirk of god ?

Quhy ar not the Lordis and vtheris, lauchfull mi=
nisteris as Johne Knor and his Complices.
th. xxxv. Quektioun.

His answer
leir wes la
schort and
obscur pat
we vnder=
stude it not

OIue Johne Knor and ze affirmis zour sel=
fis lauchful, be ressoun of zour science : ad
that ze ar pmittit alwayis, giue ze be not admit=
tit, be thay kirkis quhome ze serue : Quhy haue
ze techit manifestlie ane gret errour and schisme
in zour congregatioun, contending w tuith and
naill (as is the prouerb)sii lordis ad gentil me,
to haue gretumlie failzeit, ministrand zour com=
munioun in tymes bypaste, to thair awin hous=
hald seruandis and tenentis : sen the saidis lor=
dis and gentilmen being men of science, be thair
awin iugement, in that case wes pmittit be thair
sadis seruandis to þ office : quha affirmis þame
selfis tobe ane kirk of god ?

SChir it mote pleis ʒow, forſamekle as we
delyuerit certane articulis to ʒow, twechig
ʒour doctryne, or dour &c. Quhatrin ſpecialie we war offendit: And that pryuatlie be ane
honorabyll perſoun of ʒour awin religion: quha
of his cheritie (as he thocht) had oft exhortit ſu
of vs, tyll ane vnioun w ʒow. And albeit we only deſyrit ane anſweir thairoff in wryt pryuatlye
wout contentioun as we pponit to ʒou: Nocht-
theles ʒe haue oppinnit the ſampn in the pulpet,
and reherſit ſum thingis thairof in oure name,
nocht ſa ſinceirly, as we pponit thaim, nor ʒit in
that mynd. Heirfor we exhorte ʒou ʒit, as afore,
that we maye haue ʒour anſweir in wryit. And
giue it ſal pleis ʒou alſo to anſueir to ʒaim in ʒe
pulpet: We wald that firſt ʒe red our wryttings
fullelie and ſinceirlie: And thairefter anſweir
thairto, *Sicut ex deo, coram deo, & in chriſto.* Quhare **ɩ. Cor. ʒ.**
ʒe ſperit, quhat we menit tobe ſend of god imedi
atlie, be power of the ſpirit, or &c. This is our
trew mening and mynd: that almychtie god teſtifiis thair power geuin to ſick be his worde & ex-
preſſe ſcripture. pnunceit be inſpiratioun of the
haly ſpirit, that he ſend thaim as his trew mini-
ſteris of his worde and ſacramentis: As he teſti
fiit of S. Iohne Baptiſt, be the Prophetis Ma- **Malac ʒ. 4.**
lachias, Eſaias, and Zacharie, his father, be ʒe **Eſa. 0 4.**
Angell, and the mouthe alſo of our ſaluiour ſelf: **Luc. I.**
Or as he teſtifiit that he ſend his Apoſtolis and
seuintytwa

Discipulis be the samin his word, geuand thaim also power to wyrk wounderis. Joh. 20. Luc. 9. And sa ze sall fynd nane in the lawe of grace, sed imediatlie of god, bot be ane of thir twa wayis: of the quhilkis nane (as we vnderstande zit) conuenis to zow. And as twechinge S. Johne Baptist, we think his lauchfull vocatioun sufficientlye schawin to the People, be Gode in signis and wounderis, wrocht afore his conception, & efter his Natiuitie in Zacharie his Father, and be Elizabeth and him self in hir waimb, pat thair nedit na ma signis of his lauchfull office: sen thay wounderis wes knawin and keipit

in memorie as it is wryttin Luc, I. *In tota montana Iudee diuulgabantur omnia uerba hec. Et posuerunt oes qui audierat, in corde suo dicentes: Quis putas puer iste erit? Etenim man° domini erat cu eo.* Bot se ze haif harpit sa lang on that ane string, tweching zour lauchfull vocatioun: we exhorte zow to schaw it iustlie toneit, or ze leif it. Quhilk geue ze may do, & assuir the peple and vs heirof, it is the radiast waye, to psuade al zour aduersaris to delyte in the rest of zour melodie. *In Christo vale, & opera da, ut ueritas, & non homo uincat.* 3. Mart. Be zours in all godlines.

Niniane vvinzet at the desyre of his afflictit brether.

☞ Geue ony wryttingis be put furthe onywayis contrare zow or zouris without subscriptioun, impute nocht that to me. For: I testifie to zow that I wes neuir participat of sic wryttingis to yis hour.
Idem Ninianus.

Swa it is wryttin on the bak as on the vtheris.
Rare eruditionis facumdiæq; uiro Ioanni Knox.

Sir it mot pleis zow be rememberit, that
we declarit zow i our laſt wzytting at zour
deſyze, quhat we meanit to be imediatlye
callit of god, tobe ane lauchful Paſtour : quhilk
is ony man to haue the ſpeciall cõmand of godis
wozd at the leſt, chargeand him to that vocatiõ:
Oz ellis to haue the ſampn cõmand with power
to wyzk ſignis and wounderis : ₹ ſchew that S.
Iohne Baptiſt (be quhois exemple, ze apperit to
intend to pzeue zour lauchfull vocation) had the
auctozie of godis wozde : ãd that ſignis alſo wat
ſchawin be god, that he wes ſend be him.   Bot
quhair ze denyit ỹ S. Iohne. wzocht ony ſigne:
ze affirm ỹ wt the Iowis : quhilk albeit be trew,
of ỹ exteriour ſigne requirit be Infidelis, zit in ỹ
ſampn place, ze maye collect, that he wzocht that
ſigne ſufficient to ane faithfull: quhilk wes that
al thing quhilk he ſpak in ye ſpirit of Pzophecie
of Chziſte, wes trew. Quhair ze intendit to pzeue
zour lauchfull vocatioun be exemple of the Pzo-
phet Amos : ỹ pzoffetis zow na thig. Foz quhat
chziſtiane man may dout but Infidelitie (as all
mẽ may dout of zour doctryne but al perrell)bot
the Pzophecie of Amos is the wozde of god? Foz
the ſcripture teſtifiis yat Amos wes ſend begod,
₹ that viſible ſignis wes ſchawin to him be god.
And ane ſufficient ſigne to ye peple wes, that al
thing quhilk he fozeſpak, come to pas. And ſup=
poſe Amos, as the reſt of ye pzophetis: war ſend
namelie, to ſchaw ſum ſpeciall thing off goddis

Io. 10.

Amos. 7.
& . 8.

wyll cóforme to the tyme : Zit he vſurpit not tha auctoꝛitie of the hie Biſchope in Hierusalem, as ʒe do at this pꝛeſent of the pꝛimat of Scotlande in Edinburgh. Quharefoꝛ chearitie moueis vs to aduertis ʒou of thꝛe thingis : The firſt is of y̌

Numi.16.
terrible puniſement of Coꝛe, Dathan, & Abiron, being of that tribe appoyntit onely of God tobe pꝛeiſtis, ád allegeand the ſcriptur alſo foꝛ yaim,

Exod. 19.
ſapand : *Sufficiat vobis quòd omnis multitudo ſácta eſt, & in ipſis eſt dominus* : As ʒe do this place off the ſcrip-

Apoca.I.
ture foꝛ ʒow, *Fecit nos (chriſtus) reges et ſacerdotes deo & patri*, with ſiclyke. Be ye quhilk auctoꝛitie gi-ue ʒe be ane lauchfull pꝛeiſt oꝛ biſchope in Edin-burgh, ʒe ar be the ſampyn auctoꝛitie alſo lauch-full king of Scottis. The ſecund is to remèber

Iaco.3.
ʒow, *quòd ſapientia quæ eſt deſurſum, a patre luminú, pudica eſt, pacifica, modeſta, tractabilis, &c. & nihil ſimulans. Et quòd domini ſeruú non oportet litigare, ſed placidú eſſe ad oës,*

2.Timo. 2.
propenſum ad docendum, patientem, cum modeſtia corripientè eos, etiam, qui reſiſtunt veritati : And ſen we alllegeit na thing in our laſt byll, bot ſinceirlie the expꝛes woꝛd of god, but wꝛyſtig, wꝛyig, gloiſſig, oꝛ clo-kig as ʒe culd not pꝛeue y̌ ſtrate : yat ar ſidꝛy of-fendit w̌ zour terrible exclamatioun towart vs, quhilk wes, *Progenies viperarum &c.* The thꝛid is, that we exhoꝛt ʒow, and adiuris ʒow alſo, in thee name of our Loꝛde Jeſus, giue ʒe haue na mair teſtimonie, foꝛ ʒour lauchfull vocatioun imedi-at, than ʒe haue ſchawin, to deſcend from the hie ſkyis, but ferder contentious cauillation, amáng men : And ſchaw ʒour power gewin ʒow of yaim

foz vtherwayis we freindlie aduerteis zow, that
zour awin scoleris thinkis, ӯ that ane mistoneis
string confoundis all zour harmonie. The lozde
of peace mot geue zou his peace and veritie, ԝ
bs, and mynd to wyll, that veritie win the victo
rie. Io. Marc. 1561, Be zours in all godlines.

Niniane vvynȝet at the desyre of his brether.

Ane vther delyuerit the xii. of Marche. ꝛc.

Sthir it mot pleis zour pzudence to haue in
mynd ӯ we send zow ane wzytting this last
twisday : exhoztyng zow to testifie tyll vs,
mair planelie zour ozdinatioun tobe lauchfull.
Of the quhilk ze spak na thing in zoure nixt ser=
mon. Heirfoz sen ze by our first desyze and coun=
sell, hes spokin sa bzaid thairof in the pulpet, ӑ
as ȝit not assurit not only not vs, bot nocht zour
awin best learnit scoleris of the sampyn : we pzay
zou and exhoztis zou, and als be al power geuin
to mony of vs be ye auctozitie of pzeisthed, com=   I. *Timo.* 4.
mandis ӑd chargeis zou in the name of our lozd
Jesus, ꝛ in ye power of his maist mychtie spirit,
that ze other mak demonstration to the people ӑd
vs, of zour lauchfull ministerie geuin be god im
mediatlie, as had the Ipostolis. Oz be man in ӯ   Io. 20,
cause haifand the power of God, as S. Paule   I. *Timo.* 4.
ozdinatit Timothe and Tite : Oz be baith, as ye   2. *Timo* I,
said S. Paule wes first callit be god, and syne   Act. 9,
ozdinatit be men. Oz vtherwayis that ze aluter=   ꝛc. Iȝ.
lie desiste, fra the vsurpyng of

ane vther mannis office, quhill ʒe be lauchfullie
callit thairto : and heir ʒit the Apostill sayand,
Nec quisquã vsurpat sibi honorẽ, nisi qui vocatur a deo. The
Hebre.5.
Numi.16,
seueir punisment of Coʒe Dathan and Abiron, ⁊
the feirfull Plaige that come on thay people,
quha fuleschelie assentit to thair pʒydefull arrogance (as we sũpart schew in our laste wʒytting)
thunderis swa thʒow al our sensis, and peirsis vb
feir oure heartis, that we dar nocht bott in com-
patience bʒotherlie aduerteis ʒow, and ʒour scoleris tobe (as we think) in the perrell of the samyn punischement. We beseik ʒow also to remẽber of the plaige of the king Oʒias : quha in his
2.Paral.
26,
pʒesumptioun ingerit him self to offer the bʒynt
sacrifice at ÿ alter of god, to quhilk office he wes
not callit. And ʒit his falt wes a smal thig in respect of ʒouris, giue ʒe want godis auctoʒitie as
he did : Sen he intendit to offer the signe onelie,
and ʒe to treit the veritie self of the Sacrifice off
the kirk, at ʒour cõmuniõ cõfoʒme to our Sal-
uiouris institutioun, togidder vb all the vtheris
Sacramentis ãd mysteriis. Foʒ we can persaue
be ʒour awin allegẽce na power ÿat euir ʒe had,
except it, quhilk wes geuin to ʒow in ÿ sacramẽt
of oʒdinatiõ be auctoʒitie of Pʒeisthed. Quhilk
I.Timo. 4.
auctoʒitie geue ʒe esteme as nochtis, be reasoun
it wes geuin to ʒow (as ʒe speik) be ane papiste
Bischope, ãd thairfoʒ renunceis it, ⁊ seikis ane
vther oʒdinatioun of secularis : It followis con
sequentlic that ʒe (quhilk god foʒbid) sulde renunce ʒour Baptim also, geuin to ʒow be ane pa
pist pʒeist, as ʒe allege on lyke maner. Foʒ as S.

Augustine maist cūnigil̄e ād godlie wryttis, As
ane man thꝛow schisme and heresie amittis nocht
the sacrament of Baptim : siclyke, sayis he, foꝛ þ
sampn faltis, he amittis nocht the Sacrament
to geue baptime, quhilk is ꝑe sacramēt of oꝛdina
tioun: conferring the ꝑꝑetuitie of the ane sacra=
mēt anis ressauit wᵗ the vther. mairouer that ȝee
may be pꝑuadit, that we speik vnfenȝetlie, ād sin
ceirlie of cōscience, we pꝛay the oīpotent tobe ꝫ̄
cꝑfull tyll vs all, and to dit and close ꝑe mouthis
of ȝow oꝛ ws, quha speakis iniquitie in dowble
mid. Vale, & in de sapiētia vince, aut respisce. Iᵹ. Mart.
1561. Be ȝouris in all godlines,

Niniane vvinȝet at the desyre of his brether.

THE THRID TRACTAT.

Niniane Winȝet to the reidar wyssis grace & peace.

Q Uhen it come to my earis, gentill reidar,
of the seditious calking of the buith dur=
ris of certane catholiks in Edinburgh at the cō=
mand of the reularis thairof, on Pasche monu=
day last passit: And quhowat that nycht at euin
the durris of certane Caluinianis wes calkit al=
so with sum notes of dishonour, I wes panceād,
quhou happy ane thing it wat, giue euerie man
mycht leuc accoꝛding to his vocatiō, at ane tran
quillitie in godlines. And thꝛow that reuolueād
iu mynd ꝑat maist flurissād part of my aige, spēt
I ꝑe teching of ꝑe grāmar soule of linlychtquow,
about the space of ten ȝeris, I iugeit the teching
of the ȝoutheid in vertew and science, nixt efter ꝑe

O

auctoritie w $\tilde{y}$ ministers of iustice vnder it, $\mathfrak{r}$ eft $\tilde{y}$
angilicall office of godlie Pastours, to obtene $\tilde{y}$
th$_2$id principal place maist commodious and necessare to the kirk of god.... ze, sa necessar thocht I it, that the dewe charge and office off the
p$_2$ince and p$_2$elate woute it, is to thaim efter my
iugement, wōnderous pynefull and almaist ipo$_2$-
table, $\tilde{s}$d zit lytle cōmodius to y^e cōmoun welth,
till vnfenzett obedience aud trew godlines, quhē
the peple is ruid and igno$_2$ant: and cōtrarie be
the help of it to the zouthed, the office of all Po-
testatis is lycht to thaim and plesand to the sub-
iectis. Fo$_2$ the mynd of man of ane gude inclina-
tion (asane auncient w$_2$yttar rycht warly notis
obeyis no.trio$_2$ submittis not y^e self willinglie to
ony cōmandar o$_2$ techear, bot to sik quhōe it is
$p$suadit, to cōmand iustlie fo$_2$ vtiliteis cause.
Quhilk $p$suasioun th$_2$ow igno$_2$ance it maye not
weill haue, woitt the lycht of vnderstanding.
Bot as vnderstāding w sciēce is maist spetialye
$\mathfrak{r}$ happelie $_2$quest in zouthe sua nane doutis it at
pat tyme obtenit, maist firmlie tobe reserūit I me-
mo$_2$ie, $\mathfrak{r}$ maist fruit to cū thairof. The singūlar
vtilitie thairof to the cōmoun welth causit me to
muell gretūlie, quhou in tymes passit amāng sa
gret liberalitie, $\mathfrak{r}$ ryche dotatiōs maid i scotlād
of sind$_2$y fundationis to religiō $\mathfrak{r}$ science, that sa
litle respect hes euir bene had to the grāmar scu-
lis(quhairi cōmonlie $\tilde{y}$ maist happy $\mathfrak{r}$ first sedis
of y^e said cōmou welth ar sawin) $\tilde{y}$ in mony tow-
nis thair is not sa mekle puidit thairto, as a cō-
mō house: And in nane almaist of al ane sufficit-
ēt life to ane techear: Albeit ma be requirit to vn

Cice. li. I.
offic.

tak ŷ euir deualie, as beckis of ony a ſcuil. And
gaue quhou it mȳ be, ŷ at ŷis time, quhē mē pȝe
is to reforme al caualis of ignoȝāce ⁊ abuſe, ŷ ſa
ew childer war haldin at ŷ ſtudie of ony ſciēce ⁊
ſpecialie of grāth. The ȝt̃ept heirfor of ŷis ſinal
nieres to ſciēce, wout ŷ quhilk na ferder pgres
nay be had ŷairto, I ȝiectutit tobe ane gret poȝ
ct ⁊ foȝetatkig of ignoȝāce ⁊ ma ȝfuſit errouris
(quhilk god auert)ſchoȝtlie tocū:namelie ſē now
al mē wilbe theologis, ⁊ curius ſeircēris of the
ŷe myſteriis of god. In remēbȝing ŷir thigis, I
allit thā to memoȝie, quhou be ŷ mcyful puidē
e of ŷe almȳtie (quha de in all ⁊ for euer pȝaiſit)
air wes ſūtyme ſubmittit to my techemet(albeit
my erudiciō wes ſmal)humane childer of happy
ȝȳnis, mair able to leir than I wes to teche: to
quhō I vſit to pporte almaiſt dalie ſū theme, ar
gumēt, oȝ ſētence, of ŷ quhilk I wald haif ŷaim in
ȝding to maid oȝiſone oȝ epiſtil in latin tōg : ād
rhȝeht ŷis inat of ſediciō afoȝe namit had bene
ane beȝap ȝuenient ⁊ metū ŷ putpoſe. Heirfor I
being dȝery ⁊ doloȝus foȝ ŷ ſchiſme ⁊ diuiſiō pȝe
ſentlie i godis kirk, ⁊apperᵏis tēpoȝal calamite
is to bpȝyſe patthȝou, ⁊ alſ killiſad affectiō tomy
kynd diſcipulis, ⁊ my glaid ⁊ godlye exerciſe ſū
tyme ẅ ẏmȝ, beȝaif Falliuaiſt foȝ paſtyme, ⁊ ſū
mitigatiō of my diſpleſūt to wȝit ŷis declamaciō
follouig aᵭ is cuit tā of dremēe wald foȝ cauſ
of exerciſe, ⁊ phiſal ſtudie, ĩt Oſld tobe in ſculis,
Netheles qẏe mie of dut bȝeiȝer chacȝit to retṙ
it be diuulgatiem ⁊ cuinered my māme, bot ſub
ſcriuit, as eŷ foȝeuiſ ⁊ eair copiis ŷairof alſ ȝ
had beneiw euiſk ntȝwod ẅ quhen ŷ eȝ ſul
ſtude that ſum wes offendit thair ẅ ⁊ ẅ me alſo

forit, I seik the copye thairof & considderis it.
And as I plaue rethorik thairof verray small:
swa I cā espy na thing thairin abhorring fra ye
treuth. Of the quhilk I (geuing the honour of
learning tyll vtheris) inteyding to be ane faithful Chzistiane, & ane sone of ye haly kirk vniuersale, hes only regaird. Heirfor sen I neuer sett
furth ony wrytting cōtrare the Protestātis, sup-
pressing my name, that I maye saue me zit in ye
innocence, void of all detraction. I confesse me
to haue wrytting the samin tractate ād na thing
penitēt thairof as zit, except that I strenthit noght
my purpose w ma sufficient ressonis and auctoriteis. Quhilkis I differ quhill oure aduersaris
mak answeir heirto: Praying god maist grattius
to moue thame w the spirit off humilitie, ye thay
be not eschamit to recant yair errour in yis mater and all vtheris, bot thay be aluterlie groundit to maling in ane iote aganis the knawin veritie. I nameit the twa psonis following by v-
theris, because the ane is knawin tobe the principall deformare of his allegeit reformatioun
And to certifie the vther, that erar oz I condem-
nit of idolatrie Hieromē ād Augustine as leand
wytnesses, & the haill kirk of God i yis a poynce
ẅout cause: that I had leuir be banisfit furthe
of Europe as be his assistence I wes banisfit fra
Linlychtquow, for not assenting to his factioun
generalie in all poynctis. This far gentyll re-
dar haue I schawin, that I may be clein fra all
smot of blame in ye putting furth of priuat wryttingis ẅout subscriptiō: Praying ye to fairweil
in ye Lord, Of Edinburgh ye 24. of may 1561.

To the honorable Proueſt baillies and counſell of Edinburgh.

Uhen I remember, honozabyll ſchiris, ꝑ Solon ꝑ law maker of Athenis amangis the reſt com-mandit ꝑis i ſpecial, ꝑ gif ony of ꝑ toun in ane publict ſeditioun oz tumult, quhē on baith ſydis that can to armour, hid him ſelf, as ane cowart at ha me, not takand part ᵗᵒ the ane ſyde, he ſould be denudit of his gudis ꞇ baniſſit the Citie: it ſtry-kis me not ᵗᵒ lytle feir, that I ſiclyke in this con-trouerſie of religioun, as ane ſoldiour of ye kirk of Laodicea, ꝑat is, nother haet noz cauld, be ex-pellit (quhilk god fozbid) out of my citie of he-uinlie Hieruſalē, foz not aſſiſting to ꝑ aſſurit be citie, in gainſaping leis, the father thairof ye de-uyll, and all his mēberis. Quhairfoze quhē I ſe the ſedittioun amāgis 30u ꞇ 30ure Citizanis, foz the celebzatioun of the ſolennitie off Paſche, ād quhou 3e cōmand to calk the cloſit buith durris, at this tyme of certane nocht diſtonit fra ye haly kirk vniuerſale ᵗᵒ 30u, and haldis ye ſamyn mē Idolatouris ꞇ wozthy of puniſmēt, it apperis to my waik iugemēt, that to attempt ſic pzoude mif ozdour, ſall not only big vp ane wal betuix vs ꞇ 30u in religioun, bot alſo ſall engener(quhilk ye mercy of god ſtay) mair tempozal ſeditioun, cū-meris, ād debait, I thocht that I ane pziuat mā could do na better at ꝑat tyme, bot pzay foz peace amangis all pzofeſſing our lozd Jeſus. Quhilk quhen I did, and thairefter caſtand vp ye bukis

Apoc̄ 3.

Hiero. 3. pre
epist. epist.
80. & pre.
I. episto. ad
Marcellam.

Aug. ad Ia-
nuarium. li.
I.& 2.reid
pir workis
and be not
distault.

Aug.de cini
tate, del. li.
10, ca. 4.

of sū aūciet fatheris, to seik ȝ mid of godis kirk
i pis mat. I fynd maist cleir witnessing of famous fatheris, & specialie of S. Hierome & Augustine, ȝ ye hail kirk of god w aue ȝent, hes ꝓe-
lie celebratit ye solennitie of ȝule & pasche. w v-
theris reistis of our saluiour, & siclyke kepit ȝe ȝe
trlie abstinēce of fourty dayis afoȝe pasche, callit
lentren, in al cōntreis in ye warld, ꝓfessing chꝛist
afoȝe pir dayis: & affirmis ȝ yir, & siclyke thingȝ
vniuersaly obseruit, & ȝit not expresslie cōtenit in
scripture, ar traditiōs of ȝ Apostolis, oȝ decreis
of gñral tunselis, & thairfoȝ na wayis be ony ꝑ
ticulare cūtre tobe changeit. The notable cause
of pir solennit dayis geuis the said renownit fa
ther Augustine, & woȝthy tobe lokit in ye memo
rie of thaim, quha knawis thaim selfis to be wen
in pis flesche, & waik & fraill as ȝit in pis warld.
Ne curricula temporū (sayis he) ingrata subrepat obliuiō
yat be ye proces of tyme vnthākful foȝȝettiijnes
steill not vpon vs. Quhēn I reid pis maist cleir
testimonie of sa renownit fatheris, of ye vniuer
sale ȝent of godis kirk i this mater, sen our sal-
uiours dayis, I begin to muel at ye arrogāt te-
Joh. Knox
in his buke
of discipli-
ne.
meritie of ȝour haly ꝓphete Johne Knox, quha ȝ
mādis to abolise pir solēniteis as papistric: be ye
quhilk name he vnderstādis, as I cā collect, idola-
tric supstitiō, oȝ doctryne ȝtrar ȝ scriptur. And
gif he vnderstādis yat vices be pis name: I thik
ȝ yat is na treu chꝛist ꝛ̄e, bot he dar affirme bald
ly in ȝ face of al ye warld, ȝ i pis mat (quhair he
callis ȝ saids solēniteis idolatrical, supstitius oȝ
ȝtrarȳ to gods law) he speaks blasphemie aganis ye haly gaist, & agais ȝ essētial Dietie our loꝛd

& kīg christ Jesꝰ: quha ꝓmittit his said spirit of
treuth to teche his kirk ād be wt it to the warldis
end: For Johne Knox & his scolers schrynkis not Matth. vlt.
to rail, & lie yt it hes bene eũ in idolatrie i yis case Io.14.
of yir festual dayis amāgis vtheris ma. Bot I
misknaw not sũ of zow to obiect ye ꝯmād, charg
and *Sex dayis to labour, & the seuint day to sanctifie to ye
lord*, thairfore I desyre yt doutsũ mā to cause his
doctour & ꝓphete foresaid, wt all ye assistence of
his best learnit scolers, to ansueir in writ, quhat
scripture hes he or vther authoritie, by ye ꝯsẽt of
ye haly kirk vniuersal to sāctifie ye sonday tobe
yt seuint day. And gif he abolissis wt vs ye sater-
day, as ceremoniall & not requisit i ye law of the
euangel: quhat hes he by ye ꝯsent of godis kirk,
to sāctifie ony day of ye vii. & not to labour al ye
seuin days: ye sext day, because it is sua ꝯmādit,
& yt sabbaoth, because it is abolissit be ye euāgel?
& gif he cā schaw na expres scriptur yarfor: quhi
abolissis he not ye sonday, as he dois zule pasche
& ye rest vniuersalie obseruit be al christianis as
ye sōday? Bot note honorable schirs (yt yt witie be
not losit be alkatiō) ye historie of Judith, quhow
ye Jowis by ye selēniteis of yai dayis geuin yaim
afore i ye scriptur, istitute ane zeirly solēnitie to Iudith. vlti.
glorifie god for yt deliuerig Bethulia & yaim fra
ye crudelitie of Holofernes. Reid also yt Mardo-
cheus, Hester, & ye rest of ye Jowis captiues vn
der yt king Assuerꝰ, istitute sic zeirly solēnitie of blyth- Hester. 9.
nes, in remēbrāce yt be ye mychtie hand of god thay wer
delyuerit fra ye tyrannie of wikit Ammon. Gyf sic zeir-
lie memorial in blyithnes & thankis geifing wes haldin
for yt delyuerāce of yair bodeis: had not yt Apostolis, ād
the hail kirk of

god gydit bnduottitlie be the haly gaist, siclyke
auchozitie to institut sic festual dayis foz the de-
lyuering of thair bodeis and saulis, not fra twa
eirdlie tyzannis, Holofernes & Ammon, bot frō
the deupll, hell, and syn, : not be twa wemē Judith and Hester, bot be the pzetious blude of the
immaculat lamb the Sone of God & ze reid sick-
lyke the fest of the dedication callit Encenia, in-
Io.Io.)stitute be the Hebzeuis without ony cōmand cōtenit in ony canonicall scripture : quhilk solennt
tie wes appzouin and decozit be our Salutours
awin pzesence. Sall the haill peple of god heirfoz of al aiges, in the libertie of ye Euangel haif
les libertie in the lyke materis, thā had ƥ Jowis
bnder the zok of the Mosaical law & ze may re-
2.Para. 7.id also that Salomon at the dedicatioun of thee
tempyll celebzatit in gret solennitie sewin festuall dayis together, and trow ze, that he bzak the
cōmād thairthzow, Sex dayis sall thou laubour ? quhē
we heir zour pzophete cast in dout, sayand quha
wat quhat day Chzist wes bozne on & Can ze thik
hi in ony vther gre, bot nyxt eft to speir gif chzist
be bozne & O mad mā and maist fulische wald he
psuade ane faithful chzistiane, that ye haill bni-
uersall kirk, is mair bnthankfull, ād les mynd-
full of the byzth of hir spouse and king the sonne
of God, thā ony realme is of thair tēpozal king:
quhais day of Natiuitie, na cōntre fozzettis, in-
during his lyfetyme & Bot our kyng and maiste
sweit spouse leuis foz euer. Quhairfoze euer sall
ye day of his blissit natiuitie, circumsitiō, passiō,
resurrectioun, ascensioun, and his manifestatiō

to the warld callit Epiphanie in the dispyte of ye
deuyll and all his furius memb;eris (quha * euer
hes laboꝛit to abolish his name out of ꝑis warld)
be i freche memoꝛie of his deirbelouit spouse his
haly kirk vniuersall. Bot allace quhow mony in
ꝑir dayis repetis ꝑis haly kirk vniuersal, as ane
necessare articule of ꝑar beleif (as it is but dout)
and ʒit othir thꝛow ignoꝛance dissault, oꝛ thꝛow
malice blyndit, impugnis the trew vnderstanding ꝑairof? Amãgis mony materis rycht wechty
lat this samyn grosse exemple of the abolitioun
of thir solennit dayis, as idolatricall, be ane cõ-
trate the vnifoꝛme cõsent in all tyme ãd place of
the samyn kirk. Bot allace foꝛ pietie, honoꝛable
schiris, quhy remẽber we not, ꝑ foꝛ ꝑ abusing of
thir dayis, amangis vtheris faultis, God is at
wꝛayith w vs, and not foꝛ the institutioun and
godlye obseruauce of the samyn : bot because we
haue mispent thaim fra the seruice ef our god, to
the seruice of our Belliis, and of thap memberis
vnder the bellie : fra ye honour of our loꝛd chꝛist
to the vaine gloꝛious pompe of our awi bodyis:
froime cheritie, to carnalitie, bestowand that per-
tenit to the pure nedy mẽberis of Chꝛistis bodye
on our sinfull flesche w the ryche Glotton: And
sa fra humilitie, to pꝛyde : fra sobꝛiete, to dꝛukin
nes : fra peace and lufe, to contentioun ꞇ debait,
fra louing of God, to mãsuering of his name: fra
godly talk of pace, amitie, ꞇ frendschip, to scurri-
litie, stryfe, ꞇ detracttioun. Finallie fra al the ser
uice of god, requirit on the haly daye, to the ser-

E

uice of Sathan, oꝛ of the warld. And laſt of all,
quhē we ſould lamēt foꝛ our impietie, ⁊ returne
to god and the rycht vſe of this ſolenniteis,ꝛe eik
this miſcheif to all ꝛour foꝛmer wickitnes, quhē
ꝛe pnunce ꝑis blaſphemie to the ſpirit of god, af
firming that his haly kirk vniuerſall hes bene
euer pollutit ꝯ idolatrie in the obſeruing of thir
Dayis. O ſkcꝑful god wꝑl ꝛe not remēber quhay
ſpekis ſa mekle of the ſcripture, that god foꝛ the
wickitnes of the peple, wes not appleſit ꝯ thay
feſtuall Dayis, quhilks he in the ſcripture afoꝛe
had cōmandit be ꝑe Iowis to be obſeruit, quhill
the cūming of Chꝛiſt:⁊ that foꝛ thair abuſing of
ꝑe ſampn to ane vther fine, thā he inſtitute ꝑame
On this maner he complenis be his pꝛophete, I
haue hatt (ſapis the loꝛd) ꝛour feſtuall dayis: I
wꝑl not haue ꝛour bꝛunt Sacrifiteis. And iane
vther place, I ſall turne ꝛoure ſolennit dayis in
murnꝑng, and ꝛour canticulis in ſobing. The
pꝛophete Hieremie lamentis, that god foꝛ ꝑe impietie and ſinnis had cauſit the feſtuall and ſolennit Dayis in Hieruſalem to be foꝛꝛet,and in ꝑe
wꝛath ⁊ idignatiō of his fury (be quhilk we vnd
ſtand his Iuſtice aganis the wickitnes of man)
had geuin the king and ꝑe pꝛeiſte to be deſpyſit,
his temple ſanctuarie and altare to be deſtroyit.
Be the quhilk place allane it is euident, that as
the king, and all lauchfull ſuperiour poweris,⁊
pꝛeiſte biſchope, and all authoꝛitie oft he kirk,
wes contemnit foꝛ ane tyme, accoꝛding to ꝑe inſtice of god, botꝛit be the wickit ād repꝛobat ous

Amos,5.
⁊.8.

Thren.2.

He: that on lyke maner the ordinance of god tueching the saidis dayis in that tyme, quhil Christis passioun amang ye peple of god wes to be observit, according to the law geuin thaim : zit for the abusing of the samyn, the Lord be ÿ mouth of his prophete repellit yair solénnteis ād Sacrificeis. The cause thairof is declarit : because thair cōgregatiō wes iniuste & wickit, and thair handis full of blude. And zit as he wald at that tyme nane of his belufit peple to be disobedient and nott reuerence king and preist not only ye gude bot also the euyl, nor zit his peculiar peple to dispyse his sanctuarie, temple, altare, nor his haly dayis : swa he wyil but dout his belouit to obserue ye ordinance of his haly kirk vniuersal, twccheing thir samyn Solénnteis, quhilkis ar now in cōtrouersie : albeit thay be dispysit be the wickit. Giue dew obedience and reuerēce be had to kingis, quenis, princes, & prelatis, at this tyme : lat vper mē iuge. For a thig specialy exhort J zour prudence, at this present to cōsider, honorable schiris, that ze be not of ye noumber of that wickit ghtratiō, quhō ye propheterebukis on this maner, *All thair generatioun said this in thair hart, lat vs mak all the festuall dayis of the Lord to cease out of the eird.* For except ze be wylligly blind, ze may psaue yir dayis, quhairof we speik, tobe the festuall dayis of the lorde. For as zour prophetis be auctoritie of the kirk, without expresse Scripture thairfor, appreuis with vs the Sondaye to be the Sabaoth daye to all Christianis : Swa be aucthoritie of the samyn kirk in all

Esai. I.

I. Petr. ij.

Psalm. 73. Reid this Psalm for this mater and vthers at this tyme. quhilk in the inglis Bibill is the 74.

côutreis and aiges, and be the exemplis also of
the scripturis aboue wryttin, appreue ẜ affirme
we baith the ane and the vther. And that ze may
be mair assurit in conscience, that thair is na errour cômittit be the kirk in this mater, bot zour
pphetis to haue fallin arrogâtlie in ane blynd,
arrogant and wylfull errour, quhê thay dar oppone thaim sa proudlie or erar impudêrlie to the
haill kirk of god: reid in the C. rvii. Psalme,
quhare the spirit of God cômâdis ẙ kirk i blith-
nes and thankisgeuing, for hir redemptioun bee

Mar.12.
Christ (quhare he exponis him self tobe ẙ corner
or band stane, quhilk ẙ bigaris refusit) to reiose
ẜ institute solenntie of tyme thairfor in thir wor-
Psalm. 117
dis : Hęc est dies quã fecit domin⁰, exultemus & lœtemur in
ea. And againe, Constituite diem solennẽ in condensis vsq
ad cornu altaris. Twa thingẛ remanis, quhilk J of
my small learning bot of ardêt lufe beseikis zow
Schiris to consider: first that ze be not ye scurge
of god (as wes the wickit in the dayis of Hiere-
Thren.2.
mie) to dispyse king, quene, bischope, ẜ al lauch
full auctorite, to gidder ẞ thir solennit festuall
dayis cuir obseruit in goddis haly kirk vniuersall: and lir to prefer the sampn kirk to the Jugement of ony ane mâ, Citie, Prouince, realme
or ony ane aige of mê of ane vther spirit, ze, albeit it wer ane Ingell frome heuin, and knaw zour
fragilitie and fall ẜ returne hame agane to zour
awin moder godis kirk. Secundly giue ye tuid-
nes of my dptemêt haistely wryttin in feruour of
spirit.but eloquence may not dissuade zow fra ye
obstinate puersitie of zoure erroure, J exhorte ze

cause zour pphete Johne Knox, and zour supintendent Johne Spotiswod, to impreue Sanctz
Hierome ād Augustine as leand witnessis in the
premissis. And cause thaim delyuer thair ansuer
in wryt, for thir haly fatheris bukis ar patēt ty l
vs and thaim. And sum of our faithfull brether
hes wryttin sindry tymes to thaim baith, & gettis
na ansuer in wryt, bot waist wynd agane. Bot paduenture albeit thir twa zoure kempis dar nott
for schame ansuer in this mater, ze wyll appeill
to ý rest of zour lernit theologis of a gret nūber i
Scotland ād Geneua. Bot to thaim we oppone
all the Christiane catholikis in Aphrik Asia and
Europa. Bot zit, pchance ze wyll allege zour priuate misordour to haue auctoritie, as establissit
be ane lāg space, bow, almaist thre zeris in scotland: heirfore to that we oppone the vniuersale
ordour throw all the warld beleuand in Christe,
thir xv. c. xxvii. zeris as the saidz Sz. Hierome,
and Augustine witnesses afore thair tyme, ād al
histories sen syne. Desist heirfore Schiris maist
derbelufit, desiste I pray zow in ye sycht of god
fra zour furius rage & wylful blyndnes. Think
quhat it is to maling cōtrare christ, his haly kirk
vniuersall, our souerane Lady ād zour lauchful
pastouris. Be war to moue distructiō to zour selfis, and seditioun in this nobyll town be zoure
calking, and keling, and puerst mynd to puneis
the Innocent contrare all lawis of god and mā.
The potent spirit of god mot humpll zour hertis
and giue zow grace that this tumult tak rest w=
out extreme damnage. At Edinburgh ye last of

Marche. be zouris M.

☞ Quhais name ze sal knaw, quhen ze sa
knaw zoure Errour, oz quhen Johne Knox
oz his Bzether answeris heirto in wzit.

FINIS.

☜ (❀) ☞

NINIAN WINZET
The Last Blast of the Trompet
1562

THE

LAST BLAST OF THE TROMPET OF
Godis worde aganis the vsurpit auctoritie of
Iohne Knox and his Caluiniane brether
intrudit Precheouris &c.

☞ (✱) ☜

Put furth to the Congregatioun of the
Protestantis in Scotlãde, be Niniane Winzet, ane Catho-
lik preist borne in
Renfrew:

(✱✱)

☞ At the despre and in the name of his afflictit Catholike brether of ye inferiour
ordoure of Clergie, and laic men.

(‡)

Vir impius procaciter obfirmet vultum suum: qui autem
rectus est, corrigit uiam suam.
Prouerb. 2I.

Edinburgi vltimo Iulij. 1562.

THe caus quhy we haif intitulit þis tractate on the maner preceding, is : that we
first soundit the trompet of godis word,
twiching this purpose in thre questions
specialie, amangis mony ma proponit to Johne
Knox and his brether, & delyuerit to him in name
of þam al. Quhilkis we iugeit sufficiet occasio to
ony man in quhome had bene the feir of god, to
examinat him self, and to wdraw him fra þe rolkis of errour and arrogance in this mater. And
secundlie quhen this fornamit Johne wes nott
mouit thairby, bot erar puft vpe w mair pryde,
intendit to preue his vocation planelie in þ pul
pet (bot quhat strenth had his armour of defen-
ce thair, lat cuning men iuge quha hard him) we
blew the sampyn trompet againe in thre wryting-
is according to his preching on sindry dayis : and
þat verray schortlie as it had bene be thre sindry
sondis blawin almaist at ane tyme. Be þ quhilks
albeit he wes abaissit, and woundit in conscience
afore god (quhais worde is mair peirceand thã
ony twa aigeit sworde &c.) zit þe wylfull blyndnes & obstinat arrogance leidand all puersit erroneus men as captiuis and bunde presoneris,
haldis him and his brether sa fetterit, as it war
w certane strang chenis of Irne, that thay wyll
not zit descend in thaim selfis to humilitie & pen-
nance : bot indurit as Pharao whaldis the peple of god in thraldu aganis his expres comãd
and approuin ordinance. Quhairfor þ the blynd

Hebre. 4.

of thaim and thair scoleris be not impute tyll vs
in ye secht of god, for not schawing our brother
lie lufe to thaim, in admonissing of thair erroure
& perrell: we put furth this thrid and last blaste,
to call abak the scoleris frome ye plaig of godis
iustice, as we callit (as we mycht) thair techa-
ris afore: thinkand this to be sufficiēt aduertis-
mēt to al thaim quha hes earis to heir ye treuth,
yat we neid not in this mater ony ofter to sound
this trompet.

Reid and Iuge.

To the Congregatioun of the Protestantis
in Scotlande.

VHILL we ar aluterlie irkit, honorable and deirbelouit, we haif
kepit silence, almaist aganis our
cōscience, sen the twelft of Marche, awaityng on Johne Knox
answeir in writt, of his lauchfull
vocatioun, accordinge to his promis maid in the
pulpet to our last writtyng, delyuerit to him yat
day thairupon. Quhilk promis sen he nother
fulfyllis (nother anctis this, nor our vther questionis) nor zit he nor his brether desistis fra v-
surpinge sa hie ane office, to the quhilk thay can
nocht schaw thaim lauchfullie callit conforme to
godis ordinance, nor zit mak ony answeir thairin Wout thair schame (as we ar psuadit,) except
thay godlie schaw thair repentāce: We may not
bot pray and beseik zour prudence for the health

A

and saifing of zour awin saulis, that ze reid, cõ-
sidder and auge sinceirlye wuthoute all affectioun
our questionis & answeris maid to Johne Knox
declaratioun thairupon.   And exhortis zow al-
swa gif ze may collect furth of the Euangell ony
defece be precept or exemple, to assure vs of zour
precheouris lauchfull vocatioun: that ze assiste
to thaim thairwith, and mak the samyn patent
tyll vs: Quhais by that ze and we sum tyme brether of ane kirk, may be togidder, zit sobedient
brether but schisme and discorde, to the Prophetis and ministeris of god (of zoure precheouris
we meine) fra thay be knawin vndouttitlie to be
send be him. Bot failzeing thairof (as we hope
ze sall) we exhorte zow in the bowellis of IESVS
Christe oure onelie Saluiour & Mediator that
ze set aspde all blynd affectioun, and auert zoure
earis fra the sweit venum of deuyllish eloquence of wordis, and begin to feir and trimble at the

Num. 16.
feirfull exemplis of Deid in Core ãd his cumpa-
2.Par.26.
nie, and of ye proude king Osias quha temerus-
lie in his arrogance ingerit him self, to mak sacrifice at the altare of God, woute all lauchfull
vocatioun thairto. For of thir dais now present
Iuda. 1.
aduertissis zow, nocht we, bot the Apostle Iude.
Woo be to thaim (sayis he) quha in the rebelli-
oun ãd tressoun of Core hes perissit. And giue
ze think thir exemplis nocht sufficiét to persuade
zow, quhilks we haif writtin to Johne Knox in o-
theris tractatis: remêber alsua maist effectuous-
I.Kng.13.
lie we zou pray, þ for vsurpyng Samuelis office,
as for ane falt in special, king Saule wes repel-

lit fra his kingdome. The mercy of god stayis, þ
we and ʒe for defending of sic inistordour, be nott
repellit fra our natiue possessionis heir, aō efter
fra our kingdome eternale. Quhat⸳ sulde nocht
the arrogance & murmuring of Maria the sister
of Moyses, with Jaron,& þ foule lippre quhair-
with scho wes plagit thairfor, stryk ʒow to feir⸳
Quha murmuring aganis Moyses, & aseriuing
auctoritie to his self, wout all lauchfull vocatioun thairto, (as ʒour precheouris dois presētlie) Num. 12,
said this : hes god spokin be Moyses onlie⸳ hes
he not spokī siclik to vs⸳ Eui as ʒour pphetʒ saiʒ
now.Haue we not science knaulege,& vndēstādig
þ gyft of god⸳ Quhy ar we not thairth;ow, but
farder auctoritie orordinatiō, lauchfull pastoris 3.Reg.14
Bischoptis aō prelatis⸳ Reid and cōsider siclyke Ibid.12, &
to quhat miserable end Hieroboam wes brocht 11.
for his wickit consaitis and doingis, causing ye
Isralites nocht to passe to Hiersualem, to make
sacrifice to god, quhair the Arcke, Tabernakle,
and prestis (as in the town quhilk god peculiar-
lie had elect) wes appoyntit than to remane;and
nocht chesing the prestis of the tribe of Leui according to godis speciall command, bot passing
with the peple to Bethel and Dan,and thair offerit sacrifice to straînge goddis, electing be his
auctoritie ag-inis the ordinace of god, ane con-
fusioun of wickit prestis of quhat sumeuer Tribe thairto. Mark and obserue with al diligence
we exhort ʒour prudence in the name of our lord
Jes⁹,gif ʒe haif folowit Hieroboā i lykemaneror
nocht

Cant. 6.

vincent.
Lirinen,

2. Timo. 4.

Io. 20.
Act. 2, 6.
13,14.
I. Timo. 5.
Tit. I.

Hebre. 5.
Psalm. 2. &
109.

nocht: drawing ye peple and zour selfis, fra our trew Hierusalem godis haly kirk vniuersal (out of ý quhilk pair is na sacrifice of prayer, louing, or rychteousnes plesand to god) to Bethel & dan to the priuat conuenticules of Schismatikis ad heretikis: ad giue ze haue thair maid sacrifice to fals godis: ý is alsua (as ancient fatheris godlie exponis it) hes embraceit fals and erroneus doctryne, for the treuth: hes worschippit, and ad ornit erroures, hereseis and lets for the eternall veritie of godis word: & that ze mycht haif zoure awin consaitis wicketlie fulfyllit, consider giue ze *prurientes auribus* hes not electit preistis and precheoures, *& heipit vp masteris to Zour selfis*: not discending of the tribe of Leui: That is not succeding to the Apostles and thair successouris efter ý ordinace appoyntit be the word of god. And gyf al thir terrouris may nocht mollifie zour hartis to knaw oure iust motiones: and that ordinare auctoritie ad obedience thairto quhilk Chryste hes left i his kirk be his Apostlis & yair successours: Aduert we praye zow and mark the office of ane bischope to be la hie & sa excellent, that our Sal uiour self tuke not that office vpon him without the lauchfull vocatioun of his heuinlie fader, as S. Paule writtis, *Euin sa Christ alsua glorifeit not him self tobe maid the hie preist: Bot he that said vnto him: Thou art my sonne this day haue I begottin the: glorfeit him. As he sais in ane vther place. Thou art ane preist for euer efter the ordour of Melchisedech.* And sen ze reding the haill new Testamět sen Christ, & ý historiis of al cuntreis, sensyne, findis na bischope, preist, nor dearone inftitute, ⁊ ordanit be þ laic peple in ye haly catholike kirk bot be the Apoftlis and thaire fuccefouris bifchopis alanerlie: Infameble that þ fewin Diacones electit be the peple to be fteuartis fpecialie to þ pure in godis kirk, wes prefentit afore the Apoftlis ad tuke thair ordinatioun and power of thaim: At ʒe not affrait to auante fameble that ʒe haue godis worde for ʒow, ⁊ not we: and contrare the worde of god fa erprefle ad falargelie put afore ʒour eine to manteine ad defend fic mifprdoure? Wyll ʒe not fchaw ane auctorittie of godis word for ʒour minfters vocatiö? Quhair find ʒe euer ony of the Apoftlis writting to the Romanis, Corinthianis, or ony vther multitude cömanding thaim to conftitute ⁊ ordinat bifchope or vther minifter, as ʒe may reide yat he geuis erprefle cömad to ye bifchopis, Timothe and Tite, to vfe that power euery ane off thaim feueralie. Quhair reid ʒe euer in the apoftolis dais amang fa mony thoufande Chriftianis turnit to the faith, or ʒit fenfyne ony multitude of laic people allane to haue ordinatit ane bifchope, preift, or diacone? Bot that we appeir nocht to deprtue ony part of the kirk, mebris off Chrift of ony dignitie appoyntit tó thaim in the fcripture. We confefle (and to that glaidlye we aflent) that the laic peple fumtyme hes electit fic perfones, as the fewin Diaconis afore namit: ⁊ in the prefence of the peple the bifchopis to haue bene ordinatit: quha afore had bene cömonlie in the law of grace, electit ad prefentit to the Comprouinciall Bifchops be thaim, geuing to thaim

Act. 6.

I. Timo. 3.
& 4.
Tit I.

Act. 6.

Num. 20.

Art. I.

Cyp.li. I.
epist. 4.

testimonie of thair godlie conuersatiõ, & present of thair fauour to thaim: as to suc psonis quhõ est thay suld reuerêce, baith for thair office ad haly leuing. *Sa institute Moyses the Bischope Eleazarus on the hyech montane Hor before the haill multitude: as before thaim quhay sulde testifie alvvayis of his haly lyfe. Sa vves Mathias ordinatit in the place rf Ludas in the middis of the discipulis : quhome afore ye Ioseph that hed elestit.* On the quhilk place the haly martyr Cypriane writtis this : *Quód vtique idcirco tam diligenter & caxtê, conuocata plebe tota gerebatur, ne quis ad altaris ministerium, vel ad sacerdotalem locum indignus obreperet.* That is, quhilk thing verilie yairfore wes done sa diligêtlie and warlie the haill peple being callit to gidder, yat na vnworthy psoun mycht quietlie creip to the ministerie off the altare : or to the preistis roum. And in the sampn place contendis he : yat be ye auctoritie cf godis word it suld be obseruit, that the preist or bischope be admittit, in ý psence of all the peple, that he be haldin be the iugemêt and witnessing of all to be worthie ad apt to yat office: Sê ý peple (sais he) hes special power to elect the worthie preistis, & to refuse the vnworthie. Heirfore sen the princes in our dayis takis on thaim the haill power of electioun vote & suffrage of the peple, presenting quhat psoun thay pleis, wald god yat thair presentation war void of all symonie, ambition, & inordinat affection: And yt it wer adiunit alsua, ye testimonie & psêt of ý peple in euery Diocesie & parrochin, according to the auctoriteis abone rehersit. Sa we think, that thair suld nocht be sa mony *Blynd cru-*

Ioh. Knox
quha taltat
is this? ad
quhat preist?

Electioun,
ad ordina-
tioun ar not
ane as it is
talkt abone

Act. 6.

kit, & seik, smottit, mutilat, markit, deformit, scabbit, Mo-Leuit. 21.
dites, Amonites, and sclanderous, Mamzeres, contrare the & 22.
leuu of god presentit, offerit, and maid preistis ãd prelatis in Malach. I.
the kirk, Giue ony of 3ow wyl obiect that the p2e-Deut. 23.
sts bischopis ãd pe clergie in oure dais hes bene
blekkit w the saidis deformiteis and sa ignorãt
o2 vitious, o2 baith, ãd alsua scladerous. y thay
ar vnwo2thie pe name of Pasto2es. Allace we ar
rycht so2ie that this is trew fo2 the maist part, ãd
mair. Bot wald 3e consider the cause thairof to
be our iniquitie, vngodlines & abominable lyfis
fo2 the quhilk god is at w2aith with vs, and fo2
the quhilkis in reuenge of our sinnis, acco2ding
to his iustice, he sufferis, Hypoc2ites to haif cure ouir Iob. 34.
vs, as he causis, Sum tyme vitious, or tyrane princes, su-Esa. 3.
tyme effeminat personis, or babis, impotet to defẽde vs throu Eccle. 10.
iustice in quietnes ãd rest, sumtyme Infidelis to haue domi-Hierem. 38.
nioun abone vs. We wald seik ane vther remeid thã As the ba-
to heip vp sin vpon sin in pe defending of sa vn-bilonianis
godlie miso2dour agains y o2dinance ãd reuelit had vpõ pe
wyl of god i his scripture sa exp2esse & salargely Iowis and
setfurth. Quhat remeds speir 3e ? Bnt dout to the Turke
turne vnfenzeitlie of al our hart fra our idolitri-now vpon
call and insaciable auarice, p2oude feirles p2esũ-mony chri-
ptiõ, fra maist auaricio9 * p2odigalitie (we me-stianis.| ✝
ine specially of pe glo2ious bo2douring of 3oure Antithetox.
garmentis with the blude of pure) fra the deuo-Hiere. 2.
ring of the patrimonie of the kirk, pe tressour of Act. 2.
indigent, fra fleschelie libertie ãd b2utale irreli-
giosiitie, fra vaine babling of godis wo2de but
feir and reuerence thairof in contentioun and

curiositie, fra proude ignorāce, fra ȝ abominatiō of wychecraft & schameles mantening thairof in contempt of god and his law, fra fals fenȝeit hypocrisie of halines, fra ingratitude and vtheris deuylische monstres of vice regnād at this tyme: to our maist mercyfull god and trew seruing

Psalme.2. of him in haly feir and brothelie lufe and in reiosing in him be humill dredour and reuerence. Bot of the twa proude prinçes dame Heresie and hir sister we wyll not talk, knawing that our maistres faithfull simplicitie, ād lufe and lawtie, ȝ thair seruandis, be thaim wyl nocht be hard, bot repellit & schot to the dure as sillie thingis wantand craft to circumuene, flatter, & lie. For now quha seis it nocht cum to passe, quhilk god com-

Ezechi.33. plenis be his Prophete: quhilk is, That mony heris and knauis his vvorde (in ane part) and dois not thairefter, bot turnis it in ane sang of yair mouth, yair hartis beĩg geuin

☞ ty! auarice, & ye vvord of god is to thaim, as ane ballat of mestralie, quhilk hes ane sueit tone, & plesand to sung. Lat vs

Luc.10.
Psalme.79 turne I say and pray, that the Lorde of the vvineȝarde send vs lauchfull treu vvorkmen thairto baith to schute oute the vnclene baris, quha be filthie leuing ād sueinge-ting in thair stinkande styis, infectis the tender burgeounis of the ȝong wynis and to schut out or cut of allua, the wyld sanglerie, ȝ is ye proude Schismatikis and obstinat heretikis na wayis

Of doctrine & ordor we meane maist speciallie. sociale to ȝ cōpanie of christiāe catholiks. Quha in hic arrogance of thair maister, Lucifer trampis down the heuinlie incres and all decent policie of the sampyn winȝarde, drest and deckit, be ye former workmen vnfenȝeit policiaris of ye samin,